Transforming Psychology

TRANSFORMING PSYCHOLOGY

Gender in Theory and Practice

STEPHANIE RIGER

OXFORD
UNIVERSITY PRESS

2000

OXFORD

Oxford   New York

Athens   Auckland   Bangkok   Bogotá   Buenos Aires   Calcutta
Cape Town   Chennai   Dar es Salaam   Delhi   Florence   Hong Kong   Istanbul
Karachi   Kuala Lumpur   Madrid   Melbourne   Mexico City   Mumbai
Nairobi   Paris   São Paulo   Singapore   Taipei   Tokyo   Toronto   Warsaw

and associated companies in
Berlin   Ibadan

Copyright © 2000 Stephanie Riger

Published by Oxford University Press, Inc.
198 Madison Avenue, New York, New York 10016

Oxford is a registered trademark of Oxford University Press.

Library of Congress Cataloging-in-Publication Data

Riger, Stephanie.
Transforming psychology :
gender in theory and practice / Stephanie Riger.
p.   cm.
Includes bibliographical references and indexes.
ISBN 0-19-507466-1
1. Feminist psychology.   I. Title.
BF201.4.R54   1999
150'.82—dc21   99-045366

1 3 5 7 9 8 6 4 2

Printed in the United States of America
on acid-free paper

for Dan

Contents

Acknowledgments

ALL AUTHORS KNOW THAT their name alone on the cover of a book is a lie. Every book is the product of a dialogue, with contemporary and prior authors and others. I have been blessed with a community of scholars who are also friends, who have read numerous iterations of these pieces and given words of praise, helpful suggestions, insightful criticisms, and support in tough times. Foremost among these is Dan A. Lewis, to whom I am indebted for everything from endless conversations about postmodernism to more-than-his-share of parental duty at our children's sports events. Others to whom I am grateful include Faye Crosby, Cynthia Fuchs Epstein, Margaret T. Gordon, Christopher Keys, Jane Mansbridge, Shulamit Reinharz, Susan Saegert, and numerous anonymous reviewers. Students have stimulated these arguments, assisted in research, and in other ways made these chapters possible. Among others, I am grateful to Courtney Ahrens, Kathleen Beety, Amy Blickenstaff, Jennifer Camacho, Julie Nelson-Kuna, Maryann Krieglstein, Debra Pinsof, Megan Sullivan, and Sharon Wasco of the University of Illinois at Chicago, Pat Galligan of Northwestern University, and Randi Cartmill of Stanford University.

I have also been fortunate to be associated with institutions that have nurtured my work. The Institute for Research on Women and Gender at Stanford University gave me a year in which to think and colleagues to stimulate that thought; I am deeply grateful to Iris Litt, Karen Offen, Marilyn Yalom, and other members of the Affiliated and Visiting Scholars Seminar. The Great Cities Institute at the University of Illinois at Chicago gave me time in which to complete the manuscript—and a model of patience and good humor, Helene Berlin, to help prepare it for publication. The Women's Studies Program at the University of Illinois at Chicago continues to give me colleagues who inspire and help me in many ways: Sandra Bartky, Judy Gardiner, Peg Strobel, and others too numerous to mention. The Association for Women in Psychology has twice given me its Distinguished Publication Award, for articles on which the chapters on feminist epistemology and women in management are based, and the Society for Community Research and Action of the American Psychological Association has given me its award for Distinguished Contributions to Theory and Research. I am grateful to them all. Finally, I thank Joan Bossert of Oxford University Press for her forbearance over the many years it took to bring this project to fruition.

The essays in this volume have been previously published, in some cases in earlier form. I thank the publishers for their permission to reprint the following:

Riger, S. (1999). Working together: Challenges in collaborative research on violence against women. *Violence against Women, 5*, 1099–1117.

Riger, S., & Krieglstein, M. (2000). The impact of welfare reform on men's violence against women. *American Journal of Community Psychology, 5.*

Riger, S. (1997). From snapshots to videotape: New directions in research on gender differences. *Journal of Social Issues, 53*, 395–408.

Riger, S. (1995). Rethinking the distinction between sex and gender. In L. Bender & D. Braveman (Eds.), *Power, privilege, and law: A civil rights reader* (pp. 232–240). St. Paul, MN: West Publishing Co. Reprinted with permission of the West Group.

Nelson, J., & Riger, S. (1995). Women's agency in context. In J. K.Gardiner (Ed.), *Provoking agents: Gender and agency in theory and practice* (pp. 169–177). Urbana, IL: University of Illinois Press. Copyright 1995 by the Board of Trustees of the University of Illinois.

Riger, S. (1994). Challenges of success: Stages of growth in feminist organizations. *Feminist Studies, 20*, 275–300. Reprinted by permission of the publisher, Feminist Studies, Inc.

Riger, S. (1993). What's wrong with empowerment. *American Journal of Community Psychology, 21*, 279–292.

Riger, S. (1992). Epistemological debates, feminist voices: Science, social values, and the study of women. *American Psychologist, 47*, 730–740.

Riger, S. (1991). Gender dilemmas in sexual harassment policies and procedures. *American Psychologist, 46*, 497–505.

Riger, S. (1990). Ways of knowing and community-organizational research. In P. Tolan, C. Keys, F. Chertok, & L. Jason (Eds.), *Researching community psychology: Integrating theories and methodologies.* Washington, DC: American Psychological Association.

Riger, S. (1988). Comment on "Women's history goes to trial: EEOC v. Sears, Roebuck, and Company." *SIGNS: Journal of Women, Culture, and Society, 13*, 897–903. Copyright 1988 by the University of Chicago. All rights reserved.

Riger, S., & Galligan, P. (1980). Women in management: An exploration of competing paradigms. *American Psychologist, 35*, 902–910.

PART I

Knowing Gender

I

Introduction

YEARS AGO, I HEARD A prominent scholar admonish her audience to "think against the grain" of traditional beliefs. Whether in response to that intellectual challenge or out of my own perversity, I have attempted to follow that advice in my journey through psychology. The essays contained in the two parts of this book map that journey. In part I, I challenge the underlying assumptions and methods of psychology as they apply to the study of women, and I offer alternatives. In part II, I spotlight various policies and practices that affect women, such as sexual harassment policies or programs to increase the numbers of women in management, that are rooted in traditional beliefs about women, and reframe them in light of feminist critiques.

Challenging traditional assumptions in a discipline is like tugging at a loose thread. If you pull hard enough, the whole piece unravels. Just so, one criticism of psychology—that it has largely omitted women and girls in research studies—leads to questioning deeply rooted disciplinary views not only about women but also about all of human behavior, and about science. If psychology's findings about women reveal bias, then psychology's stance as an objective, value-free science is in contention. Once objectivity is questioned, basic assumptions that underlie psychological research become problematic. But what do we do once we illuminate the flaws in traditional approaches? Chapter 2, "Epistemological Debates, Feminist Voices," tackles this problem.

Chapter 3, "Rethinking the Distinction between Sex and Gender," challenges not only traditional psychology but also feminist psychology. The success of feminism means that today there is a well-established feminist psychology (or rather, feminist psychologies). To my surprise, today "thinking against the grain" sometimes means contesting feminist thought. One of the core assumptions—at first "against the grain" but by now almost part of a feminist canon—is that sex (our biological heritage) and gender (what societies make of that heritage) are distinct. This distinction was critical to formulating a new psychology of women several years ago. But it is time now to reconsider it.

Deeply rooted in American psychology is a firm belief in individualism—that who we are and what we do is bounded by our skins. Our actions and beliefs are the products of our individual choices and history. But research and theory about women's lives challenge this view, revealing the shaping quality

3

of the social contexts that surround us. Contesting the belief in individualism led me to consider not only the impact of the immediate setting on people's actions, as traditional social psychologists do, but also how the larger social and historical context impinges on our beliefs and actions. Chapter 4, "From Snapshots to Videotape" proposes a new way to study women that includes these overlapping contexts in which we lead our lives.

Recognizing the shaping power of social contexts on women's lives is an important contribution of feminism to psychology. Yet social contexts are not the only determinants of behavior and consciousness. The famous dictum of the 1960s, "the personal is political," reformulated women's personal problems as socially caused. However, considering women's actions only as the product of their social circumstances denies them the ability to be seen as originators of their own actions, or "agentic" in psychological terms. Chapter 5, "Women's Agency in Context," reconceptualizes theories of agency in order to attribute agency to women while recognizing the importance of context.

Feminism in psychology has contributed not only to what we study, but also to how we conduct research. In part because of a desire to create egalitarian relationships, but also because funders and others mandate collaboration, many research projects on violence against women attempt to involve advocates, service providers, and subjects of research in all aspects of the project. Such collaboration may yield useful knowledge for improving services and understanding, but at the same time it presents difficulties. Different stakeholders may vary in their expertise and interests. For example, researchers may want to address long-term questions that arise from prior studies, while advocates may want answers to immediate problems prompted by the pressing needs of their clients. I discuss challenges in collaborative research in chapter 6, "Working Together: Challenges in Collaborative Research on Violence against Women."

Studying women in new ways challenges the traditional scientific methods (which mirror the natural sciences) that psychology has long favored. Changing methods does not mean simply gathering data in new ways. Rather, it shifts the epistemological ground on which we stand—from hypothesis-testing to discovery; from confirming to exploring; from considering those we study as objects to seeing them as subjects, actively creating their realities, as I discuss in chapter 7, "Ways of Knowing and Community Research."

The consequences of our assumptions about gender are significant not only for individual women but also for the way that society is organized. Both the personal and the political, both individual lives and social systems, are rooted in beliefs about gender. Despite their apparently gender-free rhetoric, policies and procedures that do not take gender into account may not be fair to women. Part II of this book addresses that dilemma. For example, sexual harassment policies that do not consider power differentials between men and women may discourage women from reporting harassment, as I discuss in chapter 8, "Gender Dilemmas in Sexual Harassment Policies and Procedures."

Hidden in notions of equality for women is the belief that women should be more like men. Separation, individuation, and personal control—all values traditionally associated with men—underlie much of psychological theory. But emphasizing these values may overlook aspects of human existence that are important not only to women, but also to men as well. The current emphasis in ameliorative policies and practices on "empowerment" may be rooted in notions of power and control that ignore the traditionally female world of relationships and community, as I discuss in chapter 9, "What's Wrong with Empowerment." Moreover, increasing people's feelings of empowerment may do little to increase their actual power.

The "glass ceiling" and the "sticky floor" are metaphors often invoked to describe women's lack of progress at work. Although success stories abound in newspapers and other media, women's advancement up the organizational chart seems to have stalled. Individualistic explanations, founded on a premise that people get what they deserve, attribute women's stalled success to their lack of preparation, or (more recently) their difficulty in combining work and familial obligations. But reframing the issue as an organizational rather than a personal problem puts the spotlight on discriminatory practices in organizations as the cause of women's lack of success. Chapter 10, "Women in Management: An Exploration of Competing Paradigms," discusses the implications of shifting blame for women's lack of achievement from personal deficits to organizational dynamics.

A famous court case in the 1980s illustrated the important practical consequences of this shift. The Equal Employment Opportunity Commission had charged Sears, Roebuck and Co. with sex discrimination by channeling women into lower-paid and less prestigious jobs than men. Sears argued that women's life circumstances led them to choose these jobs, while the opposition countered that women's choices were circumscribed by the opportunities available to them. Research on the interpersonal dynamics of the workplace sheds light on these issues, as I discuss in chapter 11, "Low-Paying Jobs for Women: By Discrimination or by Choice?"

Women may face discrimination at work, but gender issues may cause problems even in all-female organizations. I have been a member, observer, consultant, gadfly, and so on, to many feminist organizations; I am sometimes called in when the organizations face problems in functioning well. The typical "grain of thought" in this situation blames problems on interpersonal dynamics or personal shortcomings. Rather, I reframe these problems, in chapter 12, "Challenges of Success: Stages of Growth in Feminist Organizations," as difficulties that often arise when organizations grow. Shifting the perspective from blaming the person to understanding organizational dynamics illuminates new solutions that go beyond replacing one "bad" worker with a better one.

Perhaps the most significant social-policy change in our lifetimes is the recent welfare reform legislation. Such changes as time limits for welfare receipt and no increases in welfare funding if the family size increases are likely to disproportionately affect women with abusive partners, since rates of violence against women on welfare are alarmingly high. Traditional theories would suggest that, if loss of welfare prompts women to get better paying jobs (as some authors of welfare reform claim), then violence against women should decrease. But feminist perspectives challenge this prediction, as I discuss in chapter 13, "The Impact of Welfare Reform on Men's Violence against Women." If the dynamics of abuse center on the need for control and domination, then a man might become more abusive should a woman's income increase.

Anger prompted me to write the earliest of these chapters, on women in management. I found infuriating the endless stream of media stories exhorting women to remedy their deficits—dress for success or learn to talk like men—if they want to get ahead. This advice ignores the presence of sex discrimination at work, a potent force that no amount of correct speech or tailored dressing can remedy. In using writing to challenge public discourse on women's success, I discovered that writing is a means of channeling emotion, of pouring my anger into a form that would broadcast it widely. Laurel Richardson describes writing as "a method of inquiry, a way of finding out about yourself and your topic."[1] To her, writing is a means to learning and to discovering. To that, I would add that writing is a vehicle for protest, a way to make others see the world my way and in so doing, to challenge their views. Emotion is rarely written about in social science unless it is the object of study, but emotion has propelled me to write these essays.

Postmodernists tell us that language does not mirror reality, it creates reality. We construct a world in the telling of it. If so, these essays hope to manifest a world remade. Social change is the motivating force behind feminism. Lighting the way to a world transformed is the goal of feminist psychology.

2

Epistemological Debates, Feminist Voices

Science, Social Values, and the Study of Women

MODERN SCIENTIFIC METHODS, invented in the sixteenth century, represented not only a stunning technical innovation, but a moral and political one as well, replacing the sacred authority of the Church with science as the ultimate arbiter of truth.[1] Unlike medieval inquiry, modern science conceives itself as a search for knowledge that is free of moral, political, and social values. The application of scientific methods to the study of human behavior distinguished American psychology from philosophy, and enabled it to pursue the respect accorded the natural sciences.[2]

The use of scientific methods to study human beings rests on three assumptions:

(1) since the methodological procedures of natural science are used as a model, human values enter into the study of social phenomena and conduct only as objects; (2) the goal of social scientific investigation is to construct laws or law-like generalizations like those of physics; (3) social science has a technical character, providing knowledge which is solely instrumental.[3]

Numerous critics have challenged each of these assumptions in recent years. Some charge that social science reflects not only the values of individual scientists but also those of the political and cultural milieus in which science is done, and that there are no theory-neutral "facts."[4] Others claim that there are no universal, ahistorical laws of human behavior, only descriptions of how people act in certain places at certain times in history.[5] Still others contend that knowledge is not neutral; rather, it serves an ideological purpose, justifying power.[6] According to this view, versions of reality not only reflect but also legitimate particular forms of social organization and power asymmetries. The belief that knowledge is merely technical, having no ideological function, is refuted by the ways in which science plays handmaiden to social values, providing an aura of scientific authority to prejudicial beliefs about social groups and giving credibility to certain social policies.[7]

Within the context of these general criticisms, feminists have argued in particular that social science research neglects and distorts the study of women in a systematic bias in favor of men. Some contend that the very processes of positivist science are inherently masculine, reflected even in the sexual metaphors employed by the founders of modern science.[8] To Francis Bacon, for example, nature was female, and the goal of science was to "bind her to your service and make her your slave."[9] As Sandra Harding summarizes:

> Mind vs. nature and the body, reason vs. emotion and social commitment, subject vs. object and objectivity vs. subjectivity, the abstract and general vs. the concrete and particular—in each case we are told that the former must dominate the latter lest human life be overwhelmed by irrational and alien forces, forces symbolized in science as the feminine.[10]

Critics see science's insistence on control and distance of the knower from the known as a reflection of the desire for domination characteristic of a culture that subordinates women's interests to those of men.[11] Some go so far as to claim that because traditional scientific methods inevitably distort women's experience, we need a new method based on feminist principles.[12] Others disagree, claiming that the problem in science is not objectivity itself, but rather *lack* of objectivity, which enables male bias to contaminate the scientific process.[13] The first part of this chapter summarizes feminist charges against standard versions of science; the second part explores three possibilities for a distinctly "feminist" response to them: *feminist empiricism, feminist standpoint epistemologies,* and *feminist postmodernism.* (By "feminist," I refer to a system of values that challenges male dominance and advocates social, political, and economic equity of women and men in society.)

Bias within Psychology in the Study of Women

Since Naomi Weisstein denounced much of psychology as the "fantasy life of the male psychologist" in 1971,[14] numerous critics have identified the ways that gender bias permeates social science.[15] For many years, subjects of relevance to women, such as rape or housework, have been considered either "taboo topics" or too trivial to study—marginal to more central and prestigious issues, such as leadership, achievement, and power.[16] Women's invisibility as subjects of research extends to their role as researchers as well, with relatively few women in positions of power or prestige in science.[17] Although more than half of all psychology doctorates since 1986 have been earned by women, only 34 percent of full time faculty in doctoral-degree-granting departments of psychology are women. Only about twenty percent of full professors are female, while women make up sixty percent of lecturers, the lowest-status position.[18] The proportion of editors of psychology journals who are female has remained at 15 percent for years.[19] When women are studied, their actions often are interpreted as deficient compared to those of men. Even theories reflect a male standard.[20] The classic example dates back to Freud's formulation in 1925[21] of the theory of penis envy.

Over the last two decades, critics have compiled a long and continually growing list of threats to the validity of research on women and sex differences.[22] For example, a great many studies include only male samples. Sometimes women are included only as the stimulus, not the subject of study—they are seen but not heard—but conclusions are generalized to everyone.[23] Sex-of-experimenter effects contaminate virtually every area of research,[24] and field studies yield different findings than laboratory research of the same phenomenon.[25] Multiple meanings of the term "sex" confound biological sex differences with factors that vary by sex (i.e., sex-*related* differences) and are more appropriately labeled "gender."[26] Sex is treated as an independent variable in studies of gender difference, even though people cannot be randomly assigned to the "male" or "female" group.[27] When a difference is found, it is usually small, but the small size is often overshadowed by the fact that a difference exists at all.[28] The emphasis on a "difference" model obscures gender similarities;[29] this emphasis is built into the methods of science because experiments are formally designed to *reject* the null hypothesis that there is no difference between the experimental group and the control group. A focus on between-gender differences and a lack of attention to within-gender differences reflects a presupposition of gender polarity that frames this research.[30]

Findings of the magnitude of sex differences have diminished over time, perhaps because of an increasing willingness to publish results when such differences are not significant,[31] or perhaps because of a reduction in operative sex role stereotypes. For example, findings of differences in cognitive abilities appear to have declined precipitously over the years,[32] and researchers have found greater influenceability among females in studies published prior to 1970 than in those published later.[33] Carol Jacklin points out that the more carefully a study is carried out, the less likely it is that gender differences will be found: "With fewer variables confounded with sex, sex will account for smaller percentages of variance. Thus, paradoxically, the better the sex-related research, the less useful sex is as an explanatory variable."[34] The decline in findings of difference suggest either that increasing care in designing studies has eliminated differences that were artifacts of bias, or that historical factors—rather than ahistorical, universal laws—shape behavior,[35] whether it be of subjects or experimenters. In fact, so many studies find no sex differences that this research might more appropriately be called the study of sex similarities.[36]

Psychological research on women often contains another source of bias, the lack of attention to social context. The purpose of the laboratory experiment is to isolate the behavior under study from supposedly extraneous contaminants so that it is affected only by the experimental conditions. The experimental paradigm assumes that subjects leave their social status, history, beliefs, and values behind as they enter the laboratory, or that random assignment vitiates their effects. The result is to abstract people's action from social roles or institutions.[37] Instead of being "contaminants," however, these factors may be critical determinants of behavior. By "stripping" behavior of its social context, psychologists rule out the study of sociocultural and historical factors, and implicitly attribute causes to factors inside the person. Moreover, the absence of consideration of the social context of people's actions is not limited to laboratory research.[38] In an ironic reversal of the feminist dictum of the 1960s, when social context is ignored, the political is misinterpreted as personal.[39]

Ignoring social context may produce reliance on presumed biological causes when other explanations of sex differences are not obvious, even when the biological mechanisms that might be involved are not apparent.[40] Social explanations become residual, although sociocultural determinants may be just as robust and important as biological causes, if not more so.[41] Although biological differences between the sexes are important, it is critical to distinguish between biological difference and the social meaning attached to that difference.[42]

Alice Eagly[43] raises a different objection to experimentation. She disagrees that the psychological experiment is context-stripped, and contends instead that it *constitutes* a particular context. An experiment typically consists of a brief encounter among strangers in an unfamiliar setting, often under the eye of a psychologist. The question is whether this limited situation is a valid one from which to make generalizations about behavior. To Eagly, the problem is that social roles (such as mother, doctor, or corporation president) lose their salience in this setting, bringing to the foreground gender-related expectations about behavior.

Cynthia Fuchs Epstein states that "Much of the bias in social science reporting of gender issues comes from scientists' inability to capture the social context or their tendency to regard it as unnecessary to their inquiry—in a sense, their disdain for it."[44] In psychology, this disdain has at least two sources.[45] First, psychology focuses on the person as he or she exists at the moment. This leads the researcher away from the person's history or social circumstances. Second, the cultural context in which psychology is practiced (at least in the United States) is dominated by an individualistic philosophy.[46] The prevailing beliefs assume that outcomes are due to choices made by free and self-determining individuals; the implication is that people get what they deserve.[47] Assumptions of individualism, and those of male dominance, are often taken for granted so much that we are not aware of them. Recognition that supposedly "scientific" assertions are permeated with ideological beliefs produces, in Shulamit Reinharz's words, a condition of "feminist distrust."[48] Perhaps one of the most difficult challenges facing social scientists is to disengage themselves sufficiently from commonly shared beliefs so that those beliefs do not predetermine research findings.[49]

Feminist Responses to the Criticisms of Science

Challenges to the neutrality of science have long been a concern to those who study women, and such challenges have prompted three different reactions among feminists.[50] Some remain loyal to scientific traditions, attempting to rise above the cultural embedment of these traditions by adhering more closely to the norms of science.[51] Others seek to redress the male-centered bias in science by giving voice to women's experience.[52] Still others abandon traditional scientific methods entirely.[53] Philosopher of science Sandra Harding[54] labels these three approaches *feminist empiricism*, *feminist standpoint science*, and *post-modernism,* respectively (see also Morgan's[55] distinction among positivist, phenomenological, and critical/praxis-oriented research paradigms). Next I shall examine the manifestations of these three positions in the study of the psychology of women.

Feminist Empiricism

The psychologists who identified the problem of "experimenter effects" did not reject experimentation. Instead, they recommended strategies to minimize the impact of the experimenter.[56] Likewise, feminist empiricists advocate closer adherence to the tenets of science as the solution to the problem of bias. From this perspective, bias is considered error in a basically sound system, an outbreak of irrationality in a rational process. Scrupulous attention to scientific methods will eliminate error, or at least minimize its impact on research findings.[57] Once neutrality is restored, scientific methods, grounded in rationality, will give access to the truth.

Maureen McHugh and her colleagues[58] present a set of guidelines for eliminating bias. In addition to obvious corrections of the problems just described, other steps can be taken to insure that the impact of the researcher's values is minimized, such as specifying the circumstances in which gender differences are found (because contexts tend to be deemed more appropriate for one sex than the other) and assessing experimental tasks for their sex-neutrality (because many tasks are perceived to be sex-linked).[59] The sex composition of the group of participants in research also may affect behavior because individuals act differently in the presence of females or males.[60] Finally, attention ought to be paid to findings of sex similarities as well as sex differences, and to the magnitude of such differences reported.

These suggestions are intended to produce gender-fair research using traditional scientific methods. A truly neutral science will produce unbiased knowledge, which in turn will serve as a basis for a more just social policy.[61] Yet the continuing identification of numerous instances of androcentric bias in research has led some to conclude that value-free research is impossible, even if it is done by those of good faith.[62] Technical safeguards cannot completely rule out the influence of values; scientific rigor in testing hypotheses cannot eliminate bias in theories or in the selection of problems for inquiry.[63] Hence critics assert that traditional methods do not reveal reality, but rather act as constraints that limit our understanding of women's experiences.

Feminist Standpoint Epistemologies

Feminist empiricism argues that the characteristics of the knower are irrelevant to the discovery process if the norms of science are followed. In contrast, feminist standpoint epistemologies claim that we should center our science on women because "what we know and how we know depend on who we are, that is, on the knower's historical locus and his or her position in the social hierarchy."[64] There are several justifications for this viewpoint.[65] First, some argue that women's cognitive processes and modes of research are different than men's. A contrast has been suggested between a supposedly "feminine" communal style of research, which emphasizes cooperation of the researcher and subjects, an appreciation of natural contexts, and the use of qualitative data, and a supposedly "masculine" agentic orientation, which places primacy on distance of the researcher from the subjects, manipulation of subjects and the environment, and the use of quantitative data.[66] Evelyn Fox Keller[67] attempts to provide grounds for this position in a psychoanalytic view of child development. She argues that the male child's need to differentiate himself from his mother leads him to equate autonomy with distance from others.[68] The process of developing a masculine sense of self thus establishes in the male a style of thinking that both reflects and produces the emphasis in science on distance, power and control. Keller identifies an alternative model of science based not on controlling but rather on "conversing with" nature.

Keller's argument that science need not be based on domination is salutary, but her explanation is problematic. She presumes, first, that males and females have quite different experiences in infancy, and second, that those early experiences shape the activities of adult scientists; she does not, however, substantiate these claims. The supposedly masculine emphasis on separation and autonomy may be a manifestation of Western mainstream culture rather than a universal distinction between females and males. Black men and women who returned from northern U.S. cities to live in the rural South manifest a relational as opposed to an autonomous self-image,[69] and both Eastern and African world views see individuals as interdependent and connected, in contrast to the Western emphasis on a bounded and independent self.[70] Identifying a masculine cognitive style as the grounds for scientific methods seems to doom most women and perhaps nonwhite men to outsider status. Furthermore, an emphasis on cognitive style ignores the role played by social structure, economics, and politics in determining topics and methods of study.[71] Experimental methods in psychology characterized by control and objectivity are accorded prestige partly because they emulate the highly valued physical sciences.[72] Within social science, the prestige of a study mirrors the prestige of its topic.[73] Sociocultural factors such as these seem more likely to be determinants of the shape of science than individual psychology.

A more plausible basis for a feminist standpoint epistemology is the argument that women's life experiences are not fully captured in existing conceptual schemes. Research often equates "male" with the general, typical case, and considers "female" to be the particular—a subgroup demarcated by biology.[74] Yet analytical categories appropriate for males may not fit women's experience. Dorothy Smith[75] argues that women are alienated from their own experience by having to frame that experience in terms of men's conceptual schemes; in Smith's terms they have a "bifurcated consciousness"—daily life grounded in female experience but only male conceptual categories with which to interpret that experience. Starting our inquiries from a subordinate group's experience will uncover the limits of the dominant group's conceptual schemes where they do not fully fit the subordinates.[76] Accordingly, a science based on women's traditional place in society not only would generate categories appropriate to women, but also would be a means of discovering the underlying organization of society as a whole.[77]

In contrast to traditional social science in which the researcher is the expert on assessing reality, an interpretive/phenomenological approach permits women to give their own conception of their experiences. Participants, not researchers, are considered the experts at making sense of their world.[78] The shift in authority is striking. Yet phenomenological approaches are limited by the requirement that the subjects studied be verbal and reflective.[79] In addition, such approaches run the risk of psychological reductionism (attributing causation simply to internal, psychological factors).[80]

Carol Gilligan's[81] theory of women's moral development is the most influential psychological study in this tradition. Her work asserting that women stress caring in the face of moral dilemmas (in contrast to men's emphasis on justice) has been criticized because other researchers have found no sex differences in moral reasoning using standardized scales.[82] Gilligan retorts that women's responses on those scales are not relevant to her purposes: "The fact that educated women are capable of high levels of justice reasoning has no bearing on the question of whether they would spontaneously choose to frame moral problems in this way. My interest in the way people *define* moral problems is reflected in my research methods, which have centered on first-person accounts of moral conflict."[83] Although standardized scales might tell us what women have in common with men, they will not reveal the way women would define their own experiences if given the opportunity to do so. The absence (and impossibility) of a comparison group of men in Gilligan's definitive study of twenty-nine women considering abortions, however, raises questions about whether moral orientations are sex-linked.[84]

The feminist standpoint epistemologies aim not simply to substitute "woman-centered" for "man-centered" gender loyalties, but rather to provide a basis for a more accurate understanding of the entire world. Howard Becker[85] claims that "in any system of ranked groups, participants take it as given that members of the highest group have the right to define the way things really are. . . . Credibility and the right to be heard are differentially distributed through the ranks of the system." Feminist standpoint epistemologies argue that traditional methods of science give credibility only to the dominant group's views. Listening to subordinates reveals the multifocal nature of reality.[86] The term "subjugated knowledges" describes the perspectives of those sufficiently low on the hierarchy that their interpretations do not reflect the predominant modes of thought.[87] Giving voice to women's perspective means identifying the ways in which women create meaning and experience life from their particular position in the social hierarchy.

Moreover, women (and minorities) sometimes have a better vantage point on society than majorities do because minority status can render people socially invisible, permitting them access to the majority group that is not reciprocated.[88] Accordingly, incorporating subordinates' experience will not only "add" women and minorities to existing understandings, but will add a more thorough understanding of the dominant group as well. For example, bell hooks[89] describes African-Americans in her small Kentucky hometown as having a double vision. They looked from the "outside-in" at the more affluent white community across the railroad tracks, but their perspective shifted to "inside-out" when they crossed those tracks to work for white employers. Movement across the tracks was regulated, however: whites did not cross over to the black community, and laws ensured that blacks returned to it.

The arguments for a feminist standpoint epistemology have stimulated rich and valuable portrayals of women's experience. Yet there are problems with a feminist standpoint as the basis for science. First, assuming a commonality to all women's experience glosses over differences among women of various racial and ethnic groups and social classes.[90] The life experience of a woman wealthy enough to hire childcare and household help may have more in common with her spouse than with a poor woman trying to raise her children on a welfare budget. Standpoint epistemology can recognize multiple subordinated groups demarcated by gender, race, social class, and so on. Yet carried to an extreme, this position seems to dissolve science into autobiography. A critical challenge for feminist standpoint epistemology is to identify the commonalities of subjugated experience among different groups of women without losing sight of their diversity. Moreover, those who are subjugated may still adhere to a dominant group's ideology.

Furthermore, we each have multiple status identities.[91] The poet Audre Lorde describes herself as "a forty-nine-year-old Black lesbian feminist socialist mother of two, including one boy, and a member of an interracial couple."[92] Each of these identities becomes salient in a different situation; at times, they conflict within the same situation. The hyphenated identities which we all experience in different ways—black feminist, lesbian mother, Asian-American, and so on—call into question the unity of the category of woman, making it difficult to generalize about "women's experience."[93]

Nonetheless, feminist standpoint epistemologies do not claim that social status alone allows the viewer clarity. Reasonable judgments about whether views are empirically supported are still possible. Rather than proclaiming the "one true story" about the world, feminist standpoint epistemologies seek partial and less distorted views. These partial views, or "situated knowledges," can be far less limited than the dominant view.[94]

Feminist Postmodernism

A number of perspectives, including Marxism, psychoanalysis, and postmodernism, share a challenge to the primacy of reason and the dignity and autonomy of the individual. Here I focus on postmodernism, and, in particular, poststructuralism, because of its influence on an emerging stream of feminist psychology.[95] A traditional social scientist entering the terrain of poststructuralism at times feels a bit like Alice falling into a Wonderland of bewildering language and customs that look superficially like her own yet are not. Things that seem familiar and stable—the meaning of words, for example—become problematic. What once were nouns (e.g., privilege, valor, foreground) now are verbs. Even the landscape looks different, as words themselves are chopped up with parentheses and hyphens to make visible their multiple meanings. What is most unsettling, perhaps, is the fundamental poststructuralist assertion that science does not mirror reality, but rather creates it—that is, that science is a process of invention rather than discovery.[96] Many scientists would agree that an unmediated perception of reality is impossible to obtain and that research findings represent (rather than mirror) reality. These scientists would, however, maintain that some representations are better than others. The traditional scientific criteria of validity, ability to generalize, and so forth determine how close research findings come to actual "truth." In contrast, poststructuralists reject traditional notions of "truth" and "reality;" they claim instead that power enables some to define what is or is not considered knowledge. Expressing our understanding of experience must be done through language, but language is not a neutral reflection of that experience because our linguistic categories are not neutral:

> If statements and not things are true or false, then truth is necessarily linguistic: if truth is linguistic, then it is relative to language use (words, concepts, statements, discourses) at a given time and place; therefore, ideology, interests, and power arrangements at a given time and place are implicated in the production of what counts as "true."[97]

Or, as Humpty Dumpty said to Alice in *Through the Looking Glass*:[98]

> "When I use a word," Humpty Dumpty said, in a rather scornful tone, "it means just what I choose it to mean—neither more or less."
> "The question is," said Alice, "whether you *can* make words mean so many different things."
> "The question is," said Humpty Dumpty, "which is to be master—that's all."

The central question in poststructuralism is not how well our theories fit the "facts," or how well the "facts" produced by research fit what is "real." Rather, the question is which values and social institutions are favored by each of multiple versions of reality (i.e., discourses). Of critical concern is whose interests are served by competing ways of giving meaning to the world.[99] Feminists of a postmodern bent claim that positivism's neutral and disinterested stance masks what is actually the male conception of reality; this conception reflects and maintains male power interests.[100] As legal scholar Catherine MacKinnon puts it, "Objectivity—the nonsituated, universal standpoint, whether claimed or aspired to—is a denial of the existence of potency of sex inequality that tacitly participates in constructing reality from the dominant point of view."[101] In MacKinnon's view, the law, rather than being neutral, "sees and treats women the way men see and treat women."[102] The same criticism can be made about traditional social science in its exclusion, distortion, and neglect of women.

The social constructionist stance, as poststructuralism is known within psychology,[103] offers a particular challenge to the psychology of women. In contrast to feminist empiricism, the central question no longer asks whether sex/gender differences exist. Knowing the truth about difference is impossible.[104] Varying criteria of "differentness" can produce divergent findings, for example, when conclusions based on averages contradict those based on the amount of overlap of scores of males and females.[105] When an assumed difference is not scientifically supported, the argument simply shifts to another variable.[106] And similar findings can be interpreted in opposing ways. Given the impossibility of settling these questions, poststructuralism shifts the emphasis to the question of difference itself:[107]

> What do we make of gender differences? What do they mean? Why are there so many? Why are there so few? Perhaps we should be asking, What is the point of differences? What lies beyond difference? Difference aside, what else is gender? The overarching question is choice of question.[108]

One goal of a feminist constructionist science is "disrupting and displacing dominant (oppressive) knowledges" in part by articulating the values supported by alternate conceptions of reality.[109] An analysis of two contrasting perspectives on sex differences demonstrates the relationship among values, assumptive frameworks, and social consequences. According to Rachel Hare-Mustin and Jeanne Maracek,[110] the received views of men and women tend either to exaggerate or to minimize the differences between them. On the one hand, the tendency to emphasize differences fosters an appreciation of supposedly feminine qualities, but it simultaneously justifies unequal treatment of women and ignores variability within each sex group. The consequence of emphasizing difference, then, is to support the status quo. On the other hand, the tendency to minimize differences justifies women's access to educational and job opportunities, but it simultaneously overlooks the fact that equal treatment is not always equitable because of differences in men's and women's position in a social hierarchy. Gender-neutral grievance procedures in organizations, for example, do not apply equally to men and women if men are consistently in positions of greater power.[111]

Researchers have widely different interpretations of the implications of poststructural critiques for social science methods. Some employ empirical techniques for poststructuralist ends. Social constructionists see traditional research methods as a means of providing "objectifications" or illustrations, similar to vivid photographs, that are useful in making an argument persuasive rather than in validating truth claims.[112] Traditional methods can also help identify varying versions of reality. For example, Celia Kitzinger[113] used Q-sort methodology to distinguish five separate accounts of lesbians' beliefs about the origin of their sexual orientation. Techniques of attitude measurement can also be used to assess the extent to which people share certain versions of reality. Rhoda Unger and her colleagues used surveys to assess belief in an objectivist or subjectivist epistemology, finding that adherence to a particular perspective varied with social status.[114]

Others propose that we treat both psychological theories and people's actions and beliefs as "texts," that is, discursive productions located in a specific historical and cultural context and shaped by power, rather than as accounts (distorted or otherwise) of experience.[115] Methods developed in other disciplines, particularly literary criticism, can be used to analyze these texts. For example, through careful reading of an interview transcript with an eye to discerning "discursive patterns of meaning, contradictions, and inconsistencies," Gavey[116] identifies cultural themes of "permissive sexuality" and "male sexual needs" in statements by a woman about her experiences of heterosexual coercion.[117] A particular technique of discourse analysis, deconstruction, can be used to expose ideological assumptions in written or spoken language, as Martin[118] does to identify forces that suppress women's achievement within organizations. Deconstruction highlights the revealing quality not just of what is said, but rather of what is left out, contradictory, or inconsistent in the text. Deconstruction offers a provocative technique for analyzing hidden assumptions. Yet it is a potentially endless process, capable of an infinite regress, since any deconstruction can itself be deconstructed.[119]

The absence of any criteria for evaluation means that the success of accounts of social construction "depend primarily on the analyst's capacity to invite, compel, stimulate, or delight the audience, and not on criteria of veracity."[120] This raises the possibility that what Grant said in another context could apply here: "Such theories risk devolving into authoritarian non-theories more akin to religions."[121] The relativism of poststructuralism can be countered, however, by the identification of moral criteria for evaluation.[122] Theory and research can be assessed in terms of their pragmatic utility in achieving certain social and political goals rather than the allegedly neutral rules of science.[123] However, because feminists disagree about whether celebrating women's difference or emphasizing the similarity of the sexes is most likely to change women's basic condition of subordination,[124] agreement about criteria for evaluation seems unlikely.

What poses perhaps the greatest dilemma for feminists is the view of the subject advocated by poststructuralist theory. Poststructuralists consider the attribution of agency and intentionality to the subject to be part of a deluded liberal humanism, complicit with the status quo. The multiple discourses of selfhood, intentionality, and so forth, which are present in our culture, compete for dominance; those which prevail constitute individual subjectivity. Social cognition on the part of the individual is channeled into certain ways of thinking that dominate society (although resistance is possible). Those discourses antedate our consciousness, and give meaning to our experience which otherwise has no essential meaning.[125] In contrast, feminist standpoint epistemologies consider individuals to be the active construers of their reality, albeit within a particular social and historical context. Women's subjectivity is considered an important source of information about their experience. Poststructuralism's rejection of intentionality on the part of the individual seems to deny the validity of women's voices just at a time when women are beginning to be heard.[126]

Poststructuralism offers a provocative critique of social science and makes us critically aware of the relationship of knowledge and power. Yet the focus on "problematizing the text" of our disciplines, while admirably self-reflexive, can lead to an inward emphasis that neglects the study of women in society. In a parallel manner, poststructuralism's emphasis on language as determining consciousness can lead to the disregard of other determinants, such as women's position in a social hierarchy.[127] Furthermore, Unger identifies a dilemma for social scientists who reject traditional empirical methods:

> The attempt to infer cause-and-effect relationships about human behavior using the tools of empiricism is one of the few unique contributions that psychology as a discipline can offer to the rest of scholarship. If such tools may not be used by feminist psychologists there is little likelihood that their insights will be taken seriously by the rest of the discipline.[128]

Feminist foremothers in psychology such as Helen Thompson (Woolley) and her colleagues at the start of the twentieth century used traditional scientific methods to contest social myths about women;[129] these methods may still serve that purpose today. Poststructuralists would likely retort that the fact that Thompson's insights have had to be repeatedly rediscovered (or, rather, reinvented) demonstrates that power, not "truth," determines which version of reality will prevail.

Is There a Feminist Method?

On the basis of multiple critiques of the social sciences, some propose an alternative research method based on feminist values. The lack of consensus on what values are feminist makes this a daunting project, yet many would agree on the need for more interactive, contextualized methods in the service of emancipatory goals.[130] A feminist method should produce a study not just *of* women, but also *for* women, helping to change the world as well as to describe it.[131] Mary Gergen advocates the following as central tenets of a feminist method:

1. recognizing the interdependence of experimenter and subject;
2. avoiding the decontextualizing of the subject or experimenter from their social and historical surroundings;
3. recognizing and revealing the nature of one's values within the research context;
4. accepting that facts do not exist independently of their producers' linguistic codes;
5. demystifying the role of the scientists and establishing an egalitarian relationship between science makers and science consumers.[132] (See also Wilkinson.[133])

Joan Acker and her colleagues[134] attempted to implement feminist principles in a study of women who had been primarily wives and mothers and were starting to enter the labor market (see also Lather[135]). Interviews became dialogues, mutual attempts to "clarify and expand understandings." Often friendships developed between researchers and the women in the study. Acker and her colleagues discovered that these methods are not without problems. The researcher's need to collect information can (perhaps inadvertently) lead to the manipulation of friendship in the service of the research. Methods that create trust between researchers and participants entail the risk of exploitation, betrayal, and abandonment by the researcher.[136] Acker's study took place over a number of years, and each participant's interpretation of her life was constantly changing in hindsight, raising problems of validity in the research. The desire to give participants an opportunity to comment on researchers' interpretations of the interviews became a source of tension when disagreements arose. The solution to these dilemmas reached by Acker and her colleagues— to report the women's lives in their own words as much as possible—was not satisfactory to the women in the study, who wanted more analysis of their experience. Finally, it was difficult to determine if this research experience had an emancipatory effect on participants. Intending to create social change is no assurance of actually doing so.

The conflict between the researcher's perspective and that of the participants in this study raises a critical issue for those who reject positivism's belief in the scientist as expert. Since a feminist method (at least according to the principles just listed here) assumes that there is no neutral observer, whose interpretations should prevail when those of the researcher and the people under study conflict? Feminism places primacy on acknowledging and validating female experience,[137] yet postmodern perspectives challenge the authority of the individual.[138] Consider, for example, Andersen's 1981 study of twenty corporate wives.[139] She disbelieved their claims of contentment and attributed their lack of feminism to "false consciousness," a Marxist term meaning that these women identified with (male) ruling class interests against their own (female) class interests. The women wrote a rebuttal rejecting Andersen's interpretation. In response, Andersen revised her position to accept the women's statements of satisfaction with their lives. Instead of treating them as deluded or insincere, she looked for sources of their contentment in their position in the social hierarchy. Lather[140] recommends this kind of dialogic process to avoid imposing on research participants interpretations which disempower them (see also Kidder[141]). Without it, we grant privilege to the authority of the researcher, even if on postmodern rather than positivist grounds.

Conclusion

Although the strategies intended as a "feminist method" overcome some of the objections to traditional social science, they raise as many problems as they solve.[142] No method or epistemology seems devoid of limitations, or perfectly true to feminist values, which are themselves contested.[143] Feminism is more useful as a set of questions—a course of "strategic heresy" that challenges the prevailing asymmetries of power and androcentric assumptions in science and society—rather than as a basis for a unique method.[144] Feminism thus identifies "patterns and interrelationships and causes and effects and implications of questions that nonfeminists have not seen and still do not see."[145]

The psychological study of women emerged from the field of individual differences. Dominated by the question of sex differences, this tradition assumes that an inner core of traits or abilities distinguishes women from men.[146] Such a conceptualization no longer seems useful. Few gender differences in personality or abilities have been reliably demonstrated,[147] and factors other than individual dispositions influence our interpersonal behavior.[148] A more appropriate strategy for the study of women would consider the ways in which gender is created and maintained through interpersonal processes.[149]

From this perspective, gender does not reside within the person. Instead, it is constituted by the myriad ways in which we "do" rather than "have" gender; that is, we validate our membership in a particular gender category through interactional processes.[150] Gender is something we enact, not an inner core or constellation of traits that we express; it is a pattern of social organization that structures the relations, especially the power relations, between women and men:[151] "In doing gender, men are also doing dominance and women are doing deference."[152] Transsexuals know well that merely altering one's sex organs does not change one's gender. Membership in the category of "male" or "female" must be affirmed continuously through processes of interaction.[153]

Each of the epistemological positions described here can contribute to this perspective. An interactional conceptualization of gender recognizes that the behavior and thoughts of men and women are channeled into certain sociocultural forms, as poststructuralism claims. As Manicas and Secord explain: "Social structures (e.g., language) are reproduced and transformed by action, but they preexist for individuals. They enable persons to become persons and to act (meaningfully and intentionally), yet at the same time, they are 'coercive,' limiting the ways we can act."[154] The dominant ideology of a society is manifested in and reproduced by the social relations of its members.[155] Unlike poststructuralism, however, an interactional view of gender also acknowledges individual agency in the production and transformation of social forms. Such a perspective would regard the person as an initiator of action and construer of meaning within a context composed not only of varying modes of interpreting the world but also of structural constraints and opportunities,[156] as standpoint epistemology claims.

Diverse methods are needed to capture the rich array of personal and structural factors that shape women and girls and which, in turn, are shaped by them.[157] What is critical is that we are aware of the epistemological commitments—and value assumptions—we make when we adopt a particular research strategy.[158] Moreover, the systematic examination of assumptions and values in the social order which shape scientific practices can strengthen objectivity, rather than abandon it.[159]

Epistemological debates in recent years have shattered the traditional picture of science as neutral, disinterested, and value-free, and have replaced it with a view of knowledge as socially constructed. Feminists' contributions to this debate highlight not only the androcentric nature of social science, but also its collusion in the perpetuation of male dominance in society. To assume that the multiple voices of women are not shaped by domination is to ignore social context and legitimate the status quo. On the other hand, to assume that women have no voice other than an echo of prevailing discourses is to deny them agency and, simultaneously, to repudiate the possibility of social change. The challenge to psychology is to link a vision of women's agency with an understanding of the shaping power of social context.

3

Rethinking the Distinction
between Sex and Gender

THE STUDY OF SEX DIFFERENCES has a long history in psychology. Beginning
with the emergence of experimentation at the end of the nineteenth century, researchers (many of them women) attempted to identify empirically the
"true" differences between men and women.[1] At least three obstacles stymied
these projects: Some studies found inconsistent results; many studies found no
differences between the sexes; and it was impossible to create a nonsexist environment in which the essential natures of males and females could emerge un-
tainted.[2] One way out of the impasse was to shift from the study of cognitive and
behavioral sex differences to the exploration of "masculinity" and "femininity"
as opposite and complementary substrates of personality. Anne Constantinople's[3]
argument that femininity and masculinity were neither unidimensional nor
bipolar led to a further shift to the study of androgyny. Acknowledging that an
individual could be high in both "masculinity" and "femininity," the concept of
androgyny freed personality traits from a corporeal base, although it continued
to label some traits as "masculine" and others as "feminine."[4] Moving beyond a
focus on personality traits, contemporary approaches highlight the importance
of status and power in determining sex differences in behavior and attitudes.[5]

Critical to the evolution of this stream of research is the conceptual distinction of sex (i.e., one's biological properties) from gender (i.e., the cultural expectations of those in a certain sex category).[6] John Money and his colleagues provided one of the earliest distinctions between sex and gender in pointing out that
gender identity, one's sense of oneself as male or female, is not bound to biological sex.[7] Separating gender from sex clarifies the assumption that behaviors or
personality traits are not inextricably linked to biology; that is, that sex differences may be as much a product of culture as of nature and that there are as
many ways of being "female" as there are different cultures. The replacement
of the term "gender differences" by the currently popular usage "gender-related
differences" further emphasizes the uncoupling of gender from sex. Confusion
of the terms "sex" and "gender" reflects conflicting and muddled views about
the underlying causes of phenomena linked with female or male status.[8]

In psychology, Rhoda Unger[9] advocated the adoption of the dual vocabulary
of sex and gender, not only to limit assumptions of biological causality associated
with findings of sex differences, but also to highlight the importance of gender
as a stimulus variable, that is, how the label "male" or "female" alters others' ex-

pectations and perceptions. Feminist psychology currently emphasizes the way gender is negotiated through interpersonal interactions that reflect and reinforce an unequal distribution of power and resources in society.[10] Sex is important primarily as a static cue that assigns people to a particular gender category; hence, biological properties are relevant only as they are socially meaningful.

Distinguishing gender from sex has facilitated feminist research on the social construction of gender, that is, the cultural, social, political, and economic forces that shape relations between men and women. Eschewing biological determinism, much of this research treats culture as if it were completely separate and distinguishable from biology. Some claim that all sex differences other than those engaged in reproduction are socially constructed, suggesting that these differences are infinitely plastic and culturally malleable.[11] From this perspective, bodies are neutral or merely blank slates on which culture inscribes its dictates. This view risks overlooking important, biologically linked aspects of women's (and men's) experience. A woman's breastfeeding may affect her attitude toward her children, while a stressful occupation may affect women's and men's physiology in different ways. Certainly bodies are subject to cultural interpretation, but an emphasis on gender to the exclusion of sex (or on culture to the exclusion of biology) may disregard potentially important aspects of people's lives.[12] A belief that biology is irrelevant may indeed hold women to a male standard of behavior. For example, many organizational policies ignore the fact that a woman's career-building years coincide with her childbearing years. These policies are not neutral; they are instead designed with the expectation that employees are male.

Including biology in a feminist psychology of women requires that we make explicit the assumptions underlying our conceptions of sex and gender. In this chapter, I examine problems with the concepts of sex and gender. I then criticize the assumed separation between sex and gender that stems from what I will argue is a false distinction between nature and nurture. Simple dichotomies such as "male/female" or "culture/nature" obscure the complex connections between their two poles while typically giving primacy to one of the pair. I conclude by advocating the use of a transactional model of the relationship between biology and the social environment as a strategy for including biology in the study of women and men.

Problems with the Conceptualization
of Sex and Gender

Much of the research using the distinction between sex and gender assumes not only that sex is based on biology and gender on culture, but also that both are dimorphic. That is, two genders are assumed to parallel two sexes. These assumptions are problematic.

Five Sexes, Not Two?

As Unger[13] noted, the division of sex into dichotomous categories is not always self-evident. The hormones associated with sex—androgen, estrogen, and progesterone—exist in both males and females, albeit in different proportions. People who have ambiguous or contradictory sex characteristics also challenge our assumption of sexual dimorphism. The external genitalia and internal sex characteristics that occur congruently in most individuals may conflict in as many as 4 percent of the population.[14] Intersexed individuals provide so many combinations of male and female sex characteristics that geneticist Anne Fausto-Sterling has created three more sex categories to facilitate proper classification.[15] She adds to "male" and "female" the categories "merms" (for those who have testes and some aspects of female genitalia but no ovaries), "ferms" (for those who have ovaries and some aspects of male genitalia but lack testes) and "herms" (hermaphrodites: for those who have one testis and one ovary). Although Western culture rejects the notion of more than two sexes (and supports that rejection with surgical intervention), some societies, such as the Sambia of Papua New Guinea or those in the Dominican Republic, have a third social category for intersexed "females" who become male at puberty. These societies have three sexes (e.g., male, female, and *guevedoche* or "penis at twelve" in the Dominican Republic) but only two genders.[16]

The need to identify the infant's "true sex" as male or female is a fairly modern invention. In the Middle Ages, individuals with hermaphroditic characteristics were free to decide at adolescence which sex to belong to, although they had to stick to that choice or be punished. Today, a general assumption in Western culture is that people have a "primary, profound, determined and determining sexual identity," discoverable at birth.[17] In cases of intersexed infants, doctors assign sex based on the length of the penis, a literal example of phallocentrism. As Suzanne Kessler[18] pointed out, physicians who treat the intersexed engage in a curious semantic reversal. They do not consider the ambiguous genitalia that are present at birth to be natural; rather, surgery restores the body to a "natural" state.

At the heart of the need to identify "true sex" is the belief that one's sex "hides the most secret parts of the individual: the structures of his fantasies, the roots of his ego, the forms of his relationship to reality."[19] Hence, "proper" identification of the intersexed child's biological nature is necessary not only for purposes of sex classification but also because one's psychological essence resides in sex. Not only is the blending of bodies prohibited but also the blend-

ing of minds. Without assignment as male or female, and without surgical intervention to reinforce that assignment, an intersexed child has been thought
in the modern era to be doomed to be a psychological misfit.[20]

Kessler[21] has argued that physicians undertake genital reconstruction of intersexed infants not because ambiguous genitalia are life-threatening to the
child, but because they are threatening to a culture founded on a two-sex system. As Fausto-Sterling[22] points out, laws governing the military draft, marriage, the family, and sexuality are posited on a two-sex system; hence the state
and the legal system have an interest in maintaining the belief in sexual dimorphism. But such a belief defies nature, since almost all biological aspects
of gender exist on a continuum rather than in discrete categories.[23] Males have
relatively more "male" sex hormones while females have relatively more "female" ones, yet some individuals have hormone levels below those of their assigned sex but above those of the other sex. Even Fausto-Sterling's[24] categories
of "merms" and "ferms" treat as disjunctive differences that actually are continuous.

Perhaps the recognition of multiple sex categories will help break down the
dichotomous thinking that pervades attitudes about the sexes. In a five-sex system, it is impossible to talk about the "opposite" sex. Parents of two children
tend to describe their children in contrasting terms: one is a leader, the other
a follower; one is shy, the other aggressive. But parents of three or four children focus on unique aspects of each child in their descriptions, emphasizing
diversity rather than opposition.[25] Recognizing that the variables that make
up biological sex exist on continua rather than in mutually exclusive categories
may help break down the conceptualization of the sexes as paired opposites.

Many Genders—or None?

Gender, likewise, is not a simple dichotomy. Some cultures have a third gender that, like the Zuni "berdache," allows men to combine elements of male
and female social roles,[26] although few cultures permit females to act out the
male gender role.[27] The prevalence of a belief in a two-sex system obscures the
perception of cultural systems that are not binary.[28] In addition, gender is
fluid; its salience varies with the social context.[29] Furthermore, gender must
be viewed in the context of other demographic variables that have social im-
port, such as race and ethnicity. Feminist theorists have long recognized that
we cannot talk about "women," only about women in the context of their ethnicity, social class and so forth (e.g., African-American women, young women,
poor women, etc.)[30] The expectations and life experience of women may be
defined as much by other demographic factors—such as race or poverty—as
by gender. Even the capacity to bear children, sometimes thought a common

denominator among women, is not shared by all. Yet women who are infertile are no less women. Ultimately this stream of thought should dissipate "woman"—or any other demographic variable—as a unitary category of analysis.

Many behaviors thought to be related to gender might actually be associated with status or power. What is considered feminine is frequently the product of powerlessness and low status.[31] For example, although Carol Gilligan[32] linked with gender an emphasis on rationality compared to relatedness in moral decision-making, Rachel Hare-Mustin and Jeanne Maracek[33] reframed Gilligan's distinction, making status rather than gender the determining factor. Those in higher positions tend to advocate rules and rationality, while those lower in the hierarchy must focus on connection and communal goals to survive. From this perspective, gender is not the sum of individual personality characteristics attributed to males and females, but the product of interactional processes occurring within particular contexts that reflect and reinforce the distribution of resources in society.

Problems with the Nature-Nurture Distinction

Problems in understanding the relationship between sex and gender stem from an underlying assumption that nature is distinct from culture. This belief is deeply imbedded in our society and in our science. As philosopher of science Sandra Harding observed, "the culture/nature dichotomy structures public policy, institutional and individual social practices, the organization of the disciplines (the social versus the natural sciences), indeed the very way we see the world around us."[34]

The distinction between nature and culture—itself a product of culture— has been attacked on several grounds. First, some argue that our views of nature impose cultural stereotypes on the natural world: what we consider to be the "facts" of biology are actually the interpretations generated by culture. Others make the opposite argument, that culture is simply the manifestation of biology. In a third position, which I will argue is the most useful for the study of women and gender, nature and culture are inextricably entwined. Here I examine each of these positions briefly.

Biology as Culture

Some argue that rather than mirroring or even reflecting nature, biology (and indeed, all science) is permeated by cultural stereotypes of male and female that mediate and distort how we see reality. From this perspective, the "facts" purported to be discovered by biologists are merely cultural interpretations invented by them.[35] Critics have challenged the disinterestedness of scientists on many grounds.[36] Science is embedded in, not distinct from, society, and the values and interests of the times affect scientists. In biologist Ruth Hubbard's words, "Science is made by people who live at a specific time in a specific place and whose thought patterns reflect the truths that are accepted by the wider society."[37] Feminist critics have pointed out the ways in which theories and practices in science reflect and reinforce a belief in male superiority.[38]

Take, for example, research on the egg and the sperm. As eighth-grade biology class taught us, the egg and the sperm unite to create a fertilized egg, the basis of human life. But anthropologist Emily Martin[39] has drawn a convincing picture of how, when scientists study fertilization, they view that process through a lens of stereotypes of masculinity and femininity that colors what they see. Males are seen as *producing* sperm while females *shed* eggs, a less active process; the sperm is described in active terms, such as "burrow" and "penetrate", while the lowly egg "is transported" or even "drifts." The heroic sperm ventures up a dark passageway to find the dormant egg, the prize of its perilous journey. The female is seen as passive in this process, although as biosociologist Alice Rossi reminds us, "inert substances such as dead sperm and even particles of India ink reach the oviducts as rapidly as live sperm do."[40] In short, biologists describe the process of fertilization in terms that "feminized" the passive egg and "masculinized" the active, aggressive sperm.[41]

Recently, however, this fairy tale has taken a modern twist: Current research suggests that adhesive molecules on the surface of the egg trap the sperm. Rather than a passive maiden, the egg now is depicted as an aggressive sperm-catcher, and fertilization the result of interaction between the two. But this picture too taints new data with old stereotypes: the egg is now portrayed as engulfing and devouring rather than passive and waiting. The common thread running through these interpretations is the stereotypes about women that they reflect.[42]

Certainly biology is a product of culture, but it is not simply limited to reproducing cultural stereotypes.[43] The socially constructed nature of biology allows the possibility of bias, but it does not mean that bias will predominate. As Fausto-Sterling[44] pointed out, "The activities of scientists are self-deluding *and* self-correcting; they are at once potentially progressive and retrogressive." Strategies exist for minimizing the impact of cultural blinders on science. Biologist Ruth Hubbard,[45] for example, proposed making explicit the implicit assumptions that underlie scientific descriptions and interpretations, while philosopher of science Sandra Harding[46] advocated starting scientific inquiry from the perspective of women and other subordinate groups in order to reduce the distorted vision that comes from a position of dominance.

Culture as Biology

The opposite of the claim that science simply reproduces culture is the proposition that culture is always biologically bound. One meaning of this claim is that social as well as biological influences are always mediated through the central nervous system. Because the elements of culture that shape our biological beings are themselves experienced biologically, culture is always mediated by biology. Accordingly, as Money[47] acerbically put it, the opposite of our biological selves is not culture, but rather our astral beings.

Biological determinists take a further step, claiming that biology inevitably and inescapably determines relations between the sexes. Drawing on evolutionary theory, for example, sociobiologists claim that social behavior has a biological basis in the need of a surviving organisms to perpetuate their genes. As Richard Dawkins puts it, "we are survival machines—robot vehicles blindly programmed to preserve the selfish molecules known as genes."[48] Sociobiologists' claims about rape illustrate this view. Applying a form of cost/benefit analysis, they argue that males are genetically programmed to rape when the potential reproductive benefits outweigh the cost of punishment.[49] Yet there is no evidence that rape contributes to the reproductive success of the rapist. Indeed, the examples of same-sex rape in prison, rape-murders that obviously leave the victim unable to reproduce, and rape of girls not of childbearing age or of elderly women counter the argument that rape is reproductively beneficial or motivated.[50]

Some sociobiologists claim that human universals, such as the sexual division of labor, demonstrate a biological basis for behavior. Such a claim has two major flaws. First, the universality of social phenomenon may be the product of ubiquitous social environments. Second, the universality of many behaviors is in dispute. Even though all societies divide labor by sex, for example, the form this division takes varies considerably both within and across cultures. In some societies, men earn the bread while women bake it, but in other cultures women are the merchants and financiers.[51] Certainly some physical capacities and experiences of the sexes differ universally: only women experience menstruation, pregnancy, miscarriage, parturition, lactation, and menopause; mothers typically take care of their very young children; and men are, on average, larger and stronger than women.[52] Yet these define only central tendencies among human capacities, while the form that these capacities take is heavily dependent on social and cultural conditions. The amazing diversity of social arrangements across cultures and across time, particularly in conditions of rapid technological change, makes generalization fraught with danger.[53]

Perhaps most damning to biological determinism is the shrinking or disappearing of the group differences purported to be explained by biology as our techniques of measurement became more sophisticates. For example, Feingold[54] found that differences between boys and girls on tests of cognitive abilities (other than mathematics) declined precipitously over a number of years; Hyde[55] reported a decline in the magnitude of differences in mathematics performance. Furthermore, cross-cultural examination of intellectual abilities has identified no consistent pattern of differences between males and females, suggesting that such differences, should they exist, are not universal.[56]

Twenty years ago, many feminist social scientists rejected the idea of innate sex differences in thought or emotion, emphasizing instead the cultural construction of gender. A hallmark of this perspective was the publication in 1974 of Eleanor Maccoby and Carol Jacklin's encyclopedic *The Psychology of Sex Differences*.[57] In their careful scrutiny of hundreds of studies of personality and abilities, Maccoby and Jacklin identified only a very small number of sex differences that could be considered scientifically reliable. Today, using meta-analytic statistical techniques, even the small number identified by Maccoby and Jacklin has shrunk.[58] But by a decade after the publication of Maccoby and Jacklin's work, a strand of feminism had emerged that celebrates women's difference, exemplified by Carol Gilligan's 1982 book, *In a different voice*.[59]

Although Gilligan did not attribute difference to biology, other feminist social scientists such as Alice Rossi began to raise the question of biology's role in determining women's behavior. Rossi asserted that social factors as well as biology determine behavior,[60] although most of the evidence she presented suggests biology as causal.[61] Others seem to suggest a biological determinism centered on female's procreative capacity or on male's supposedly innate propensity for violence. Whereas sociobiologists and social Darwinists appeal to biology to justify the status quo, some radical feminists look to biology as the basis for challenges to the existing social order.[62] Their arguments, focused primarily on male control of women's sexuality, seem to attribute men's potential for violence and aggression to an innate biological flaw. Ironically, other feminists had deemed sexist the attribution of a personality trait or behavior to women's biology when there is no evidence to support such causality.[63] Unsubstantiated attributions from a reductionist perspective about the impact of male biology on behavior seem no more persuasive.

Nature versus Culture: A False Opposition

Perhaps the biggest problem in the nature-nurture distinction is the assumption that these are two independent domains, with biology providing the foundation on which social experiences are overlaid. From this perspective, gender is the social phenomena, diverging widely over place and time, that is imposed on biological difference, whereas biology typically is seen as the First Cause, more primary in its impact than other factors.[64] This "bedrock" view of biology is illustrated in the following claim about sex differences in the brain: "The die is cast *in utero*; that's when the mind is made up, and the luggage of our bodies, and of society's expectations of us, merely supplements this basic biological fact of life."[65] This perspective incorrectly implies that social effects are modifiable, while nature is immutable (surgical interventions not withstanding). Anthropologist Clifford Geertz summarizes this "stratographic" metaphor:

> Man [*sic*] is a composite of "levels," each superimposed upon those beneath it and underpinning those above it. As one analyzes man, one peels off layer after layer, each such layer being complete and irreducible in itself, revealing another, quite different sort of layer underneath. Strip off the motley forms of culture and one finds the structural and functional regularities of social organization. Peel off these in turn and one finds the underlying psychological factors—"basic need" or what-have-you—that support and make them possible. Peel off psychological factors and one is left with the biological foundations—anatomical, physiological, neurological—of the whole edifice of human life.[66]

Rather than a set of separate levels, however, the relatively general response capacities of human beings are given shape and meaning by culture:[67] "Gender is neither simply the manifestation of sex nor simply an easily dispensable artifact of culture. It is, instead, what a culture makes of sex; it is the cultural transformation of male and female infants into adult men and women."[68] In a parallel fashion, all humans are born with a motor capacity to smile, but what they smile at is shaped by culture.[69] The biological and social aspects of human experience constitute a unitary system, although they can be measured and analyzed separately. There is no such thing as a human nature independent of culture; that is, culture is just as essential an ingredient in human nature as biology, and vice versa. Accordingly, gender and sex are inextricably entwined.

Models of Biological Influence

How, then, do biology and social experience influence each other? Sameroff and Chandler[70] differentiate three models of constitutional-environmental (nature-nurture) relationships in developmental disorders that Ehrhardt[71] has applied to the study of gender. The first two models contain flaws that limit their usefulness; the third provides a promising conceptual framework for the study of women and gender.

The Main-Effect Model

In the main-effect model, one factor is presumed to determine a particular behavioral outcome regardless of other influences. For example, Huntington's disease and sickle-cell anemia are due to single genes that produce disease regardless of environmental circumstances.[72] Conversely, a certain social environment could produce a particular psychological condition or pattern of behavior, no matter what the individual's biological makeup. The central premise of this model is that nature and nurture exert effects that are determinant and independent of one another. But considerable research demonstrates that reductionistic and deterministic explanations, whether centered on biology or environment, fail to account for complex behavior.[73]

Both the pure constructionist and biological determinist positions reflect a main-effect perspective, albeit in opposite ways. On the one hand, a pure biological determinist would conclude that gender differences in our social world were a direct manifestation of biological factors, while environmental influences are of little or no importance (or are misguided attempts to distort what is "natural"). However, the diversity of gender arrangements makes these claims questionable. As Hoyenga and Hoyenga forcefully concluded after reviewing the evidence on gender differences, "Pure biological determinism for any behavioral or psychological trait, including one's identity as a biological male or female, is a myth."[74] An extreme environmentalist, on the other hand, would consider constitutional factors irrelevant other than for purposes of procreation; in this view, all differences other than reproduction would be socially constructed.[75] But people do not just accept cultural stereotypes; they create them as well, and their actions may affect their biology.[76]

Although their contents differ, the underlying assumptions of pure biological determinism and environmentalism are the same.[77] Both of these views consider human beings as passive and reactive; both view agency as impossible or at least constrained to forms of resistance to either "natural" tendencies or to the social order. Both deny the considerable evidence that the two domains influence each other, and that most complex human phenomena, like aggression or gender identity, have multiple causes.

Increasingly we find evidence of a continuing interplay of influence and counterinfluence between the organism and its environment.[78] Certainly studies of both males and females support the idea that the social environment influences constitutional factors, and vice versa. Martha McClintock[79] found that the menstrual cycles of females living together in a college dormitory came to be more closely synchronized as the academic year progressed. McClintock suggested communication by means of pheromones as a possible mechanism underlying menstrual synchrony; personality factors and the amount of time spent together may also play a role.[80] The day of onset of the menstrual flow came to coincide markedly among roommates who were also close friends; the effect was less strong but significant among women who were close friends but not roommates. Nor are men immune to these effects: changes in social rank influence men's testosterone levels, and their testosterone levels influence their social rank.[81] A naturalistic study of male doctors on a sailing trip found that testosterone levels increased among those who achieved the highest positions of dominance during the trip, while those who became least dominant had the lowest testosterone levels at the end of the trip.[82] Social conditions probably have an impact on human biology in many situations that have not yet been tested.

Large-scale studies of the relationship of hormones and behavior in children and adolescents show considerable complexity with respect to differences between women and men. A particular hormone that is related to behavior in one sex may have no relationship or even the opposite relationship in the other sex.[83] Furthermore, the direction of causality in these studies is not yet understood: social factors can influence biology, just as biology can influence behavior. The principle of reciprocal determinism—that influence flows in both directions—best describes the relationship of biological and social factors at all stages of development[84]; consequently, attempting to assign causality to either biology or culture is futile.

The Interactional Model

The interactional model considers a variety of constitutional and social environmental factors and predicts the individual's behavior from any combination of two factors.[85] For example, variations in environments can affect behavioral characteristics. As Sandra Bem has commented, "whereas the sex-differentiated aspects of human biology are relatively constant, the cultural context varies a great deal, sometimes exaggerating the influence of biology, sometimes counteracting the influence of biology, and sometimes—in a more neutral fashion—simply letting the influence of biology shine through without either exaggerating or counteracting it."[86] Although some would dispute Bem's contention that sex-differentiated aspects of biology remain constant, they might agree that culture can amplify or minimize biological difference. Differentiation of males and females occurs in all known cultures, but masculinity and femininity are loosely constructed categories, forming clusters of attributes that vary considerably depending on the particular cultural context. Furthermore, behaviors thought to be associated with masculinity and femininity are highly subject to situational influence.[87]

Variations in social environments and life circumstances can have physiological as well as behavioral consequences. In other words, biological properties can be dependent as well as independent variables. A culture that emphasizes thinness in women may encourage certain behaviors that in turn affect females physiologically, such as anorexia and bulimia. Being a single parent may elevate stress-related blood chemicals. Indeed, even physical environments have biologically measurable effects on people.[88]

Although the interactional model overcomes some of the problems of the main-effect model by taking more influences into account, it contains two deficiencies. First, it assumes that constitutional and social factors remain stable over time, when in fact they are constantly in flux. Second, it does not permit reciprocal determinism.[89]

The Transactional Model

The third model allows the possibility of mutual influence. It considers the person not simply as a reactor to environmental stimuli or as a product of biological factors, but also as an active agent selecting and constructing an environment that in turn may affect biology.[90] R. A. Hinde articulates the following principles that have emerged from biologists' studies of development. First, behavioral characteristics exist along a continuum "from those that are relatively stable with respect to environmental influences to those that are relatively labile."[91] Assigning any particular form of sexual dimorphism to a point on this continuum is problematic because a behavior that appears stable, such as mothers taking care of very young children, could either be so regulated by biology that it appears across a wide range of circumstances, or it could be the product of ubiquitous social circumstances. The considerable controversy about behaviors that appear sexually dimorphic—namely, whether such behaviors are the product of cultural assignment or linkage with biological sex—asks a question posed misleadingly in either/or terms, and denies the possibility of mutual influence between biology and culture.[92]

Second, according to Hinde, "organisms are constrained by what they can learn, and have predispositions to learn some things rather than others."[93] This proposition has been amply demonstrated in such species as songbirds. Biologists consider it probable that similar constraints exist for humans, and that the same environment may have different effects on people depending on individuals' predispositions. The difficulty in assessing this proposition lies in assuring that the environment remains constant. Anke Ehrhardt[94] observed that girls exposed prenatally to unusually high levels of androgen engaged in more physically energetic outdoor play and less nurturing compared to other girls who had not been so exposed. But knowledge that the former group of girls was endocrinologically atypical may have influenced the attitudes and behaviors of those around them. Rossi suggested that biological predisposi-tions make it easier for women than men to learn certain parenting skills.[95] Again, the problem in testing this proposition is that the social environment does not equally reinforce male and female parenting. From the time they are given their first baby doll, females are encouraged to care for young children more than males are. The intertwining of biology and culture renders futile in most cases the attempts to identify sex differences in biological predisposi-tion to parent.[96] Moreover, predisposition to learn a certain behavior does not mean that the behavior will inevitably be performed; the culture may not re-inforce it. Nor does it mean that individuals without the predisposition can-not achieve the behavior. Training and encouragement may override differ-ences in predispositions.[97]

A third principle of the transactional model is that individuals shape their environments as well as being shaped by them.[98] Maccoby[99] has observed the tendency among children to gravitate toward same-sex peers. She points to dominance relations as a possible explanation: Among young children, girls have difficulty influencing boys, whereas in same-sex pairs, influence is mu-tual. Girls may avoid interactions with boys and instead seek out those envi-ronments in which they can establish control, while boys may look to other boys for rough-and-tumble play, leading to sex-differentiated groupings. Children may shape their own environment in this and other ways. Because people behavior differently with different partners,[100] as Jacklin cogently puts it, "we are the company we keep."[101]

Alternative explanations of the correlation between testosterone levels and occupational status illustrate the transactional model. Purifoy and Koop-mans,[102] assessing the hormone levels of fifty-five normal females, found that women in professional, managerial, and technical occupations had higher lev-els of androgens than women clerical workers and housewives. They proposed a complex relationship between hormones and occupation over time to ac-count for these findings, rather than a simple main effect of testosterone on oc-cupation.[103] Perhaps some women had high levels of androgen prenatally that predisposed them to energetic play while young, and they were encouraged to play in this way, giving them more exposure to team play and competition. This in turn promoted their assertiveness and competitiveness, which led them to professional careers. On the other hand, hormones and play in early life may have been irrelevant. Perhaps their social environment encouraged a professional career, which in turn affected their endocrine system in the pro-duction of testosterone. Or perhaps the repetition and tedium of low status oc-cupations inhibits androgen secretion. Various paths between biology and the environment could account for these findings.

Hinde[104] has proposed a dialectical model in which physiological factors, individual behavior, short-term interactions among individuals, ongoing relationships, social groups, and societies composed of overlapping groups affect and are affected by each other. Each of these levels is also linked reciprocally to the sociocultural structure and to the physical environment. Offsetting the complexity and difficulty of measuring the multiple factors in this model is its greater accuracy in describing the relation of constitutional and environmental factors. Including biology in this model does not invalidate the role of social factors in shaping behavior.[105] Training scientists to conduct multifactorial research of this complexity will require broad, interdisciplinary education.

The transactional model suggests multiple research strategies for the study of women and men.[106] For those interested in sex differences, longitudinal studies that measure both biological factors and social and structural variables are best. Or one could work backward, first assessing biological differences among individuals and then examining whether those differences vary with sex and social experience. Another possibility is to identify social environments that differ systematically and compare individuals' biologically measurable properties. Conclusions that differences are due to biological sex ought not to be made without replication with a different subject population, such as individuals from another culture, or with those from different social categories, such as various age or status levels.[107] The selection of experimental and control groups in scientific research is not simply a methodological issue; it also reveals implicit theories of causation.[108] A focus in research on differences between women and men and a lack of attention to differences within each sex category reflects the presupposition of gender polarity that pervades research on women.[109]

A Cautionary Note

Jacklin[110] has observed that a "threshold-of-convincibility" leads researchers to accept a conclusion more readily if it is congruent with their own beliefs. Like many social scientists, those who study women and men may more readily accept explanations of behavior that favor the social environment rather than biology as causal and may dismiss or fail to pursue biological explanations. Social scientists' resistance to considering biological explanations stems in part from the connection between biological determinism and social and political conservatism. They may fear, sometimes correctly, that conservatives might misinterpret the causal significance of biological variables to mean that sex differences are immutable, and use that misinterpretation to justify discrimination.

Biological explanations for group differences have had a varied history in American social science, at times gaining ascendancy, as in the social Darwinism of the late nineteenth century, and at other times losing ground. The "threshold-of-convincibility" for biological explanations seems to vary not only with one's personal beliefs but also with the larger social and political climate. In times of political and social conservatism, dispositional theories of behavior predominate, only to be replaced by environmental explanations during periods of reform.[111]

Historian Carl Degler[112] argues that many social scientists of the mid-twentieth century rejected biological explanations because they contradicted then-prevalent liberal beliefs that social groups should be equal. Assuming innate differences among groups seemed somehow to undermine the traditional American commitment to equality of respect. Ironically, many of the original social Darwinists were also liberals, believing that by finding the biological basis of social superiority we could breed out undesirable traits and therefore perfect human nature.

In Degler's view, biological explanations have come back into fashion in social science, but without the pejorative connotations attributed to group differences. Others are less sanguine; they see Victorian assumptions of social inequality reflected in contemporary studies of the biological basis for group differences.[113] Because of this, many are wary of biological explanations, assuming that they will inevitably lead to proclamations of the inferiority of certain social groups in the name of science and eventually to genetic manipulation. Current attempts to add "Premenstrual Dysphoric Disorder" (a label that turns women's biology into a mental illness) to the *Diagnostic and Statistical Manual of Mental Disorders* (American Psychiatric Association) provide evidence that this fear is grounded in reality.[114]

The role of biological factors in behavior may be less subject to misinterpretation today not only because the political climate is less amenable than in the nineteenth century to biological determinism, but also because complex models of reciprocal influence preclude reductionistic and deterministic explanations. We also know now that compensatory strategies and training can mitigate or even reverse the effects of biological factors on difference. Yet even sophisticated research may be misinterpreted. Scientists who study the inheritability of behavior emphasize the role of both environment and genes,[115] but the popular media seem eager to jump on any suggestion that biology is causal. Witness the publicity given to Simon LeVay's[116] study of the differences between homosexual and heterosexual men in the size of an area within the corpus collosum. Despite its many flaws (such as lack of verification of the sexual orientation of its subjects), this correlational study has been widely (and inaccurately) reported as providing conclusive evidence of a biological basis for homosexuality. Scientific caution about multiple causes and reciprocal influence may get knocked aside in the political frenzy that surrounds such research.

Conclusion

An inclusive psychology of women and gender that considers the reciprocal influence between biology and culture will permit questions more sophisticated than simply whether biology or culture causes difference. As Evelyn Fox Keller[117] admonishes, we need to learn to count past two in our thinking. An analysis that cuts across biological, psychological, social, structural, and cultural phenomena and considers the relationships among such factors promises the deepest understanding of behavior, although examination of phenomena within each dimension is also of value.[118] Simply ignoring factors other than those one prefers to emphasize risks reductionist conclusions. Furthermore, differences based on factors other than sex classification, such as variations within each sex category or among myriad social groups, may be equally or more important than differences between women and men. Now that more and more social scientists are reporting the size of sexual differences as well as the simple fact of statistical significance,[119] it is time for explicit comparisons of the size of these differences with the size of similar differences between classes and cultures. Typical research strategies in psychology emphasize differences in central tendencies among groups and arrange these differences in hierarchical order. In contrast, we can begin to appreciate—and recognize—diversity both among and within groups when our focus is on variation and similarity rather than simply difference.

The study of sex differences began years ago with the assumption that biology caused behavior. In repudiating such simple biological determinism, we need not reject biology. Nor need we give biology causal primacy; the effects of the social environment on biology and behavior are equally and often more important. Biology is no less immutable or complex than the social environment, and consideration of biological influences does not invalidate the impact of situational, structural, or cultural determinants of behavior. Research on gender has just begun to investigate the multiplicity of influences that shape men and women's lives. To develop multifactorial models, we need new terms—and new concepts—that capture not only the distinctions but also the connections between sex and gender, biology and culture. Although models based on multiple factors and reciprocal influence make our work harder, they are also likely to make it more meaningful.

4

From Snapshots to Videotape

New Directions in Research on Gender Differences

As DIRECTOR OF A women's studies program, people often besiege me with questions about sex differences. Their questions typically are prompted by stories that appear in the media reporting the latest supposedly "scientific" findings of gender differences. Is it true, they ask me, that men can park their cars better than women? That women cannot read maps? What do the experts say? Sit down, I tell them, this is going to take a while.

There are at least five different responses to the question of whether there are sex differences. These five answers derive from different traditions within psychology. The earliest tradition, an individual differences model, produced what I call "snapshot" research, that is, one-time, quick, narrowly focused studies in which people's performance is assumed to be the product of internal factors, be they biology or socialization. This model has been expanded at least to some extent by a social psychological model that incorporates situational factors as causal possibilities. I believe that both of these models are limited, and here I advocate further expansion into what I will describe as "videotape" rather than "snapshot" research, which would enable us both to capture the dynamic qualities of gendered behavior and to widen our lens to include larger cultural, historic, and economic forces as causal agents.

The Main Arguments

First, let me describe the five answers to the question of whether there are sex differences:

The "Sociobiology" Argument

Some researchers state clearly and unequivocally that there are significant sex differences, that those differences are, at least in part, biologically based, and that they affect our social lives in important ways. Perhaps the form of this argument most widely broadcast these days is the evolutionary psychology of David Buss[1] and his colleagues (vigorously popularized by Robert Wright in *Time* and *The New Republic*, among other venues). Buss[2] argues that sex differences have a biological basis in reproductive roles: women face the need for life-sustaining resources while they are pregnant and lactating, and men face the need to reduce uncertainty about the paternity of the offspring they support. These different adaptive challenges have produced different psychological mechanisms in men and women which, in turn, are moderated by social factors.

However, as Fausto-Sterling[3] points out, evolutionary theories in psychology are not grounded in actual data about human evolution. A key challenge to those who hold such positions is to identify specific links between biological mechanisms and social behavior over generations; until they do so, their theories remain on the level of speculation.

The "Differently Situated" Argument

Advocates of this position agree that there are important sex differences but consider them socially, not biologically, based. Various forms of this argument have been made, for example Eagly's[4] claim that the division of labor between the sexes produces gender-role expectations and sex-typed skills and beliefs that in turn lead to sex differences in social behavior. Miller[5] also believes that sex differences exist, but she places causal primacy on women's subordinate and men's dominant status.

These approaches identify particular antecedents of differences and put them in a theoretical context that highlights the fact that women are differently situated in society than men are, but they tend to overlook the fact that not all women are similarly situated. One challenge to these researchers is to identify particular social or structural factors that produce specific differences, whether those factors be roles, expectancies, or power positions. Lott[6] provides numerous examples of how a belief in gender differences influences behavior and social policies.

The "Contingent" Argument

Advocates of this position claim that what appear to be sex differences tend to disappear or are mitigated when other factors are taken into account; hence the existence of sex differences is contingent on situational or social factors. Feingold,[7] for example, points out that findings of differences in spatial visualization have declined by 59 percent over the years. It is possible that changes in testing methods have led to more precise measurement or that societal factors that either produced or minimized differences have changed. In this case, sex differences seem to be made up in part by cohort effects.

Brody[8] reviews research on gender and emotion that demonstrates that expression of emotion by males and females is contingent on other factors, such as culture; Americans may differ by gender more than other cultural groups.

As Epstein asserts, "what is regarded as uniquely female in one culture, group or subgroup may be regarded as male in another."[9] A great deal of research on sex differences is done on members of one culture and assumes that those findings generalize across cultures. Markus and Oyserman[10] point out that the relational sense of self as interdependent, embedded, and continuous with others, which is thought to characterize Western women, is in many ways little different from the collectivist sense of self that characterizes both men and women in some Eastern and African cultures. Furthermore, Wink[11] and his colleagues argue that conceptualizing individualism and collectivism as dichotomous and oppositional may itself be a mistake, since individuals could be high (or low) on both these dimensions.

Others make a similar point when they underscore the need to look at race, social class, and other within-sex groupings, not just differences between males and females. One key question here is the relative importance of sex compared with other variables that demarcate subgroups of populations. Unger advocates an increase in the number and kind of group differences studied: "The more differences we explore, the less important any single difference can be."[12]

In comparing group differences, however, the usual practice has been to adopt the dominant group as a standard and see how closely the subordinate group matches it. According to Hurtado,[13] this deficit model leaves the dominant group unexamined and assumes that influence is unidirectional. Instead, she advocates a model that permits examination of the fluid nature of individuals' multiple group identities.

The "No Differences" Argument

Some psychologists emphatically respond "no" when asked if there are important sex differences. For example, Tavris asserts that: "Meta-analysis of social behaviors, such as helpfulness, find that differences are due more to role than to gender, and meta-analyses of intellectual skills, such as math, verbal, and spatial abilities, find that differences have virtually vanished or are too trivial to matter."[14] To Hyde, most differences are small and unimportant, but a few differences—such as those in sexual attitudes and behaviors—are large and should be studied.[15] In her view, a key challenge is to identify which few differences are large enough to merit close inspection. Others would argue that the central task should be to identify similarities rather than give primacy to differences.

Some differences identified in past research may have been an artifact of research paradigms. Barnett[16] points out that earlier research on the relationship between work, family, and mental health assumed that social roles had a differential impact on women and men, with women more influenced by family and men by work. These assumptions influenced both the research questions that were asked and the way in which findings were interpreted. In contrast, current paradigms assume that both work and family roles influence both women and men. Barnett concludes that, as women and men occupy similar work and family roles, the relationship between those roles and mental health does not differ by gender.

The "Disadvantage, Not Difference" Argument

Those who fall into this category believe that there may be sex differences; if they exist, in most cases they are small, but they are often: (a) magnified, and (b) made into justifications for inequality.[17] To advocates of this position, a central task is to identify the social processes involved that amplify differences and interpret them as inadequacies, that is, how traits and behaviors attributed to women acquire the social meaning of deficits.[18] The emphasis here is on the consequences of difference and how social institutions interpret the ways in which females differ from males as female disadvantage. As James puts it, "The extent to which the sexes differ is far less important than the consequences of emphasizing such differences in particular contexts."[19]

Hare-Mustin and Maracek go further, suggesting that the important question is that of the political utility of either affirming or minimizing gender differences. From their constructivist perspective, there is no correct answer to the question of sex differences: "theories of gender, like other scientific theories, are representations of reality organized by particular assumptive frameworks and reflecting certain interests."[20] In their opinion, research on sex differences is part of the social processes that construct gender and support the status quo. Instead of this research, they advocate the study of "privilege, power, subordination and rebellion" among individuals and social groups.

By now, the people who have queried me for simple answers to the question of sex differences are bewildered: Why the multiplicity of answers? In part, this stems from the varying "thresholds of convincibility" among researchers,[21] making us more easily persuaded by research that confirms our beliefs. But the multiplicity of answers derives also from the different research traditions, with contradictory assumptions about human behavior, that underlie various arguments about the question of sex differences.

Two Models of Research on Sex Difference

Research on sex differences began with the "individual differences model" that goes back to the earliest days of scientific psychology. Subsequent research on sex differences has been based on other models, primarily the "social psychological" model. Each of these traditions has limits for the study of women and gender.

The Individual Differences Model

When nonprofessionals ask whether there are "truly" sex differences, they are usually referring to abilities and personality traits as studied from an "individual differences" model. This tradition goes back more than 100 years to the work of Francis Galton, a cousin of Charles Darwin. Galton set up a laboratory at the 1884 International Health Exhibition in London in which, for a threepence charge, he would measure the mental abilities of members of the public.[22] He tested about 9,000 people by the time the exhibition closed, giving them information about their relative performance. Underlying Galton's work are assumptions that permeate interpretations of research on sex differences.

First, Galton saw the individual as a bundle of traits and abilities; tests of simple motor abilities and perception provided a measure of people's mental capacities.[23] Galton believed that a quick "snapshot" at one point in time of someone's performance, taken under contrived conditions, could provide a full measure of that person on a particular dimension. Underlying Galton's work is a belief in radical individualism: that mental abilities are composed of stable and unalterable individual characteristics that owed nothing to social conditions; rather, the self is contained in the individual body. The origins of our actions (and responsibility for those actions) lies within the individual, rather than in some social group larger than the individual, such as the family or one's racial or ethnic group, or other extra-individual factors.

Today many studies of sex differences bring Galton's emphasis on mental abilities into contemporary terms by looking at particular cognitive skills, such as visual-spatial abilities and verbal and math ability, and ask whether there are sex differences in these abilities and whether these differences are large enough to be socially meaningful. But problems with this model limit its usefulness for understanding women's and men's behavior.

A key question is whether these studies are measuring abilities (i.e., what women and men are capable of doing) or simply performance (i.e., what people actually do). If what we are measuring is actually performance, then we cannot discount the effects of training and culture when considering findings. Even in the area of spatial abilities, where some of the most robust findings of difference have been identified, there is evidence that training and sociocultural experiences play a role.[24]

A further problem with the individual differences model is the assumption that groups of males and females tested are homogeneous, not heterogeneous. Indeed, this assumption is built into the very statistics we use. Typical research strategies in psychology emphasize differences in central tendencies among groups and arrange these differences in hierarchical order. Often we begin with the belief that the population falls into a bell-shaped curve, and that what is defined as "normal" falls under 95 percent of that curve. But the groups that we test may be bimodal or multimodal, not bell-shaped. Within groups of males and females, subgroups may exist that do not fall neatly into the bell-shaped curve. In that situation, the "average" score will tell us little about the actual shape of the curve, and a higher percentage than 5 percent may fall under the "not normal" part of the curve. When we assume homogeneity, we cannot detect the presence of diverse subgroups. There are statistical solutions to these problems. For example, we could look at the overall shape of the distribution or the tails of curves as closely as we look at the means.[25] Such solutions will become routine only when homogeneity is no longer the guiding assumption of our research.

Moreover, we do not know with certainty what it is we have learned when we discover the presence or absence of sex differences. Galton assumed that biology caused differences among individuals. More recently, researchers have added socialization and culture to the causal mix.[26] In the absence of tests of specific causes of difference, we are left with long lists of studies, some of which show differences and some of which do not, but we have little means of understanding why these divergent findings occur.

Nonetheless, the most serious problem with the individual differences model may be the limits it places on the kinds of things that can be studied. Some of the most interesting phenomena, such as aggression or leadership, are most clearly manifested in social situations,[27] and behavior may vary depending on whether a person is tested individually, in a dyad, or in a group. Maccoby found that pairs of young children engaged in much higher levels of social behavior when playing with a same-sex partner than when playing with a child of the other sex. Girls seldom acted passively when paired with other girls, but when paired with boys, their behavior patterns changed. "Girls frequently stood on the sidelines and let the boys monopolize the toys."[28] Distinctive styles of interaction occurred in all-boy and all-girl groups, with boys focusing more on dominance and girls on social enabling behaviors. Mixed sex groups, consequently, combine styles that may be incompatible or at least divergent. These differences in style may not be present when children are tested individually.

This research demonstrates that presenting a female with a male is not equivalent to presenting a male with another male, or vice versa. Experimental psychologists refer to this as a problem in "stimulus equivalency"; I would reframe it as a problem in the assumption of individualism. One solution to this problem is to consider that research findings may well be the product of the interaction of the pair rather than the abilities or performance of the individual, highlighting the limits of the individual differences model.

The Social Psychological Model

The individual differences model has been superseded to some degree by a view of human behavior that considers extra-individual factors as potential causal agents. In the tradition of social psychology initiated by Kurt Lewin and his colleagues (many of them female), the focus is on the person embedded in a social situation.[29] Lewin held that behavior is not solely a function of one's inner traits or abilities or preferences, but rather is partly the product of the social context that surrounds the person. In contrast to Galton's focus on the individual, Lewin took the effect of situational variation on behavior as his object of study.

A great deal of research in this tradition demonstrates that what appear to be stable sex differences in behavior may actually be the product of situational factors. Because this research has been catalogued so ably in books by Epstein[30] and others, I will give only a few examples. In studies of power relations, when status is not assigned, men tend to exhibit patterns of dominance and women patterns of subordinate behaviors. When, however, status is manipulated experimentally, both women and men act in accord with their status, not with gender expectations. The most intriguing studies are those that demonstrate that the same participants exhibit both dominant and subordinate behaviors depending on their assigned status.[31]

A social psychological approach sees behavior as the product of social interaction, as adaptive rather than fixed. The underlying theme is one of influence and counterinfluence, of being molded by the social environment and simultaneously shaping that environment rather than being free from contextual influences. But one limitation of the social psychological tradition is that, in its focus on the immediate situation, it may overlook the individual's place in the larger social system, ignoring economic or political or historical forces that shape women's and men's behavior. The ahistorical nature of social psychology conflates behaviors that are the product of contemporaneous conditions with universal, timeless principles of human behavior.[32]

At the other end of the causal spectrum, the social psychological model also ignores the potential relationship of biological factors and behavior. If, for example, social conditions have an impact on human behavior, they may also affect one's biology. Considering only social factors, while ignoring biological ones, reifies the nature/nurture distinction that wrongly treats biology and culture as separable and competing sources of influence.

In summary, both the individual differences model and the social psychological model have limitations that prevent us from settling the question of whether there are socially significant sex differences. It is important to consider why we expend so much energy on this question. For those interested in research as a vehicle for social change, I think that continuing to focus our efforts on the question of whether there are sex differences in abilities or personality traits is a mistake. Feminist pioneers in psychology, including Helen Thompson (Woolley), used traditional scientific methods at the start of the twentieth century to counter the social myths about women;[33] yet Thompson's insights have had to be repeatedly rediscovered, and still the myths persist. Scientific research itself rarely seems to create the shift in attitudes that we desire, although the interpretation of our research to the public may have an impact. Repeated demonstrations that sex differences are mostly small and contextually determined will not in itself bring about equality for women. The pervasive belief in individualism, at least in Western industrialized countries, will make it difficult for those findings to be heard.[34]

Women's place in society is different in many ways—for many women—from that of men; we need only look at the continuing wage discrepancies between male and female workers to be reminded of that fact. Accordingly, it is no surprise that, being differently situated, women and men may act differently. This does not mean that women are not capable of acting in the same ways—both good and bad—as men. Nor does it mean that intrinsic differences in abilities necessarily determine men's and women's places in society.

Equality of opportunity does not require that women and men be identical—or rather that women be identical to men, which is the subtext of many discussions of sex differences. Scott urges us to discard the belief that if we accept difference, we reject the idea of equality. She points out that equality is not needed when people are identical. Demands for equality are necessary only when groups differ. "Equality," she asserts, "might well be defined as deliberate indifference to specified differences."[35] Conversely, inequality does not necessarily stem from differences in skills and abilities.

Moreover, those who want to deny women equal opportunity will do so whether research identifies sex sameness or difference. Research may be used to justify opinions (our own as well as others) rather than to change them. Newt Gingrich, then the Speaker of the U.S. House of Representatives, did not base his curious public statement about women being unfit for hand-to-hand military combat because they get infections, and men being biologically programmed to hunt giraffes, on scientific research. I think he was trying to say he believes that sex differences are innate; that social structure is the result, not the cause of difference; and that it behooves us to make sure that social structure does not contradict those innate differences. I do not think that any number of carefully crafted research studies finding otherwise would change his mind. If we want equal opportunity for women, we should work for equal opportunity, not assume that our research findings—or perhaps more important, that our interpretations of our findings—are going to convince others that social change is needed. As academics, we place great faith in reason, argumentation, and evidence, but these tools may not be the only—or even the most effective—means of bringing about political or social change. Research demonstrating equal abilities of women and men, or even demonstrating the variability among one sex, may be useful but not sufficient to bring about social equality. But research can document precisely how society is "gendered" or unequal in expectations and opportunities (thereby identifying targets for change); research can also examine how women and others who are disenfranchised cope with inequality (bringing to light strategies for survival).

Such research would have two goals:

1. First, it would make explicit the underlying gender coding—much of it gratuitous—of social structures and situations. That is, it would identify differences based on sex in expectations, opportunities, networks, and power. As Epstein has cogently put it, "No aspect of social life—whether the gathering of crops, the ritual of religion, the formal dinner party, or the organization of government—is free from the dichotomous thinking that casts the world in categories of 'male' and 'female'".[36] The transsexual British journalist Jan Morris discovered this firsthand after her surgical change from male to "female":

> We are told that the social gap between the sexes is narrowing, but I can only report that in the second half of the twentieth century, having experienced life in both roles [male and female], there seems to me no aspect of existence, no moment of the day, no contact, no arrangement, no response, which is not different for men and for women. The very tone of voice in which I was addressed, the very posture of the person next in [line], the very feel in the air when I entered a room or sat at a restaurant table, constantly emphasized my change of status.[37]

Our research can particularize this observation by identifying how specific situations and social structures treat women and men differently.

2. Once we have identified gender-coding in social systems, we can look at how women negotiate these situations and social structures—that is, accept them or engage in varying degrees of resistance against them. I assume here that women have a degree of agency, but that their ability to act is constrained in certain ways. That is, women both create and are shaped by social structures; research can document how these processes occur.

To do this research, to tell these stories, to understand women's experience at multiple levels of social organization, we need new research methods that neither considers women as sole determiners of their fate, ignoring situation constraints, nor consider them as mere pawns of larger social forces. Videotape is a useful metaphor for discovering such new research techniques. The assumptions underlying "videotape epistemology" differ radically from those of the snapshot-type research used by Galton and others.

First, the metaphor of videotape suggests that we consider people's behavior over time, enabling us to examine how people negotiate situations in light of particular constraints and opportunities. Thorne's[38] research on school-children is a good example of this; she identifies times in children's lives when gender is salient and other times when its importance is muted. She advocates conceptualizing gender as fluid and situated rather than dichotomous and oppositional.

Second, videotape technology permits viewers to zoom in—that is, fill our field of vision with the person—and zoom out to include context and, over time, patterns of behavior in that context. In other words, the metaphor of videotape suggests that we adopt techniques that allow us to consider both micro-level and macro-level factors in understanding behavior.[39]

Third, videotape enables us to hear the views of multiple participants. It suggests that we recognize the importance of individuals' interpretations, of the stories that people tell themselves, as determinants of behavior. We should not, however, deny the role of the camera operator (that is, the researcher) in choosing the object of focus, the length of time to focus on an event, and so on. By advocating videotape as a metaphor, I do not mean to imply that the camera operator is simply a technician, recording but not framing a scene.

Fourth, videotape enables us to splice and edit, thereby comparing multiple perspectives. It enables us to capture much of the complexity of a phenomenon, so that, for example, we do not consider race, sex, and social class as isolated variables.

Let me give two examples of research that capture some of these qualities. The first is Fine's[40] study of why a rape victim would choose not to prosecute a rapist. Psychologists generally think of prosecuting as taking control of the situation, and therefore part of the process of successfully coping with rape. Fine questions the assumption that asserting individual control is the optimal form of coping. She argues that this model is appropriate only for a "small and privileged sector of society" with the social power and resources to assure that exerting control is likely to lead to successful outcomes. For those with few resources, exerting control in this manner can be delusory or even self-destructive. In the case she describes, a poor black woman on welfare chose not to prosecute her rapist, having little faith in the criminal justice system and a great fear that the rapist would harm those she loved. Fine concludes that the "systematic neglect of power relations" causes us to disregard the fact that our conceptions of taking control are not always applicable across class, race and ethnic lines.

A second example is Wittner's[41] study of why battered women often drop charges against those who have beaten them. The professionals in the court system—the judges, lawyers, and so forth—see completed cases as the measure of success of Chicago's new Domestic Violence Court. They attribute the high rate of dropped cases to battered women's weakness, passivity, dependency, fear, and low self-esteem. But from the battered women's point of view, the choice to drop a case is anything but passive. Some women had the goal of getting the man to stop beating them or to leave, and merely bringing charges against him had accomplished that goal. Once they had obtained what they wanted, they saw no need to go through the tedious and time-consuming legal process. Others saw the inevitable delays and frustrations of the criminal justice system as attempts to discourage them from prosecuting. Perhaps most imposing, the state's attorney's office is in control of the course of a case, treating the battered woman as a witness for the state. Ironically, this loss of control may produce some of those feelings of dependency and helplessness among battered women that court personnel blame for dropped cases.

Wittner concludes that the Domestic Violence Court is a major resource for poor and working-class women (the majority of the complainants), enabling these women to hold men accountable. But the way the women use the court did not always accord with the way that court personnel had decided was appropriate, that is, by following complaints through to their legal conclusion. Rather, these women used the court as one among many resources—including other family members, both their own and the batterers'—in a complex series of negotiations that ensured their survival. Wittner links women's use of the court to large-scale economic changes, in particular, men's loss of high-paying manufacturing jobs. The decline in women's economic dependence on men has shifted the balance of power in relationships; women's use of Domestic Violence Court is part of a process of reconfiguring those relationships.

Both of these examples contrast the view of professionals in a social system with that of women affected by that system; both attempt to relate individual women's experiences to larger social and economic forces. Both examples use qualitative methods, although I do not believe that qualitative methods are the only approaches able to capture needed distinctions. A provocative model of quantitative methods comes from evaluation research. Stakeholder-based evaluation research attempts to incorporate into the evaluation process questions formulated by the different constituencies that have an interest in the results of an evaluation, especially those who are the least powerful.[42] In doing so, it implicitly views organizations as political entities, composed of shifting groups with different interests, that compete for scarce resources.[43] Therefore, many situations in which men and women interact or fail to interact can also be seen as political entities, forming and reforming on the basis of changing power dynamics. The metaphor of videotape rather than snapshot methods best capture this process.

Conclusion

There were numerous attempts in the 1980s and 1990s to use research to settle the question of whether there are sex differences. Yet one can still pick up a prestigious social science journal like *American Psychologist* and find one author who writes that sex differences are large and socially meaningful while another author concludes that many if not most differences are small and have a trivial impact. One subtext of this conflict is whether immutable, biologically determined differences in abilities and personality traits exist that justify limiting the potential opportunities and achievements of one sex or another. This wrongly conflates biology with biological determinism and ignores social forces that affect women's and men's roles. Understanding that different findings emerge depending on the methods used, the variables under scrutiny, the assumptions about causality, and whether the presentation of the findings chooses to highlight difference or similarities may help make sense of why the conclusions of researchers in this field are so diverse.

Continuing the debate about whether there are "truly" sex differences in personality and abilities is no longer a useful enterprise. It is time to imagine new directions for research on women and gender. Let us unpack the black box of the variable entity "sex" by taking into account specific biological, psychological, social, structural, and cultural dimensions that are linked in a given context to being female or male and examine the specific ways in which gender is created through social relations. Cross-level research that acknowledges the reciprocal influence between individuals and social systems promises the deepest understanding of behavior, although examination of phenomena within each dimension is also of value.[44] Furthermore, similarities between males and females, or differences based on factors other than sex classification—such as variations within each sex category or among myriad social groups—may be as important or more important than gender differences.

Research that spans multiple levels of social organization goes against the grain of much of our training, in which each of these levels of analysis becomes the property of a particular discipline or a subfield within a discipline. Indeed, the thought of spanning all these levels is daunting. Level-spanning research might be less intimidating if we consider working in cross-disciplinary teams of researchers. One of the exciting possibilities of women's studies is that it brings together people from various disciplines who focus on the same question, making this sort of level-spanning possible. But working with those from other disciplines also sometimes makes apparent that the disciplines use different language, sources of evidence, argumentation styles, and research methods. We need to develop new ways of working that allow us to cross these disciplinary boundaries. Using videotape as a metaphor to guide our search for new methods can change the way we do research—and produce new stories to tell.

5

Women's Agency in Context

THE FEMINIST IDEOLOGY THAT emerged in the United States during the 1960s united women on the basis of their status as a subordinate group. This ideology required that women identify themselves as victims in order to share a sense of solidarity with other women. Yet espousing feminism was itself an act of assertion and implicitly a denial of victim status. Although there was little room for agency in a worldview that saw women as a subordinate group, dominated by patriarchy, the assertive acts of women generated the feminist movement of that era. Indeed, women have long acted to solve community and social problems and to bring about social justice in unions, neighborhoods, politics, social service agencies, and many other settings.[1] These actions challenge the idea that women are passive victims of patriarchy.

A similar contradiction confronts the postmodern viewpoints that dominate much of contemporary feminist theory. According to postmodernism, our thought and perceptions are channeled in certain ways by discourses prevalent in our society. The capacity for independent thought and action in the face of hegemonic discourses is problematic. At the same time, feminists place primacy on giving voice to women and consider that voice to be an authentic reflection of women's experience. This contradiction again centers on the dilemma of conceptualizing agency in the context of women's subordinate status in society.

The concept of agency is central not only in feminist theory but also in mainstream theories of human nature. Much of psychological theory, ignoring the influence of social context and reflecting a belief in individualism that characterizes American society, assumes that individuals are the origins of their actions. Yet accumulated research points to the importance of context as well as individual efficacy in shaping behavior. In the classic formulation of social psychologist Kurt Lewin, behavior is a function of the interaction of personality and context.[2] Yet many theories of agency have ignored the importance of context in shaping human action.

This chapter explores research on agency within the traditions of psychology in order to identify some ways out of the apparent contradictions in feminist theory. Since Freud asserted that a mentally healthy individual was one who could work and love, psychologists have considered agency in contrast to communion. David Bakan was one of the first contemporary psychologists to make this distinction. In his book *The Duality of Human Existence*, Bakan describes agency as an individual acting in self-protection, self-assertion, and self-expansion, while communion refers to an individual's sense of being part of a larger whole, at one with others: "Agency manifests itself in the urge to master; communion in contractual cooperation."[3] He further hypothesized that agency and communion are linked to gender. In his view, men's strivings for achievement are directed at agentic concerns of self-assertion, attainment of status, and mastery over the environment. In contrast, women strive to achieve communion and are motivated to work cooperatively to attain a sense of harmony with others. However, Bakan does not define the concepts of agency and communion as bipolar opposites, but as separate, independent dimensions capable of coexisting within one person.

Although Bakan's formulation of agency and communion is very broad, the sociologist Talcott Parsons's earlier distinction between instrumental and expressive activity is more specific and thus potentially more useful.[4] In Parsons's formulation, instrumental actions are goal-oriented, while expressive actions are oriented toward relationships. Parsons did not use these terms as personality descriptors. Rather, the concepts of instrumentality and expressiveness refer to the way individuals interact in social systems. Instrumental activity focuses on achievement and accomplishment outside the immediate social group. In contrast, expressive activity involves an orientation toward the relationship interactions that exist within a social system. Hence, expressive actions manifest the principles of Bakan's concept of communion, while instrumental actions manifest those of agency. Similar to Bakan, Parsons does not view instrumental and expressive behaviors as two ends of the same continuum. Rather, Parsons stresses the need for both expressive and instrumental roles in both individuals and in social groups.

Considerable research in psychology has adhered to the distinction between these two realms of behavior, namely the agentic/instrumental, "doing" realm and the communal, expressive, "feeling" realm. With the advent of feminist theorizing and the growing area of research focusing on the psychology of women, it has become obvious that this simple dichotomy is inadequate. Feminists have pointed out that the two domains are not equally valued in our society. Instrumental action is highly valued, and defines what is conventionally considered "success." Expressiveness, associated with dependency, has traditionally had a negative connotation when used to characterize individuals. In her book *Toward a New Psychology of Women*, Jean Baker Miller pointed out that women are punished for making relationships and connections central in their lives.[5] In a related vein, Carol Gilligan distinguished between autonomy and relatedness and argued that psychological theories of development give primacy to the former while disregarding the latter.[6] In contrast,

Gilligan emphasized the importance of relatedness in understanding women's moral actions. Yet this emphasis echoes the traditional concept of "separate spheres" in which woman is defined by her relationship with others,[7] ignoring the variability that exists among women (and men). Linking some behaviors to women and others to men obscures the fact that behavior itself has no gender and can be manifested by either sex.

Baruch, Barnett, and Rivers attempted, in their book *Lifeprints*, to redefine what is "well-being," or healthy behavior, for women. They identified two dimensions of well-being: mastery and pleasure. Mastery reflects the instrumental dimension or the "doing" in life, in contrast to pleasure's emphasis on the expressive domain, or "feeling" side of life. According to these authors, women frequently neglect the mastery domain and thus are prone to depression and struggles with the lack of structure in their lives. They argue that "the best preventive medicine for women against depression is fostering their sense of mastery. The confident, autonomous woman is likely to be less vulnerable to depression. If we continue to insist that we will find the answers to a woman's problems . . . only in the realm of her feelings toward others, we will keep on looking in the wrong place."[8]

Although mastery and achievement may be key to women's depression, men's emotional difficulties may lie with expressiveness. Miriam Johnson and her colleagues tested the separateness of Parsons's concepts of instrumentality and expressiveness by having people rate themselves on adjectives that represented these dimensions.[9] Johnson concluded from her research that the expressiveness dimension is a more basic aspect of gender difference than the instrumental dimension. Her findings suggest that women are able to integrate autonomous qualities with expressiveness in their self-concept, while men appear to deny the expressiveness dimension in their self-image.

These authors challenge the traditional attribution of agency to men and communion to women by maintaining that a balance of both domains is critical for all people. Yet they continue to maintain a false dichotomy. The separation of action and emotion, of instrumental and expressive activity, erects a boundary between "doing" and "feeling" that denies the interpenetration of these domains. Furthermore, considering these concepts as traits located within the person ignores the role of social context in eliciting behavior. Rather than the product of inner traits, gender-related behavior emerges in response to situational demands.[10] As Rhoda Unger forcefully put it, "Gender is created by social processes. When social demands are strong enough, people will behave in sex-characteristic ways whether or not they possess the sex-typed traits supposedly directing their behavior."[11]

A critical factor in women's mental health is the extent to which women's life circumstances permit the opportunity for agency. Stewart and her colleagues examined the levels of stress of women in five life situations: never-married employed women; married employed women without children; married mothers who did not work outside the home; married, employed mothers; and divorced, employed mothers. Although no life structure was stress-free, they varied in the risks and opportunities presented. Gaining a sense of agency was problematic for housewives, while single women without children were vulnerable to the opposite extreme: "unmitigated agency." The single working mothers had difficulty experiencing communion, while the working parents found it difficult to coordinate the agentic and communal aspects of their lives. Although not all life structures offer similar opportunities for agency and communion, the critical factor in emotional health appears to be the degree to which the opportunities provided by the life structure fit the needs of the individual's personality.[12]

In contrast, Rachel Hare-Mustin and Jeanne Maracek view autonomy and relatedness as a function not of one's gender or personality, but rather of one's position in a social hierarchy.[13] From this perspective, gender is not the sum of personality traits attributed to males and females, but rather the product of interactional processes that occur within particular contexts. Those in higher positions tend to advocate rules and rationality, while those lower in the hierarchy emphasize relatedness. The highly valued attributes that our society defines as agentic are those associated with power and status because autonomy and mastery require the freedom to make choices. Frequently, what is considered feminine is the product of powerlessness and low status;[14] those not in a position of autonomy and choice must focus on connection and communal goals to survive. Accordingly, whether individuals act in an autonomous manner or operate in a communal mode reflects their relative position in the social structure.

In our society today, men (particularly white men) are more likely to occupy positions permitting autonomy, while many women lack the institutional power, status, and economic independence to act agentically. Those characteristics traditionally viewed as endemic to being female—sensitivity, empathy, and nurturance—may be adaptive mechanisms to women's social position. Miller has claimed that women's subordinate status requires them to be aware of feelings, thoughts, and responses of others. Research by Sara Snodgrass supports the concept of interpersonal sensitivity as a function of social role rather than an innate or socialized gender difference. Snodgrass assessed one person's ability to interpret correctly another person's thoughts and feelings within interacting pairs of women, men, and mixed sex dyads. Interpersonal sensitivity did not differ by gender, but those in subordinate positions were more sensitive than leaders to the feelings of the other dyad member. Snodgrass concluded that sensitivity is affected by the respective social roles of the participants rather than by their gender.[15]

Snodgrass's research reflects the fact that behavior is a function in part of social context. This position challenges the assertion that we are independent human actors, actively controlling our lives. Psychological theories tend to alternate between two paradigms, one that claims that the "Person constructs reality" and the other that claims that "Reality constructs the person."[16] What is needed instead is a dialectical paradigm that emphasizes the reciprocal, interactive relationship between the person and the social environment.

One such model is proposed by Deaux and Major in their micro-level model of gender-related social interaction. Using a social psychological perspective, they suggest that three elements produce men's and women's social behavior: (1) a perceiver, who enters an interaction with both a set of beliefs about gender and personal goals for the interaction; (2) a target individual, who enters the interaction with his or her own gender-related self-conceptions and interaction goals; and (3) a situation, which varies in the extent to which gender issues are relevant. This perspective emphasizes the importance of the interaction of situational factors and personal beliefs regarding gender: Gender related behaviors are context-dependent, highly flexible, and multiply determined.[17]

Beliefs about gender form an important part of Deaux and Major's model. One such gender-related belief is that of self-efficacy, "people's beliefs about their capabilities to exercise control over events that affect their lives."[18] Emphasizing the role of cognition in determining behavior, self-efficacy theory claims that action is influenced by the belief that the activity or behavior can be accomplished, producing a distinction between possessing abilities and being able to enact them successfully. People will avoid situations and choose not to undertake a task that they believe is too difficult. In this way, efficacy beliefs may limit and constrict the choices that one makes in life and may result in a diminished sense of agency.

Efficacy beliefs vary by gender. Among children, girls view themselves as less efficacious than boys on intellectual activities that have been stereotypically linked with males.[19] Compared with males, females tend to have lower estimates of their abilities, performance, and expectations for future success in achievement situations, even when they actually perform as well as, if not better than, males.[20]

Carol Dweck and her colleagues have identified a possible cause of these gender differences in self-efficacy. Dweck identified differences in the way children respond to task difficulty and experiences of failure. She noted the greater tendency for girls to attribute their failures to low ability rather than lack of motivation or effort. Girls responded to failure (or threat of failure, or even intensified evaluation pressure) with motivational and performance decrements, a phenomenon known as "learned helplessness." Girls consistently underestimate their chance for future success while boys overestimate success.[21] The roots of these differences may lay in teachers' differential interactions with girls and boys. In one study, Dweck and her colleagues observed that, while girls received more positive feedback from the teacher than boys did, this feedback was more likely to concern nonintellectual issues such as neatness. Almost all of the negative feedback directed to girls concerned the intellectual quality of their work, while only about half of such feedback directed to boys concerned intellectual content of their work and the rest was directed at neatness or form. Overall, the pattern of feedback encouraged boys more than girls to feel that their success reflected academic abilities, while their failures did not.

Self-efficacy beliefs are also influenced by emotions. People's belief in their ability to cope with anxiety-provoking situations affects how much depression and stress they experience. Additionally, they will avoid potentially threatening situations because they believe they will be unable to cope with the situation. These beliefs are related to having the coping skills needed to manage a stressful situation successfully. Ozer and Bandura created a "mastery modeling" program in which women learned the skills necessary to defend themselves successfully against unarmed assailants. The mastery modeling training enhanced perceived coping and self-efficacy beliefs and decreased perceived vulnerability to attack. Women used avoidance as a safety strategy less often as their feelings of empowerment and self-assurance increased.[22]

Conclusion

In this brief overview, the limits of psychological research on agency are apparent. Much of this work ignores the larger context not only of cultural beliefs and values but also of the distribution of power and other resources that shape beliefs about efficacy as well as actual efficacy itself. Agency may have different meanings or take different forms in different contexts, or among different groups of people. Yet this overview suggests some possible directions for feminist theorizing about agency.

First, agency and communion may not be opposite ends of a single continuum; one can be high or low in both agency and communion. Mothering, for example, seems to encompass a high degree of both domains. Second, formulations that distinguish agency from communal or relatedness behavior may oversimplify by dichotomizing the two, creating a false distinction between them. Furthermore, precise definitions of agency are needed that include a cognitive component consisting of agentic beliefs. These beliefs may be a critical link between abilities and action, and they may connect the individual and the environment in a condition of mutual influence. Certainly societal views of women can influence self-efficacy beliefs, but individuals also have the capacity to evaluate their own abilities, and to change that evaluation.

The famous dictum of the women's movement in the 1960s and 1970s, "the personal is political," reformulated women's personal problems as socially caused, rather than the product of individual deficits. This dictum absolved women of personal responsibility for their low status in society, but it did not remove their responsibility to seek remedies through political action. That is, while social influences may constrain and shape women's agency, they do not remove the ability to act.

Rather than seeing women either as a product of environmental forces or as autonomous determiners of their destiny, it is critical to view women in a reciprocal relationship with their particular situational and structural environment. Agency is possible, but it occurs within a social context that frames it in certain ways. Close examination of women's lives reveals the ways in which subordinate status shapes those opportunities. Feminists are well aware that race, ethnicity, social class, and other factors that mark cleavages in our society limit women's autonomy; yet women respond to these limits in a variety of ways. Theories that incorporate a consideration of specific contexts and that recognize the multiplicity of ways of coping with those contexts will most accurately portray women's experience of agency.

6

Working Together

Challenges in Collaborative Research
on Violence against Women

COLLABORATION BETWEEN advocates and researchers working on issues of violence against women has become increasingly important in recent years for at least two reasons. First, both groups recognize that they have much to gain by working together. New knowledge and improved services require multiple forms of expertise. Whereas researchers may help answer practice-driven questions, advocates may be able to use research findings to improve services, impress funders, and change policies and public opinion.

Second, collaborations occur now not only because both groups benefit, but also (and increasingly) because funders and others mandate collaboration. Several funding agencies, such as the Centers for Disease Control and the National Institute of Justice, require collaboration in research on domestic violence. Research projects sometimes must have advisory boards composed of community members, and innovative service projects often must have an evaluation component. So it is increasingly important that advocates and researchers learn how to work together. However, even if they collaborate because they want to, not just because they have to, working together may be difficult.

In the 1970s, when many grassroots programs that respond to violence against women began, researchers and advocates were fairly distinct in interests and expertise. Today, many advocates have research training, and many researchers have experience as advocates. Although the two roles overlap considerably, even to the point where researchers and advocates occupy both roles, most place primacy either on research or on service provision or advocacy. Therefore, for purposes of discussion, this chapter portrays researchers and advocates as distinct groups.

Although they share the common goal of reducing and preventing violence against women, researchers and advocates may differ in their priorities. Researchers may be most interested in developing knowledge and theories, while advocates may be more concerned with social action.[1] Typically, advocates and researchers work in organizations with different cultures. Researchers may be rewarded for publications with promotions and research funding, while such rewards may be irrelevant to advocates. To them, successful research is that which benefits their communities and promotes social change. Advocates and researchers may differ somewhat in their professional backgrounds and expertise, and they use different terminology.[2] Moreover, differences in race, class, gender, and sexual orientation between advocates and researchers may exacerbate mistrust.[3] These differences may produce tensions that make it difficult to work together.

Collaborative research (also known as participatory research) has a long history in social science,[4] and studies on violence against women often use feminist collaborative research approaches.[5] Collaboration may range from joint development of research goals, methods, and interpretations of findings to occasional consultation with community representatives by researchers or even simply researchers' request for a letter of support from advocates. Yet two hallmarks of collaborative research on violence against women are (a) the desire to share control of the research process among all collaborators, and (b) the desire to involve all participants (be they researchers, advocates or service-providers, community representatives, or women who have been abused) in many phases of research, from designing the research questions to collecting data to disseminating findings.

Challenges in Collaboration

Trust

Researchers who come into a community, collect data, and leave—doing what some call "drive-by data collection"—have created a legacy of mistrust. This kind of research may be exploitive, benefiting only the researcher and giving nothing back to the community. At its worst, such research harms women if it is designed or interpreted in ways that "blame the victim" or are inaccurate, or that do not consider the safety and confidentiality of the participants. For these good reasons, some advocates mistrust researchers.

Advocates also fear harm to their programs from the results of evaluation research. Reflecting on an evaluation of a welfare to work project, Levin raises the question of whether evaluation will be done "with the project or 'to' the project."[6] That is, are program staff to be involved in the design of the study and interpretation of data, or will research "experts" collect data that they (unilaterally) deem important and then interpret (or possibly misinterpret) the data? Today, when so much competition exists for funds, any hint of negativity about a program may be used against it. A negative evaluation may enhance researchers' reputations for rigor but hasten the demise of a program.[7] Evaluation researchers who are not sensitive to the political environment in which a program exists inadvertently may provide fuel for the program's enemies. At the same time, advocates need to be willing to acknowledge that their programs might not have the desired impact.

Especially when dealing with violence, confidentiality and safety of clients are of utmost concern. Practitioners may fear that researchers will not be sensitive to these issues or that the process of participating in a research interview will create anxiety or distress.[8] However, clients may benefit from the opportunity to tell their stories to researchers,[9] and innovative data collection techniques can protect women's privacy. For example, a study of domestic violence among women on welfare used tape recorders to ensure privacy while conducting interviews in busy welfare offices. Women listened through headphones to questions about domestic violence on a prerecorded tape and marked their responses on an answer sheet that contained only question numbers and response categories. This technique not only enabled women to respond privately, but it also overcame literacy problems.[10] A feminist researcher in another study argued successfully against the use of tape recorders in interviews with abused women, claiming that mechanical devices would heighten women's suspicion and fear of being interviewed.[11] Tape recorders worked well in the first setting, a relatively public office of a state agency, but they were not appropriate in the second situation, which involved private interviews with battered women who had just given birth. Although they adopted opposite strategies, both studies tailored their research methods to meet the specific needs of the women being interviewed, based on advice from advocates.

Another source of mistrust, not only between advocates and researchers but also within each group, may lie in the clashing assumptions people hold about violence against women. Some assumptions stem from an individualistic perspective that assumes that causes for action lie within the individual and often ignores the role of social context in shaping behavior. Research done from this perspective, such as research that seeks to identify characteristics of women likely to be battered, isolates women from factors in their environment, such as racism or class discrimination, that may affect their response to violence. In so doing, this research may imply that women are responsible for their abuse.[12] Working with advocates aware of the importance of contextual factors may counter this individualistic bias. Other researchers consider a "contextual" approach to include examination of things that women say or do in a battering situation. Despite a disclaimer that they are not attributing causation to women, these researchers are likely to encounter considerable opposition from advocates.[13]

Overcoming distrust between researchers and advocates (or within each group) is not simply a matter of good communication or whether researchers are "good" people who do not exploit. It also is a matter of power and control.

Power and Control

Questions of control of research are particularly sensitive because researchers may be connected with (apparently) resource-rich universities, while advocates often come from small, underfunded community agencies. Rarely do community organizations have the resources to pay for, and thus perhaps control, researchers. Developing trusting relationships can create a context in which power differentials may be negotiated, but they do not negate these inequalities.[14]

Resolving questions of power is often the most difficult aspect of collaboration.[15] These questions arise in many aspects of research:

Whose Priorities Will Predominate? Researchers may be concerned with theory development or with the collection of data, while practitioners may be less concerned about theory than with the need for answers to immediate questions or with the well-being of participants in the study.[16] The emotional needs of women who have been abused may at times conflict with the data collection process. One way to deal with this is to train interviewers in advocacy and to train advocates to interview. Interviewers in a crime-related study became concerned about how to respond to women who had been raped. The interviewers did not want to be placed in the role of counselor, yet they wanted to respond to the women's needs. The solution was to have each interviewer give the respondent a list of local rape victim resources, ask her if she was familiar with them, and leave the list with her.[17] A similar compromise was reached in the previously mentioned study of battered women who had just given birth. Some researchers wanted the women to be interviewed by tape recorder or at least by interviewers who were unaware of the purpose of the research, while feminist advocates insisted that the interviewers be formerly battered women who could empathize and intervene in battering situations. The solution was to train advocates in interview techniques and to have them use a structured interview. The advocates could also offer support and information when appropriate.[18]

Collaborators in an evaluation of a domestic violence intervention in a manufacturing plant had in common a desire to reduce and prevent domestic violence. Beneath that overarching goal, however, stakeholders' interests differed. The plant manager needed to maintain a high level of production, restricting time available for the intervention, while the employer foundation that initiated the intervention wanted to use the project as a model for future programs. The employer foundation's legal advisors prohibited identification of survey respondents, hindering researchers' ability to match pre- and postintervention responses. In hindsight, the researchers should have taken more time to explain the importance of aspects of the research design.[19]

The collaborators in this project represent various constituencies that themselves were not homogenous. Although plant personnel had approved a survey, some employees criticized its language because it referred to female victims and male batterers. This caused some members of the plant's advisory committee to claim that the researchers were imposing feminist values through their research. Underlying differences in values among various collaborators had not been explored prior to implementing the research, resulting in conflict while the project was ongoing.[20]

Power struggles in a collaborative project also may be reflected in conflict over who controls the funding. A school of nursing and a domestic violence program collaborated on providing health services to women seeking shelter, but the project foundered on the question of which organization would be the primary recipient of grant funds.[21] Although these two organizations cooperate in many other ways, resolving this issue has been difficult.

Who Decides How the Study is Going to Be Done? In evaluating interventions, conflict may occur over the use of a control group of women who do not receive the new program.[22] From a research perspective, control groups may be essential in order to determine whether the program has an impact; from an advocate's viewpoint, denying participation in an effective program is unethical. There are ways to resolve this dilemma, such as giving the control group the new program after the study is done (requiring that funding or other support for the intervention also include resources to do this).[23]

Who Owns the Data? That is, Who Gets to Publish It, and Where? Collaborators may disagree about whether findings should be published as a press release, in a scientific journal article, or in some other form. A study of violence against women on welfare came up with a unique solution to this question. The collaborators developed two separate reports based on the research. The researchers' report presented the survey methodology and findings, while the advocates' report suggested policy directions based on those findings.[24] In this way, the researchers were able to maintain their preferred role as neutral fact finders while implications for policy were addressed by advocates.

If the Researchers and Advocates Disagree about Interpretation of the Data, Whose Interpretation Will Prevail? Those in different social locations may interpret research findings in strikingly different ways. A researcher studying corporate wives rejected their claims of contentment, attributing them to "false consciousness," a Marxist term meaning that these women identified with (male) ruling class interests against their own (female) class interests. The women wrote a rebuttal rejecting this interpretation. In response, the researcher revised her position to accept the women's statements of satisfaction with their lives but looked for sources of their contentment in their position in the social hierarchy.[25]

This kind of dialogic process recognizes the viewpoint of the researcher but avoids imposing interpretations on research participants.[26] Without such a dialogue, we grant privilege to the authority of the researcher, but such a dialogue must also recognize that those with varying perspectives exist within a social hierarchy. The issue, therefore, is not simply one of "different perspectives" but rather the fact of inequality. Dominant or subordinate status in a social system may shape people's points of view.[27]

In a Program Evaluation, Who Defines Success? For example, using reduction in violence as an outcome measure may be holding a program for women with abusive partners accountable for men's actions, which are beyond its control or influence.[28]

The issues of power and control discussed here are not simply matters of trust or good communication; rather, they require a clear articulation of how control (and rewards) will be distributed among those working together and the development of a mechanism for making decisions when disagreement occurs. It may be tempting to attribute conflict to insufficient understanding or lack of commitment on the part of (other) participants, but conflict is inevitable in any work group, just as in any ongoing relationship. The absence of explicit mechanisms for dealing with conflict makes it difficult to negotiate disagreements openly, leaving a group vulnerable to control by its most forceful or well-connected members, while others become frustrated or alienated from the project.[29]

As Levin[30] points out, although individual power may be lost in collaboration, group power may be gained. Shared power has the benefit of developing a sense of "ownership" of the project among many constituencies. In evaluating a welfare-to-work project, although administrative and managerial staff were consulted, line staff were not asked their opinions until problems occurred. Not having been consulted, they were unwilling to modify their actions to enhance the research. Only after repeated attempts were made to include them in improving the project design and implementation did the line staff become engaged in the research.[31]

Time Perspective

Researchers typically take a long-term time perspective. They are trained to gather complete information on a topic. They want to take time to develop research instruments carefully and test them until they are satisfactory.

Furthermore, researchers know that the results of any one study are not likely to be conclusive; they are trained to consider the preponderance of evidence from a large number of studies. Advocates, on the other hand, are used to making quick decisions based on incomplete information.[32] They want—and need—answers soon. Their time perspective may sharply contrast with that of researchers.

The pressing need for solutions to social problems may cause the adoption of policies or programs based on the findings of one or two studies when the conclusions of those studies may be called into question by subsequent research. For example, an influential 1983 study found that arresting men who were assaulting their wives or lovers led to a reduction in domestic violence.[33] Efforts by some advocates, supported by these findings, led to "mandatory arrest" laws in at least seventeen states and the District of Columbia requiring police to make arrests when called to domestic assaults or when civil protection orders are violated. However, a more recent study done by the same researcher[34] found that whether or not the men were employed made a critical difference in subsequent levels of violence. Among men who were employed, being arrested led to a decline in their rates of domestic violence in the year after being released from jail. But those who were unemployed were more likely to be violent if they had been arrested than if they had only been warned. Basing legal policy on a single study may have inadvertently raised the levels of violence against some women. Furthermore, the mandatory arrest laws may have had the unintended consequence of an increase in the number of women arrested for wounding men, even in self-defense.

Time is important in collaborative research in another way. The ongoing negotiation required to maintain a successful collaborative relationship takes a great deal of time. As Edleson points out, "Negotiating the research design, implementation procedures, interpretation, and publication of results is extremely time-consuming in general, and is even more so when the process is shared among collaborators from different disciplines who often have different values."[35] Those for whom research is a central part of their job may have more time to discuss research issues in detail. In contrast, for advocates, research may be an addition to what is already a more than full-time job, giving them little time (except overtime) for collaboration with researchers. Public agencies may be especially crisis-driven and pressed to respond to immediate needs.[36] Researchers can respect this by fitting their needs into advocates' existing schedules—for example, by attending regularly scheduled staff meetings rather than setting up additional meetings and in other ways organizing the research at the advocates' convenience.

Collaboration may become a long-term commitment that lasts beyond any particular project or its participants. Joint efforts between a school of nursing and a domestic violence program have become so embedded in both organizations that both recognize their cooperative work will continue beyond any one project. This commitment to an ongoing relationship helps to overcome temporary conflicts.[37]

A study of battered women's risk of homicide included in its advisory group representatives of six agencies, four out-of-town consultants, and four local experts. This project used a variety of means including phone calls, fax, e-mail, and letters to keep its advisory group members informed. The researchers distributed detailed minutes of meetings and found that some advisory board members who could not attend meetings would respond to queries included in the minutes. Some members would participate actively when their expertise was useful, and not at other times. More than twenty people contributed to the development of the survey used in this project, but such wide participation required many months of effort. Keeping everyone familiar with the project's progress and making sure that people received credit for their contributions helped to maintain a large and diverse group over time.[38]

The time necessary for collaboration may have extra costs for some participants. Funders and administrators (such as academic review committees seeking a large quantity of publications from candidates for tenure) may be impatient with the time that this relationship-building requires.[39] Participatory research may retard academic publication and career advancement[40] or at least require that a researcher justify the added time necessary to do community research.

Expertise

Research training and experience as an advocate both develop expertise, but that expertise may differ. (Many who work on violence against women have occupied both roles, so in practice these forms of expertise often overlap.) Advocates have a wealth of knowledge developed through direct experience with battered and abused women. Their close, day-to-day work gives them a fine-grained knowledge of these women's lives. They are likely to be particularly aware of the way that culture and ethnicity affects responses to abuse, and so they know how research instruments should be modified for particular groups of women. Because of their close involvement in women's lives, they are aware firsthand of cutting edge issues that have not yet surfaced in research and policy discussions. Furthermore, they often are knowledgeable about the politics surrounding violence and abuse policies. For example, experts in domestic violence were extremely helpful in devising questionnaires, training interviewers, and raising ethical and practical research concerns in a study of women's risk of homicide by an intimate partner.[41] Battered women also contribute to research and theory, for example by specifying outcome variables and identifying strategies to implement research safely.[42]

Research training prepares one to collect data, conduct statistical tests, draw inferences from data, and report findings. Those with research training know how to evaluate whether a finding is consistent with other studies and whether a study is scientifically sound. They know formal theories about violence and abuse, and they know how to use data to enter into theoretical and policy debates on a national level. Research can give voice to women and to a point of view, using data as support. For those who are attempting innovations in practice, evaluation research can provide guidance for program development. Moreover, findings from research may be convincing to funders and others concerned with a program's effectiveness or legitimacy.

What is essential is that all involved respect each other's expertise and contributions. One multidisciplinary violence research group gave equal weight to all participants. Researchers did not take on the "expert" role; instead, they acknowledged the value of contributions from all participants. This encouraged advocates to share their knowledge with the group and, reciprocally, to appreciate the challenges involved in doing research. Participants in this research group, some of whom were advocates and some of whom were researchers, increasingly saw themselves as occupying both roles as the group developed.[43] Working well together necessitates a shift from the role of "expert" to that of "co-learner."[44] Levin[45] describes evaluation researchers as invited guests, while another metaphor is that of translator or mediator, in which the researcher interprets the concerns of one group in terms that are understandable to another and helps to negotiate agreements. Partnership is still another metaphor for collaboration, implying that all parties benefit from the relationship.[46] Whether co-learner, invited guest, translator or partner, each of these metaphors reframes the role of researcher from that of expert to one of a participant on equal terms in a joint enterprise.

Stressful Emotions

Violence against women generates stress for both advocates and researchers. Working day after day with women who are bruised and battered takes a toll, as evidenced in the high burn-out rate among advocates. Researchers also find studying violence against women to be stressful. One project's staff stated that "constantly reading about and discussing rape and other forms of violence against women often left us anxious and depressed."[47] Stanko[48] describes "anger, frustration, fear, and pain" during her research experiences, while Moran-Ellis[49] uses the phrase "pain by proxie" to describe her emotional responses to her research on child sexual abuse. One benefit of collaboration is that experienced advocates may share with researchers strategies for coping with their own emotional distress, as they did in a study of violence against women on welfare.[50]

From an advocate's perspective, those who work at a research center may appear to have the luxury of separating themselves from immediate involvement with violence, even if they spend some time in a setting that serves abused women. Advocates who work in a shelter, or who staff crisis lines or the like, may not have the same opportunity to leave violence behind while they work. Advocates may resent what they perceive to be researchers' relative freedom from the issue of violence. And researchers may have difficulty recognizing the emotional drain of doing such practice day after day. Collaboration may reduce some of the isolation that contributes to stress for both groups.[51]

Collaborative research paradigms bring special sources of tension for those trained in traditional research methods. Traditional positivist models of research separates thought from emotion, reason from values.[52] Modeled after the physical sciences, traditional methods treat people being studied as objects, and the researcher as the source of understanding and interpretation.[53] Collaborative models, in contrast, treat those who are studied as "experts" on themselves, abolishing the distinction between the knower and the known that is central to conventional research.[54] For traditional researchers, the loss of control and authority implicit in a collaborative model may be unsettling. Those who are attracted to research because of its detached, analytic, intellectual nature may find that successful collaboration requires political and social skills that may not be part of researchers' professional training but that are necessary to develop relationships with nonresearchers.[55]

Gondolf[56] proposes an "advocacy research" role that serves the concerns of advocates much as a defense lawyer does a client's concerns. That is, the advocacy researcher uses research skills on behalf of advocates and the battered women they represent rather than to promote a research agenda. Helping to refine concerns into researchable questions, explaining the advantages and disadvantages of various research designs, and discussing interpretations of findings with advocates are some functions that the advocacy researcher can fulfill. However, an advocacy stance should not preclude using scientific strategies to minimize bias; scientific criteria of reliability and validity still apply. Not addressing traditional concerns of rigorous science would mean that research is unlikely to be taken seriously by other researchers or funders.

In contrast to an "advocacy research" approach, Gelles[57] argues: "At best, researchers can use conceptual models and statistics about extent and correlation to inform clinicians and advocates. But those are the practical limits of research." In his view, researchers are "objective and dispassionate" truth-seekers, while advocates argue for their personal point of view. He claims that attempting to mix the two roles is neither necessary nor productive.

The contrast between Gelles' position and that of advocacy research mirrors fundamental disagreements in science about objectivity. An "advocacy research" model, where researchers' values are explicit, counters the positivist assumptions of research as value-free. Feminists and others have argued that even traditional research is not value-free.[58] As Levin[59] states: "The questions that we ask and the ways that we go about answering them reflect a set of beliefs, expectations and interests." Recognizing the value-laden nature of research may be difficult to accept for those trained in the positivist model and imbued with its stance of objectivity. Mary Koss and Claire Renzetti, two prominent researchers on violence against women, reflect this struggle in referring to themselves respectively as a "recovering positivist"[60] and "reformed positivist."[61]

Conclusion

Collaborative research on violence against women presents some special problems. The imminent threat of harm to those who are the subjects of study makes high-quality, accurate research especially important. Moreover, it is critical that the policy implications not be "victim blaming."

Jacobson describes dialogues on woman abuse that range from "stimulating intellectual discourse between camps with distinct but reconcilable world views to a downright hostile shouting match between advocates of seemingly contradictory positions."[62] Shouting matches seem unlikely to help abused women. Advocates and researchers may share a desire to end violence against women, yet too often each group considers the other to be antagonistic.

On the basis of four in-depth case studies of successful collaboration, Edleson recommends that researchers spend time with practitioners, that they share decision-making power, and that they help shape practitioners' concerns into researchable questions.[63] Some researchers may work as volunteers in a program and eventually be considered "one of them." But other models of successful collaboration are also possible. Despite the recent push to identify "best practices," several factors mitigate against one "best" way to collaborate.

First, the ecology of settings varies greatly. Resources, expertise, demand, and other factors differ considerably across locales, making each setting somewhat unique. Moreover, although structural factors may provide a common context for collaborative efforts, participants may interpret phenomena in varying ways. The "indeterminacy of meaning," as postmodern theorists label it, means that different parties in a joint effort may interpret things in different ways.[64] For example, researchers may see themselves as performing a useful service for advocates while advocates may see those same researchers as exploitive. Advocates may view procedures for safeguarding participants in research as essential, while those same procedures may seem excessively burdensome to researchers. Reaching common understandings and agreements requires establishing relationships, a process that may vary depending on the participants, their history and numerous other factors. Consequently, no single collaboration strategy may best fit all settings.

Furthermore, unforeseen events occur that require partners to renegotiate their understandings and working procedures. For example, about one year into a study of domestic violence among women on welfare, the collaborative group doing the research expanded its membership. Prior to expansion, the group had developed an effective consensus-building process. Adding new members with diverse viewpoints required new efforts to come to agreement.[65] Moreover, programs being evaluated may change over time, requiring alterations in the research plan.[66] A domestic violence intervention project in a manufacturing plant used a comparison group at a neighboring plant; a month after the project began, the neighboring plant unexpectedly closed.[67]

One way to enhance the success of collaboration is to articulate expectations and goals as fully as possible before the research begins. Once a project begins, the collaborative group can create a decision-making structure that makes explicit each person's responsibilities, areas of control, and rewards. Too often, the structural arrangements between researchers and advocates are vague, leaving the arrangements open to varying interpretations by different people.[68] Addressing sources of tension before the research begins will reduce some possibilities for conflict. For example, how and by whom will decisions be made about the research design? How will the data be reported? How will women's safety and confidentiality be ensured?

Stakeholders may not always be aware of all of their expectations and goals at the beginning of a project, and those goals may change over time. Despite preliminary agreements, therefore, it is likely that these issues will need to be renegotiated as research progresses. As in any continuing relationship, renegotiation of roles and obligations is constant.[69] What may be predictable, however, is that conflict will inevitably arise and that some mechanism for dealing with conflict will be needed.

Moreover, conflict within collaboration may serve a useful purpose. As Fine claims, "The strength of feminist activist research lies in its ability to open contradictions within collaborative practices."[70] The varying perspectives of different stakeholders are not only sources of disagreement and tension, but they are also reflections of the ways people's location in a social order shapes their consciousness. As such, they become useful indicators of underlying processes; that is, the conflicts themselves are data about the phenomena of interest.

To sustain collaborative projects, we need forums in which we can begin to identify these conflicts, explore areas of agreement, and negotiate disagreement. Only by such continuing efforts will the potential of collaborative research be fully realized. A domestic violence research group, such as the one at Simmons College,[71] is one example of an ongoing opportunity for dialogue among researchers, activists, policy-makers, and community-based providers of services to victims of violence against women. This group maintains a feminist, inclusive, participatory stance and, in the process, overcomes the isolation and stress felt by many who work on issues of violence. Another example is the "collaborative table" set by the Chicago Women's Health Risk Study,[72] at which they include many stakeholders (ranging from interviewers to project funders) as participants in designing the research.

The benefits of collaboration are many, including improved research designs, enhanced research implementation, and more accurate interpretation of findings. Unexpected gains may also occur. For example, the Chicago Women's Health Risk Study unintentionally served as a pilot study for universal abuse screening in Chicago hospitals and health clinics.[73] Unfortunately, the difficulties of collaboration are numerous as well. Despite its many challenges, collaboration may be the best way to develop meaningful research findings that address the vexing problem of violence against women.

7

Ways of Knowing and Community Research

COMMUNITY PSYCHOLOGY HAS benefited greatly from adopting theories and methods developed by organizational psychology. Organizational psychologists use multiple perspectives when they analyze organizations: for example, structural theory, a human resources approach, political theories, and cultural analysis.[1] For community psychologists, then, the organizational perspective contains a wealth of frameworks with which to look at community. Typically, we have adopted these frameworks to study advocacy,[2] neighborhood organizations,[3] and the experience of people who work in social service agencies.[4] What we have in common with organizational psychologists (and others) is agreement on a basic paradigmatic assumption.[5] To understand people, you must understand the settings in which they operate.

Perhaps most important for the field of community psychology, organizational psychologists have developed constructs and measurement techniques that go beyond an individual level of analysis and that can be adapted to community research. For example, Mulvey, Linney, and Rosenberg[6] use the concept of the distribution of decision-making power with an organization in an examination of residential treatment programs for juvenile offenders. Their description of organizational control is based on Tanenbaum's[7] notion of the distribution of decision-making power in industry. Gruber and Trickett,[8] in their study of an innovative high school, also use the concept of decision-making power within an organization as a definition of empowerment. Both of these studies demonstrate the usefulness to community research of conceptualizations of the setting that have been developed by organizational psychologists.

Yet the concordance between organizational and community psychology ends when one considers the underlying values and goals of each field. Values that distinguish community psychology from organizational psychology lead us to emphasize the well-being of individuals rather than the organization's efficiency or effectiveness (see Keys and Frank and Shinn and Perkins[9] for excellent overviews of the organizational-community interface). Organizational psychology has as its purpose the identification of ways to improve organizational functioning, typically by looking at middle-level managerial strategies. Critics describe its goal as figuring out how to get more work for less pay out of fewer people,[10] whereas supporters argue that organizational psychologists are often the sole defenders of the quality of work life in organizations.[11] Although interventions that make organizations more effective may incidentally increase job satisfaction or improve working conditions,[12] that is not their primary purpose.

The values that inform community psychology ought to lead us in a different direction, with a different purpose. We ought to look at those who are on the bottom of the organizational heap—at those who are most affected by organizational practices and policies but who have not effected those policies because they are subordinates in the organization hierarchy. Our purpose ought to be to give voice to their perspective on the organization: To identify how programs and policies affect the choices that are available, and to articulate the strategies that people use to create meaning, given those options. What is critical is that, in studying their lives, we recognize that people are actors who make choices, not simply passive recipients of our interventions, who either accept or fail to see the worth of our programs. How do people with little formal power make their way within organizations? How do they navigate their way among the networks of organizations that structure modern life? What choices are available, and how do they shape those choices? The answers to these questions require that we listen in a different way than usual—indeed, they require that we listen above all.

An example of this kind of research comes from work I have done with a team of researchers at Northwestern University concerning people who have left state mental hospitals.[13] In this case, the organizations involved were the tangled network of social service agencies connected to state mental hospitals. Among other questions, we asked where people went for help when they had problems. The chronically mentally disabled living in community settings today suffer from a multiplicity of problems typical of poor, unemployed people: lack of adequate housing, a shortage of jobs, poor health care, and so on. We found that, for many people, especially those who are younger and those who are black, the family remains the primary source of help. This is true even when people have had multiple hospital admissions and are connected to a social service agency. The only public services used with any frequency were public aid or social security. Thus, from the consumers' view of the "organization" of care, social services are much less relevant as supports than are family. However, policies are usually aimed at and programs developed for the individual patient.

Policies and programs assume that those needing mental health services are autonomous individuals, floating alone through the world. Although this is true of some people, in many cases the family may be the unit in crisis. If we shift our perspective slightly and ask what the person's inability to function has done to the family as an organization, we see a different set of needs and possibilities, for example, for support groups for families of the chronically mentally ill (such as the Alliance for Mental Illness). The organizational elements under consideration may be the same, but, by shifting the perspective slightly from the program to the person, we can see different patterns and advisable solutions. In understanding what happens when people interact with policies and programs, too often an organizational approach can take the policy as a given and see if it works or does not work according to its stated goals. What community psychologists using organizational frameworks should do instead is start with people's lives and see how the policy affects what happens to them. Research from this perspective would help reduce the frequency with which we "stumble over our ignorance" of what actually happens to people affected by mental health policies.[14]

Too often, the voices of those subordinate in organizations are not heard in the debate about policies and programs. This occurs for at least two reasons. First, people who are members of subordinate groups often do not believe that they have the right to speak out. Author Richard Rodriguez presents an eloquent statement of this in his autobiography, *Hunger of Memory*.[15] Rodriguez, born to a working-class Hispanic family in California, felt that he had no right to a public persona—in his case, to speak out at school—unless and until he became a mainstream American by adopting the English language and rejecting Spanish. Only by becoming Americanized could he speak out, and only in English could his voice be heard by society.[16]

The second reason why those in subordinate positions are not heard is that those who predominate have the power to define the terms of the discussion and provide explanations for the behavior of people who are lower in a hierarchical relationship.[17] The superordinate group has more credibility in the public debate, and its explanations are accepted as "truth." Often dominant-group members have preconceived ideas of what should be happening (what we term hypotheses), listen only for whether others fit or do not fit those notions, and fail to hear what else is going on. Thus, in the mental health field, we have numerous studies that document the "failure" of deinstitutionalization because mentally disabled people leave the community so often to return to mental hospitals.[18] What goes unrecognized is the way in which the hospital and allied agencies have become "the community" for people, given the absence of other choices and resources.

Implications for Organizational Research

If we are to hear the viewpoints of those who are in subordinate positions in organizations, we must go about our research in a different way, different than business as usual. Our research methods are not well suited to this task. The values of "normal science" emphasize prediction and control for the purpose of dominating nature, and the methods embody separation and distance from that which we are studying. However, to understand another's world from his or her perspective requires empathy, sensitivity to context, acceptance of complexity, and interrelationship rather than domination. Without these qualities, we simply replicate people's everyday experience of subordination within our research; rather than reflecting objectivity, we reflect the status quo.[19]

How then shall we go about doing organizational community research? Guidelines for a new methodology come from feminist scholarship, in particular from a book entitled *Women's Ways of Knowing*.[20] The authors begin the book by raising difficult questions: "What is truth?" "What is authority?" "What counts for me as evidence?" "How do I know what I know?" Although we may frame them in different language, these questions are the central ones we grapple with as we voice our discontent with research in community psychology. Our answers to these questions define and delimit the research we do. The authors of *Women's Ways of Knowing* assert that "our basic assumptions about the nature of truth and the origins of knowledge shape the way we see the world and ourselves as participants in it." This is as true for those who do research as for the heterogeneous mix of female students who speak out in interviews in this book.

The authors argue that modes of knowing that are especially common among women differ from those that are common among men. They identify five epistemological frameworks, linked by the theme of "finding a voice." Typically, scientists use metaphors of vision and sight rather than voice to describe the process of knowledge acquisition. Evelyn Fox Keller suggests that visual metaphors require passivity on the part of the knower and that distance from the subject is needed to get a proper view. In contrast, hearing and saying implies closeness between subject and object. "Unlike seeing, speaking and listening suggest dialogue and interaction."[21] The process of finding a voice is the process of developing the ability and the confidence to participate in the creation of knowledge.

The first of the five epistemological positions identified as typical of women is silence, a condition in which women feel neither the right nor the ability to express themselves. The second, received knowledge, is a position from which women can accept knowledge from omniscient authorities but cannot create it on their own. Subjective knowledge, the third position, reflects a move from passive to active, from acceptance of external authority to a conception of truth as personal and private, in which one becomes one's own authority. Procedural knowing, the fourth position, emphasizes reason and objectivity as strategies for gaining knowledge. It is this position that describes traditional research methods in psychology. The final category, constructed knowledge, has been described as follows:

> The central insight that distinguishes this position is that all knowledge is constructed and the knower is an intimate part of the known. The woman comes to see that the knowledge one acquires depends on the context or frame of reference of the knower who is seeking answers and in the context in which events to be understood have occurred. . . . Empathic seeing and feeling with the other is a central feature of the development of connected knowing. . . . Communion and communication are established with that which one is trying to understand. Women use such images as "conversing with nature," "getting close to ideas," "having rapport with an author" in order to understand, rather than more masculine images such as "pinning an idea down," or "seeing through an argument."[22]

The key characteristics of constructed knowledge—that all knowledge is contextual, that people create knowledge, and that both objective and subjective strategies are valuable and can be integrated—seem particularly congruent with the values of community psychology. The process of "gaining a voice," of thinking that is informed by feeling rather than devoid of it, of collaborative talk in which new knowledge is developed and ideas emerge, all suggest strategies for community research that extend—indeed, even transform—traditional methodologies.

How then do we translate these ideas into research techniques? Suggestions for how to do that come from the description of women at the constructivist level:

> Question posing and problem posing become prominent methods of inquiry. . . . Women tend not to rely as readily or as exclusively on hypothetico-deductive inquiry, which posits an answer (the hypothesis) prior to the data collection, as they do on examining basic assumptions and the conditions in which a problem is cast. For constructivist women, simple questions are as rare as simple answers. Constructivists can take, and often insist upon taking, a position outside a particular context or frame of reference and look back on "who" is asking the questions, "why" the question is asked at all, and "how" answers are arrived at.[23]

Finally, constructivists identify a process of "really talking," rather than didactic talking in which the speaker simply presents ideas to others. "Real talk" is a process of dialogue in which ideas can emerge and be explored, not simply confirmed. Furthermore, the process is collaborative, not hierarchical. "Connected knowing arises out of the experience of relationships; it requires intimacy and equality between self and object, not distance and impersonality; its goal is understanding, not proof."[24] "Really talking" suggests to us a method for overcoming silence.[25] It suggests a process of "dialogue from which knowledge is an unpredictable emergent rather than a controlled outcome."[26] Moreover, it acknowledges that we are linked with those we study in a human relationship and emphasizes the need for an awareness of the ways in which we construct the knowledge that is developed in that context.

The themes that permeate constructivist thought processes are those of connection, mutuality, and reciprocity. These themes are ones that Gilligan[27] has identified as typifying the way that women (at least in this society at this time) often think about morality. Rather than basing moral decisions on an ethic of rights, women consider responsibilities and care. These themes are particularly evident in the operation of community organizations. At the local level, women are often involved as prime movers of community organizations, and the thrust of their involvement comes from a concern with their families and homes that has been extended to their neighborhoods.[28] As one organizer put it, "You start by organizing in your house and move to your community."[29]

An excellent example of this kind of study of an organization comes from Leavitt and Saegert's[30] analysis of tenant organizations in Harlem, New York, that formed in buildings that had been abandoned by their owners. Moreover, this study exemplifies many of the characteristics of constructivist knowing, of "really talking," and of empathic discourse, in its emphasis on context, on identifying the ways in which people shape the resources available to them and the reasons for the choices they make, and on the connection between knowledge and values. Leavitt and Saegert interviewed tenants who were part of a city program that permits people who manage their abandoned building to own it eventually, in a limited equity cooperative arrangement. Many of the leaders of the tenant organizations were female and elderly, and their care of the building extended to care for the sick and elderly tenants. Care for the people in the building is interwoven with care for the physical property:

. . .communication among the leaders was constant, ways of involving all tenants had been developed, responsibilities were shared maximally and a multidirectional flow of information established. More than this, the ethic of caring for your neighbors extended from relationships among the Board of Directors through the actions of the committee system to look after the sick and elderly through willingness to bear the financial costs of the inability of sick, old people to pay rent increases.[31]

The tenant co-op provided an opportunity for traditional values of women in this community—commitment to community, religious values, and an emphasis on care—to emerge as predominate. These women extended the values from the home to encompass the other tenants in a building, in what Leavitt and Saegert call a "community-household model." Neighborhood activism among working-class women often has as its objective the protection of the "welfare of the family-in-the-home-in-the-neighborhood."[32] In the community-household model, the welfare of one's own home is assured by protecting the welfare of the building as a whole, as well as the people in it.

One of the critical points Leavitt and Saegert make is that housing policy is not set up to accommodate this sort of organization. Housing policies assume hierarchical organizational structures in a situation where webs exist instead. "The personal and intensive nature of their approach contrasts with the impersonal, standardized and efficiency-oriented strategies embedded in most housing policies."[33] Existing policy assumes a bureaucratic model of tenant management with values of efficiency and effectiveness, whereas this research suggests a need for policies that are based on nurturance and caring. For example, greater emphasis on maintenance and rehabilitation of buildings rather than on new construction would enable the preservation of existing social relationships. There is little room in current policy for this approach. Furthermore, organizational research that shares the assumptions of the bureaucratic model will not illuminate the presence of supportive webs and how they work.

Both of the studies discussed here are about people in organizations—in one case, the small, personal, nurturing world of a tenants' organization, and in the other, the large, often impersonal world of the state mental hospital and associated agencies. What both of these studies have in common is an attempt to enter into the worldview of those whom they are studying, and to see how the organization is experienced from their perspective. These studies take into consideration the context in which people live their lives, the resources they have, and the choices that are available to them. They do not look simply at the effect of a particular program on people, but they also consider how that program fits into the totality of people's lives. It is this complexity that we must attempt to capture if we wish to understand the perspective of subordinate groups in organizations.

Doing so will not be easy. We will need to value discovery as well as (and as much as) hypothesis testing, to value exploratory as well as confirmatory research. Yet the biases within the field of psychology make these research strategies deviant—valued by a minority, if at all. Sherif [34] describes the field of psychology as containing a status hierarchy in which the top rung is occupied by experimentalists, who seek status by aligning their work with the more prestigious physical or natural sciences. "Applied" researchers occupy the bottom rung. Because this status and value hierarchy prevails in academic departments of psychology, those favoring nonexperimental research strategies, especially on applied topics (as community psychologists are wont to do), will probably be low in status within their departments. Furthermore, because innovations that counter a social system's values and modes of operating are not likely to be adopted,[35] attempts to broaden the range of acceptable methodologies within psychology are likely to be in vain. Indeed, those who resist inclusion of nonexperimental techniques may do so with good reason because methods such as "constructed knowing" challenge some of the fundamental tenets on which experimentalism is based. Accepting the validity of "constructed knowing" will not simply add more choices to our array of research strategies, but will also imply a shift in the value hierarchy within psychology. Given their low status within psychology departments as "applied" researchers, the pressure on many community psychologists is not to innovate but rather to demonstrate acceptability by using research methods that approximate experimental techniques as closely as possible.

Yet psychology departments are not monolithic, and techniques have been accepted in recent years that exemplify some of the characteristics of connected knowing.[36] For example, stakeholder-based evaluation research—a technique that takes consumers' priorities into account in the process of evaluating social programs[37]—can be applied to organizations. This technique attempts to incorporate into the evaluation process questions formulated by the different constituencies that have an interest in the results of an evaluation, especially those who are the least powerful.[38] In doing so, this method implicitly views organizations as political entities, composed of shifting groups with different interests, that compete for scarce resources.[39] Because stakeholders may differ, the evaluator must decide which group's (or groups') questions will be addressed, bringing the issue of values to the fore. The awareness of the choice process involved reflects an awareness of the way in which knowledge is socially constructed.[40]

The limitations of this evaluation strategy may apply to connected knowing as well. Findings may not be generalizable to other settings; the degree of involvement required by the research process may not be practical or desirable from the participants' point of view; and diverse participants may experience a setting in conflicting ways, some of which do not get included.[41] Descriptive research may limit our ability to make causal inferences. Furthermore, we need to look not only at how individuals experience an organization, but also at the organizational factors that shape and inform individuals' experience.[42] Finally, simply giving voice to the experience of the least powerful in organizations may not lead to change.[43]

Although these difficulties may place limits on the constructivist approach, transformation of research methods to include this way of knowing would bring us closer to our goal of assessing the impact of organizations on people's lives rather than simply viewing people as organizational components. Each of the major theoretical perspectives in organizational psychology examines a different set of issues. Structural theory directs us to examine the way in which jobs are organized and activity is integrated; a human relations approach focuses on individual needs, skills and attitudes toward one's job; a political approach examines the shifting set of coalitions and alliances that make up organizational life; and the symbolic approach examines organizations as a stage upon which dreams are enacted that reflect human needs and concerns.[44] Within each of these frameworks, the use of constructivist research methods will allow us to examine the impact of the organization on its members in a manner that permits consideration of the complexity of human experience. It will facilitate elucidation of the impact of the organization on those at the bottom of the organization's hierarchy, particularly those who are the recipients of its services. As Seidman[45] states, in a discussion of social problem solving: "Recipients, who are presumed to benefit in the short or long run, can no longer be excluded or incorporated in only token fashion if the process is to be truly meaningful and beneficial to them. They may have dramatically different conceptualizations." Constructivist knowing is an approach to research that will enable recipients' conceptualizations of the organization to become part of the discussion. It is a way for community psychologists to apply organizational frames to the aspects of organizational processes that we value knowing about.

The lack of adventuresome research in community psychology is deplored every few years when some of our colleagues muster the energy to review all of the articles published in one of our journals.[46] It is not simply that we lack the imagination to translate our values and beliefs into research questions. Rather, our adherence to traditional scientific methods limits what we can study and what we hear.

I do not advocate the elimination of discipline and conscientiousness in our research; nor am I suggesting that we reject quantitative methods (as the example given here of stakeholder analysis demonstrates). Rather, let us retain the best qualities of current research methods and expand them, transforming them in the process. Traditional research methods, as reflective of mainstream American culture, emphasize objectivity, efficiency, separateness, and distance. Yet objectivity need not be confounded with domination or hierarchical relations with those whom we study.[47] Let us consider as well connection and empathy as modes of knowing and embrace them in our criteria and in our work. We would do well to make room for "constructed knowing" in our adventuresome research.

PART II

Gender, Policies, and Practices

8

Gender Dilemmas in Sexual Harassment Policies and Procedures

SEXUAL HARASSMENT—unwanted sexually oriented behavior in a work context—is the most recent form of victimization of women, following rape and wife abuse, to be redefined from a personal to a social problem. A sizable proportion of women surveyed in a wide variety of work settings report being subject to unwanted sexual attention, sexual comments or jokes, or offensive touching as well as attempts to coerce compliance with or punish rejection of sexual advances. In 1980, the U.S. Merit Systems Protection Board conducted the first comprehensive national survey of sexual harassment among federal employees; about four out of ten of the 10,648 women surveyed reported having been the target of sexual harassment during the previous twenty-four months. Updates of this survey found that the frequency of harassment in 1988 and 1994 was almost identical to that reported earlier: 42 percent of women surveyed in 1988 and 44 percent of women in 1994 reported that they had experienced some form of unwanted and uninvited sexual attention compared to 42 percent in 1980.[1]

Women in occupations ranging from blue-collar workers[2] to lawyers[3] to airline personnel[4] have reported considerable amounts of sexual harassment. Among a random sample of private sector workers in the Los Angeles area, more than half of the women surveyed by telephone reported experiencing at least one incident that they consider sexual harassment during their working lives.[5] Some estimate that up to about a third of women in educational institutions have experienced some form of harassment.[6] Indeed, Garvey states that "Unwanted sexual attention may be the single most widespread occupational hazard in the workplace today."[7]

It is a hazard faced much more frequently by women than men. About four out of every ten women in the original U.S. Merit Systems Protection Board survey reported having experienced sexual harassment, compared to only 15 percent of the men.[8] Among working people surveyed in Los Angeles, women were nine times more likely than men to report having quit a job because of sexual harassment, five times more likely to have transferred, and three times more likely to report losing a job.[9] Men with less power and status, whether due to lower age, being single or divorced, or being in a marginal position in the organization, are more likely to be harassed.[10]

Sex differences in the frequency of harassment also prevail in educational environments.[11] A mailed survey conducted at the University of Rhode Island sampling more than 900 women and men asked about a wide range of behavior including the frequency of respondents' experience of sexual insult, defined as an "uninvited sexually suggestive, obscene or offensive remark, stare, or gesture."[12] Of the female respondents, 40 percent reported being sexually insulted occasionally or often while on campus, compared to 17 percent of the men. Both men and women reported that women are rarely the source of such insults. Similar differences were found in a survey of social workers, with two and a half times as many women reporting harassment as men.[13]

Despite the high frequency rates found in surveys, few complaints are pursued through official grievance procedures. After reviewing survey findings, Dzeich and Weiner[14] concluded that 20–30 percent of female college students experiences sexual harassment. Yet academic institutions averaged only 4.3 complaints each during the 1982–83 academic year,[15] a time period roughly similar to the surveys cited by Dzeich and Weiner. In another study conducted at a university in 1984, of thirty-eight women reporting harassment, only one reported the behavior to the person's supervisor and two reported the behavior to an adviser, another professor, or employer.[16] Similar findings have been reported on other college campuses.[17]

Low numbers of complaints appear in other work settings as well. In a survey of federal workers, only about one in ten victims (11 percent) reported the harassment to a higher authority, and just over one in fifty (2.5 percent) used formal complaint channels.[18] Similarly, female social workers reacted to harassment by avoiding or delaying the conflict or attempting to defuse the situation rather than by adopting any form of recourse such as filing a grievance.[19] The number of complaints alleging sexual harassment filed with the Equal Employment Opportunity Commission in Washington, DC, has declined since 1984, despite an increase in the number of women in the workforce during that time,[20] and some surveys suggest that the rate of sexual harassment has remained relatively stable.[21]

It is the contention of this chapter that the low rate of utilization of grievance procedures is due to gender bias in sexual harassment policies that discourages their use by women. Policies are written in gender-neutral language and are intended to apply equally to males and females. However, these policies are experienced differently by women than men because of sex differences in perceptions of harassment and orientation toward conflict. Although victims of all forms of discrimination are reluctant to pursue grievances,[22] females—those who are most likely to be the victims of sexual harassment—are especially disinclined to pursue sexual harassment grievances for at least two reasons. First, the interpretation in policies of what constitutes harassment may not reflect women's viewpoints, and their complaints may not be seen as valid. Second, the procedures that are designated to resolve disputes in some policies may be inimical to women because they are not compatible with the way that many women view conflict resolution. Gender bias in policies, rather than an absence of harassment or lack of assertiveness on the part of victims, produces low numbers of complaints.

Gender Bias in the Definition of Sexual Harassment

The first way gender bias affects sexual harassment policies stems from differences between males and females in the interpretation of the definition of harassment. Those writing sexual harassment policies for organizations typically look to the courts for the distinction between illegal sexual harassment and permissible (although perhaps unwanted) social interaction.[23] The definition of harassment in policies typically is that provided by the Equal Employment Opportunity Commission Guidelines:

> Unwelcome sexual advances, requests for sexual favors, and other verbal or physical conduct of a sexual nature constitute sexual harassment when (1) submission to such conduct is made either explicitly or implicitly a term or condition of an individual's employment, (2) submission to or rejection of such conduct by an individual is used as the basis for employment decisions affecting such individual, or (3) such conduct has the purpose or effect of unreasonably interfering with an individual's work performance or creating an intimidating, hostile, or offensive working environment.[24]

The first two parts of the definition refer to a "quid pro quo" relationship, often involving people in positions of unequal status, because superior status is usually necessary to have control over another's employment. Here, bribes, threats, or punishments are used. Incidents of this type need happen only once to fall under the definition of sexual harassment. However, courts have required that incidents falling into the third category, that of "an intimidating, hostile, or offensive working environment," must be repeated in order to establish that such an environment exists[25] and must be both pervasive and so severe that it affects the victim's psychological well-being.[26] Harassment of this type can come from peers or even subordinates as well as superiors.

In all three of these categories, harassment is judged on the basis of conduct and its effects on the recipient, not the intentions of the harasser. Thus, two typical defenses given by accused harassers that "I was just being friendly" or "I touch everyone—I'm that kind of person" do not hold up in court since they refer to intentions. But behavior may have an intimidating or offensive effect on some people, while others are not offended or even welcome such conduct. In deciding whose standards should be used, the courts employ what is called the reasonable person rule, asking whether a reasonable person would be offended by the conduct in question. The dilemma in applying this to sexual harassment is that a reasonable woman and a reasonable man are likely to differ in their judgements of what is offensive. However, the differences between women and men, although consistent, are small, and opinions vary considerably within each sex grouping.[27]

Definitions of sexual harassment are socially constructed, varying with not only characteristics of the perceiver but also those of the situational context and actors involved. Behavior is more likely to be labeled harassment when done by someone with greater power than the victim,[28] when it involves physical advances accompanied by threats of punishment for noncompliance,[29] when the response to it is negative,[30] when the behavior reflects persistent negative intentions toward a female,[31] the more inappropriate it is for the actor's social role,[32] and the more flagrant and frequent the harasser's requests.[33] Among women, professionals are more likely than those with secretarial-clerical positions to report the more subtle behaviors as harassment.[34]

The sex of the rater most consistently predicts variation in people's definition of sexual harassment. Men label fewer behaviors at work as sexual harassment.[35] Men find sexual overtures from women at work to be flattering, while women find similar approaches from men to be insulting.[36] Both men and women agree that certain blatant behaviors, such as sexual assault or sexual bribery, constitute harassment, but women are more likely to see as harassment more subtle behavior such as sexual teasing or looks or gestures.[37] Even when men do identify behavior as harassment, they are more likely to think that women will be flattered by it.[38] Men are also more likely than women to blame women for being sexually harassed.[39]

These sex differences make it difficult to apply the reasonable person rule. Linenberger[40] proposes ten factors that permit an "objective" assessment of whether behavior constitutes sexual harassment, regardless of the perception of the victim and the intent of the perpetrator. These factors range from the severity of the conduct to the number and frequency of encounters, and the relationship of the parties involved. For example, behavior is less likely to be categorized as harassment if it is seen as a response to provocation from the victim. But is an objective rating of provocation possible? When sex differences are as clear-cut and persistent as they are in the perception of what behavior constitutes sexual harassment, the question is not one of objectivity, but rather which gender's definition of the situation will prevail. Becker asserts that there is a "hierarchy of credibility" in organizations, and that credibility and the right to be heard are differentially distributed: "In any system of ranked groups, participants take it as given that members of the highest group have the right to define the way things really are."[41] Because men typically have more power in organizations,[42] Becker's analysis suggests that in most situations the male definition of harassment is likely to predominate. As MacKinnon puts it, "objectivity—the nonsituated, universal standpoint, whether claimed or aspired to—is a denial of the existence or potency of sex inequality that tacitly participates in constructing reality from the dominant point of view. . . . The law sees and treats women the way men see and treat women."[43] With respect to sexual harassment, this means that males' judgments about what behavior constitutes harassment, and who is to blame, are likely to prevail. Linenberger's ten factors thus may not be an objective measure, but rather a codification of the male perspective on harassment. This is likely to discourage women who want to bring complaints about more subtle forms of harassment.

Gender Differences in the Attribution of Harassment

Attribution theory provides an explanation for the wider range of behaviors that women define as harassment compared to men, and for men's tendency to find women at fault.[44] Attribution theory suggests that people tend to see their own behaviors as situationally determined, while they attribute the behaviors of others to personality characteristics or other internal causes.[45] Those who see sexual harassment through the eyes of the actor are likely to be male. As actors are wont to do, they will attribute their behaviors to situational causes, including the "provocations" of the women involved. They will therefore not perceive their own behaviors as harassing. In fact, those who take the perspective of the victim do see specific behaviors as more harassing than those who take the perspective of the actor.[46] Since women are more likely to view harassment through the eyes of the victim, they will label more behaviors as harassment because they attribute them to men's disposition or personality traits. Another possibility is that men, as potential harassers, want to avoid blame in the future, and so shift the blame to women[47] and restrict the range of behaviors they define as harassment.[48] Whatever the cause, a reasonable male and a reasonable female are likely to differ in their judgments of whether a particular behavior constitutes sexual harassment.

Men tend to misinterpret females' friendliness as an indication of sexual interest.[49] Acting on this misperception may result in behavior that is harassing to women. Tangri, Burt, and Johnson state: "Some sexual harassment may indeed be clumsy or insensitive expressions of attraction, while some is the classic abuse of organizational power."[50] Gender differences in attributional processes help explain the first type of harassment, partially accounting for the fact that the overwhelming preponderance of sexual harassment incidents involve a male offender and a female victim.

Gender Bias in Grievance Procedures

Typically, procedures for resolving disputes about sexual harassment are written in gender-neutral terms so that they may apply to both females and males. Yet males and females may react quite differently to the same procedures.

Analyzing this problem requires looking at specific policies and procedures. Educational institutions will serve as the context for this discussion for three reasons. First, they are the most frequent sites of surveys about the problem, and the pervasive nature of harassment on campuses has been well documented.[51] Second, while sexual harassment is harmful to women in all occupations, it can be particularly devastating to those in educational institutions where the goal of the organization is to nurture and promote development. The violation of relationships based on trust, such as those between faculty and students, can leave long-lasting and deep wounds. Yet many surveys find that those in positions of authority in educational settings are often the source of the problem.[52] Third, educational institutions have been at the forefront in developing sexual harassment policies, in part because of concern about litigation. In *Alexander v. Yale University* (1980) the court decided that sexual harassment constitutes a form of sex discrimination that denies equal access to educational opportunities, and falls under Title IX of the Educational Amendments of 1972. The Office of Civil Rights in the U.S. Department of Education now requires institutions receiving Title IX funds to maintain grievance procedures to resolve complaints involving sexual discrimination or harassment.[53] Consequently, academic institutions may have had more experience than other work settings in developing procedures to combat this problem. A survey of U.S. institutions of higher learning conducted in 1984 found that 66 percent of all responding institutions had sexual harassment policies, and 46 percent had grievance procedures specifically designed to deal with sexual harassment complaints, with large public schools more likely to have them than small private ones.[54] These percentages have unquestionably increased in recent years, given the government regulations previously cited. While the discussion here focuses on educational contexts, the problems identified in sexual harassment policies apply to other work settings as well.

Many educational institutions, following guidelines put forward by the American Council on Education and the American Association of University

Professors,[55] have established policies that prohibit sexual harassment and create grievance procedures. Some use a formal board or hearing, while others use informal mechanisms that protect confidentiality and seek to resolve the complaint rather than punish the offender;[56] still others use both types of procedures. The type of procedure specified by the policy may have a great impact on victims' willingness to report complaints.

Comparison of Informal and Formal Grievance Procedures

Informal attempts at resolving the dispute differ from formal procedures in important ways (see figure 8-1).[57] First, they have as their goal problem-solving, rather than a judgment of the harasser's guilt or innocence. The assumptions underlying these processes are that both parties in a dispute see a problem as existing (although they may define that problem differently); both share a common interest in solving that problem; and together they can negotiate an agreement that will be satisfactory to everyone involved. Typically, the goal of informal processes is to end the harassment of the complainant rather than judge (and punish, if appropriate) the offender. The focus is on what will happen in the future between the disputing parties, rather than what has happened in the past. Often policies do not specify the format of informal problem solving, accepting a wide variety of strategies of reconciliation. For example, a complainant might write a letter to the offender,[58] or someone might talk to the offender on the complainant's behalf. The offender and victim might participate in mediation, in which a third party helps them negotiate an agreement. Many policies accept a wide array of strategies as good-faith attempts to solve the problem informally.

	Informal Procedures	Formal Procedures
Purpose	Problem-solving or reconciliation	Judge guilt or innocence
Time Focus	What will happen in the future	What did happen in the past
Format	Usually unspecified	Usually specified
Ends	When complainant is satisfied	When hearing board decides
Control over outcome rests with	Complainant	Hearing board

Figure 8-1 A comparison of informal and formal grievance procedures.

In contrast, formal procedures generally require a written complaint and have a specified procedure for handling cases, usually by bringing the complaint to a group officially designated to hear the case such as a hearing board. The informal process typically ends when the complainant is satisfied (or decides to drop the complaint); the formal procedure ends when the group hearing the case decides on the guilt or innocence of the alleged harasser. Thus, control over the outcome usually rests with the complainant in the case of informal mechanisms, and with the official governance body in the case of a hearing. Compliance with a decision is usually voluntary in informal procedures, while the decision in a formal procedure is binding unless appealed to a higher authority. Formal procedures are adversarial in nature, with the complainant and defendant competing to see whose position will prevail.

A typical case might proceed as follows: A student bringing a complaint writes a letter to the harasser (an informal procedure). If not satisfied with the response, she submits a written complaint to the sexual harassment hearing board. The board then hears both sides of the case, reviews available evidence, and decides upon the guilt or innocence of the accused (a formal procedure). If the accused is found guilty, the appropriate officer of the institution decides upon punishment.

Gender Difference in Orientation to Conflict

Women and men may differ in their reactions to dispute resolution procedures for at least two reasons. First, women typically have less power than men do in organizations.[59] Using a grievance procedure, such as appearing before a hearing board, may be inimical because of the possibility of retaliation for a complaint. Miller suggests that differences in status and power affect the way that people handle conflict:

> . . .as soon as a group attains dominance it tends inevitably to produce a situation of conflict and . . . it also, simultaneously, seeks to suppress conflict. Moreover, subordinates who accept the dominant's conception of them as passive and malleable do not openly engage in conflict. Conflict . . . is forced underground.[60]

This would explain why some women do not report complaints at all. The second source of gender differences in dispute resolution may lie in values. When they do complain about harassment, women's values may predispose them to prefer informal rather than formal procedures. Beliefs about the appropriate way to handle disputes vary among social groups.[61] Gilligan's[62] distinction between an orientation toward rights and justice compared to an emphasis on responsibilities to others and caring seems likely to be reflected in people's preferences for ways of handling disputes.[63] Neither of these orientations is exclusive to one gender, but according to Gilligan, females are more likely to emphasize caring. Empirical support for Gilligan's theories is inconclusive.[64] Yet the fact that most victims of sexual harassment state that they simply want an end to the offending behavior rather than punishment of the offender[65] suggests a "caring" rather than "justice" perspective.

In the context of dispute resolution, an emphasis on responsibilities and caring is compatible with the goals of informal procedures to restore harmony or at least peaceful coexistence among the parties involved, while that of justice is compatible with formal procedures which attempt to judge guilt or innocence of the offender. Thus women may prefer to use informal procedures to resolve conflicts, and indeed most cases in educational institutions are handled through informal mechanisms.[66] Policies that do not include an informal dispute resolution option are likely to discourage many women from bringing complaints.

Problems with Dispute Resolution Procedures

Although women may prefer informal mechanisms, they are problematic for several reasons.[67] Since they do not result in punishment, offenders suffer few negative consequences of their actions and may not be deterred from harassing again. In institutions of higher learning, the most common form of punishment reported is a verbal warning by a supervisor, which is given only "sometimes."[68] Dismissal and litigation are almost never used. It seems likely, then, that potential harassers may view sexual harassment as low-risk behavior, while victims see few incentives for bringing official complaints.

The confidentiality usually required by informal procedures prevents other victims from knowing that a complaint has been lodged against a multiple offender. If a woman knows that another woman is bringing a complaint against a particular man who has harassed both of them, then she might be more willing to complain also. The secrecy surrounding informal complaint processes precludes this knowledge from becoming public, making it more difficult to identify repeat offenders. Also, complaints settled informally may not be included in reports of the frequency of sexual harassment claims, making these statistics underestimate the scope of the problem. Yet confidentiality is needed to protect the rights of the accused and may be preferred by those bringing complaints.

These problems in informal procedures could discourage male as well as female victims from bringing complaints. Most problematic for females, however, is the assumption in informal procedures that the complainant and accused have equal power in the process of resolving the dispute. This assumption is likely to put women at a disadvantage. Parties involved in sexual harassment disputes may not be equal either in the sense of formal position within the organization (e.g., student vs. faculty) or status (e.g., female vs. male students), and position and status characteristics that reflect levels of power do not disappear simply because they are irrelevant to the informal process. External status characteristics, which indicate macro-level social stratification (such as gender and age), help explain the patterns of distribution of sexual harassment in the workplace.[69] It seems likely that these external statuses will influence the interpersonal dynamics within a dispute resolution procedure as well. Since females are typically lower in both formal and informal status and power in organizations than males, they will have less power in the dispute resolution process.

When the accused has more power than the complainant (such as a male faculty member compared to a female student who is bringing a complaint against him), the complainant is more vulnerable to retaliation. Complainants may be reluctant to use grievance procedures because they fear retaliation should the charge be made public; for example, students may fear that a faculty member will punish them for bringing a complaint by lowering their grades or withholding recommendations. The person appointed to act as a guide to the informal resolution process is usually expected to act as a neutral third party rather than advocate for the complainant, and may hold little formal power over faculty: "Relatively few institutions have persons empowered to be (nonlegal) advocates for the complainants; a student bringing a complaint has little assurance of stopping the harassment and avoiding retaliation."[70] The victim is therefore left without an advocate to face an opponent whose formal position, age, and experience with verbal argument is often considerably beyond her own. Since the more vulnerable a woman's position within her organization, the more likely it is that she will be harassed,[71] sexual harassment, like rape, seems to involve dynamics of power and domination as well as sexuality. The lack of an advocate for the complainant who might equalize power between the disputing parties is particularly troubling. However, if an advocate is provided for the complainant in an informal process, fairness and due process require that the defendant have an advocate as well. The dilemma is that this seems likely to transform an informal, problem-solving process into a formal, adversarial one.

Other Obstacles to Reporting Complaints

Belief That Sexual Harrassment is Normative. Gender differences in perception of behavior are likely to mean that males and females involved in a sexual harassment case have sharply divergent interpretations of that case, particularly when an "offensive environment" claim is involved. To females, the behavior in question is offensive, and they are likely to see themselves as victims of male actions. The requirement that an attempt be made to mediate the dispute or solve it through informal processes may violate their perception of the situation and themselves as victims of a crime. When someone is a victim of a mugging, it is rare that the victim is required to "solve the problem" with the mugger through mediation.[72] To males, the behavior is not offensive but rather normative. In their eyes, no crime has been committed, and there is no "problem" to be solved.

Some women as well as men may consider sexual harassment as normative. Women may believe that these sorts of behaviors are simply routine, a commonplace part of everyday life, and thus not something that can be challenged. Younger women—those more likely to be victimized[73] —are more tolerant of harassment than are older women.[74] Indeed, Lott and her colleagues conclude "younger women in particular have accepted the idea that prowling men are a 'fact of life.'"[75] This attitude might prevent women from labeling a negative experience as harassment. Surveys that ask women about sexual harassment and about the frequency of experiencing specific sexually harassing behaviors find discrepancies in responses to these questions.[76] Women report higher rates when asked if they have been the targets of specific harassing behaviors than when asked a general question about whether they have been harassed. Women are also more willing to report negative reactions to offensive behaviors than they are to label those behaviors as sexual harassment.[77]

Normative beliefs may deter male victims of harassment from reporting complaints also, because males are expected to welcome sexual advances if those advances are from females.

Negative Outcomes for Victims Who Bring Sexual Harassment Complaints. The outcome of grievance procedures does not appear to provide much satisfaction to victims who bring complaints. In academic settings, despite considerable publicity given to a few isolated cases in which tenured faculty have been fired, punishments are rarely inflicted on harassers, and the punishments that are given are mild, such as verbal warnings.[78] Among federal workers, 33 percent of those who used formal grievance procedures to protest sexual harassment found that it "made things worse."[79] More than 65 percent of the cases of those who filed formal charges of sexual harassment with the Illinois Department of Human Rights involved job discharge of the complainant.[80] Less than a third of those cases resulted in a favorable settlement for the complainant, and those who received financial compensation got an average settlement of $3,234.[81] Similar findings in California were reported by Coles[82] with the average cash settlement there of $973, representing approximately one month's pay. Although a few legal cases result in large settlements,[83] these studies suggest that typical settlements are low. Formal actions may take years to complete, and in legal suits the victim usually must hire legal counsel at considerable expense.[84] These small settlements seem unlikely to compensate victims for the emotional stress, notoriety, and financial costs involved in filing a public complaint. Given the consistency with which victimization falls more often to women than men, it is ironic that one of the largest settlements awarded to an individual in a sexual harassment case ($196,500 in damages) was made to a male who brought suit against his female supervisor,[85] perhaps because sexual aggression by a female is seen as especially egregious.

Emotional Consequences of Harassment for the Victim. In academic settings, harassment can adversely affect students' learning, and therefore their academic standing. It can deprive them of educational and career opportunities because they wish to avoid threatening situations. Students who have been harassed report they consequently avoid taking a class from or working with a particular faculty member, change their major, or leave a threatening situation.[86] Lowered self-esteem follows the realization that rewards such as a high grade may have been based on sexual attraction rather than one's abilities.[87] Decreased feelings of competence and confidence, and increased feelings of anger, frustration, depression and anxiety all can result from harassment.[88] The psychological stress produced by harassment is compounded when women are fired or quit their jobs in fear or frustration.[89]

Meek and Lynch[90] propose that victims of harassment typically go through several stages of reaction, at first questioning the offender's true intentions and then blaming themselves for the offender's behavior. Women with traditional sex-role beliefs are more likely to blame themselves for being harassed.[91] Victims then worry about being believed by others and about possible retaliation if they take formal steps to protest the behavior. A victim may be too frightened or confused to assert herself or punish the offender. Psychologists working with victims of harassment would do well to recognize that not only victims' emotional reactions but also the nature of the grievance process (as previously discussed) might discourage women from bringing formal complaints.

Prevention of Sexual Harassment

Some argue that sexual harassment does not occur with great frequency, or if it once was a problem, that problem has been eliminated in recent years. Indeed, Morgenson,[92] writing in the business publication *Forbes*, suggests that professional sexual harassment counselors have drummed up the whole issue in order to sell their services. Yet the studies cited here have documented that sexual harassment is a widespread problem with serious consequences.

Feminists and union activists have succeeded in gaining recognition of sexual harassment as a form of sex discrimination.[93] The law now views sexual harassment not as the idiosyncratic actions of a few inconsiderate males but as part of a pattern of behaviors that reflect the imbalance of power between women and men in our society. Women in various occupations and educational settings have sought legal redress for actions of supervisors or co-workers, and sexual harassment has become the focus of numerous organizational policies and grievance procedures.[94]

Well-publicized policies that use an inclusive definition of sexual harassment, that include an informal dispute resolution option, that provide an advocate for the victim (if desired), and that permit multiple offenders to be identified seem likely to be the most effective way of addressing claims of sexual harassment. However, even these modifications will not eliminate all of the problems in policies. The severity of the consequences of harassment for the victim, coupled with the problematic nature of grievance procedures and the mildness of punishments for offenders, makes retribution less effective than prevention of sexual harassment. Organizations should not assume that their job is completed when they have established a sexual harassment policy. Extensive efforts at prevention need to be mounted at the individual, situational, and organizational level.

In prevention efforts aimed at the individual, organizations need to conduct education about harassment.[95] In particular, people need to learn to "think like a woman" in defining which behaviors constitute harassment and recognizing that these behaviors are unacceptable. Understanding that women find offensive more subtle forms of behavior (such as sexual jokes or comments) may help reduce the kinds of interactions that create a hostile environment. Educating personnel about the punishments involved for offensive behavior also may have a deterring effect.

However, education alone is not sufficient. Sexual harassment is the product not only of individual attitudes and beliefs, but also of organizational practices. Dzeich and Weiner[96] describe aspects of educational institutions that facilitate sexual harassment, including the autonomy afforded the faculty, the diffusion of authority that permits lack of accountability, and the lack of women in positions of authority. Research is beginning to identify the characteristics and practices in other types of work settings that facilitate or support sexual harassment; such research suggests that sexual harassment may be part of a pattern of unprofessional and disrespectful attitudes and behaviors that characterizes some workplaces.[97]

Perhaps the most important factor in reducing sexual harassment is an organizational culture that reflects equal opportunities for women. A strong negative relationship exists between the level of perceived equal employment opportunity for women within a company and the level of harassment reported.[98] Workplaces low in perceived equality are the site of more frequent incidents of harassment. This finding suggests that sexual harassment both reflects and reinforces the underlying sexual inequality that produces a sex-segregated and sex-stratified occupational structure.[99] The implementation of sexual harassment policies demonstrates the seriousness of those in authority; the language of the policies provides some measure of clarity about what behavior is not acceptable; and grievance procedures may provide relief and legitimacy to those with complaints.[100] But neither policies nor procedures do much to weaken the structural roots of gender inequalities in organizations.

Reforms intended to ameliorate women's position sometimes have unintended negative consequences.[101] The presence of sexual harassment policies and the absence of formal complaints might promote the illusion that this problem has been solved. Insuring that this belief does not prevail requires assessment of all organizational policies and practices as to whether they promote or hinder equality for women. A long-range strategy for organizational reform in academia would thus attack the chilly climate for women in classroom and laboratory;[102] the inferior quality of athletic programs for women; differential treatment of women applicants; the acceptance of the masculine as normative; and a knowledge base uninfluenced by women's values or experience.[103] In other work settings, such a long-range approach would attack both sex-segregation of occupations and sex-stratification within authority hierarchies. Sexual harassment grievance procedures alone are not sufficient to insure that sexual harassment will be eliminated. An end to this problem requires sex equity within organizations.

9

What's Wrong with Empowerment

COMMUNITY PSYCHOLOGISTS HAVE long emphasized the importance of context for understanding human behavior. Leaders in our field have persuasively argued that human actors play out their roles in particular environments that offer specific constraints and opportunities and that serve as stimuli for action. Yet, despite our awareness of context for those we study, we do not always apply that understanding to ourselves. My purpose here is to point out how our context—that is, the assumptions and values underlying the discipline of psychology in the United States—shape, sometimes without our awareness, how we define and study key ideas in our field.

To demonstrate this, I focus on the concept of empowerment, a concept at the forefront of community psychology research today. I make two points: First, psychology's emphasis on the cognitive processes of the individual leads us to study individuals' *sense of* empowerment rather than actual increases in power, thereby making the political personal. Second, the concept of empowerment, in accord with psychology's traditional emphasis on agency, mastery, and control, emphasizes concerns that have typically been associated with masculinity and men, rather than concerns typically associated with femininity and women, such as community and connections with others.

Empowerment and Power

History and culture shape the concepts that we use to explain human action. Perhaps most important of the values shaping psychology is the belief in individualism, a belief that lies at the heart of psychology's vision of human nature. A great deal of research in psychology rests on the assumption that the healthy individual is one who is self-contained, independent, and self-reliant, capable of asserting himself and influencing his environment (and I do mean *his*) and operating according to abstract principles of justice and fairness. Yet, as Sampson points out, "the individual that is psychology's research subject is the creation of a given sociohistorical system" rather than an exemplar of a timeless human nature.[1] The supposedly autonomous individual of modern psychology is the product of Western social and economic belief systems, just as our concepts of fairness are shaped by capitalist principles of equity and exchange. Recall Erik Fromm's observation: "The underlying structure of capitalism calls for people who believe themselves to be free agents while they are actually governed by [market] forces that press them this way and that, but behind their backs."[2]

Consider how the belief in individualism affects our conception of empowerment. As Rappaport presents it, empowerment refers to "a mechanism by which people, organizations, and communities gain mastery over their affairs."[3] His notion of empowerment is intended to include a psychological sense of personal control as well as concern with actual social influence, political power, and legal rights. As Zimmerman summarizes, "Psychological empowerment includes beliefs about one's competence and efficacy, and a willingness to become involved in activities to exert control in the social and political environment. . . . Psychological empowerment is a construct that integrates perceptions of personal control with behaviors to exert control."[4]

Although these definitions of empowerment include actual control and influence as part of the concept, in a great deal of research actual control is conflated with the *sense of* personal control. For example, in a study of the development of community leaders, Kieffer describes "the fundamental empowering transformation . . . from sense of self as helpless victim to acceptance of self as assertive and efficacious citizen,"[5] while Bandura and his colleagues consider empowerment to be a manifestation of people's belief in their efficacy.[6] Sampson has pointed out psychology's tendency to reduce complex phenomena to individual psychological dynamics:

> Effort is expended in developing precise ways to measure and assess individual psychological states and perceptions and to evaluate individual behavioral outcomes. The social context within which these individual perceptions and activities take place is put off to the side, occasionally alluded to, but rarely if ever systematically addressed."[7]

Sampson here was criticizing psychological research on justice, yet his comments apply as well to the predilection in community psychology to assess empowerment through individuals' perceptions.

This proclivity stems from a deeper unresolved tension within psychology between two views of human nature, one which holds that "reality creates the person" (as reflected, e.g., in behaviorism) and the opposing view that "the person creates reality" (as reflected, e.g., in cognition).[8] Many agree that the cognitivist perspective currently dominates American psychology.[9] Central to this viewpoint is the belief that structures and processes within the individual's mind are the primary determinants of behavior: "For cognitivism, it is more important to understand what is going on within the person's head as she or he confronts an objective stimulus situation than it is to understand the properties of the situation itself."[10]

The consequence of the cognitivist perspective is to ignore or downplay the influence of situational or social structural factors in favor of a focus on individual perceptions. But this view artificially disconnects human behavior from the larger sociopolitical context, resulting in a search within the self for solutions to human problems.[11] In the context of empowerment, if the focus of inquiry becomes not actual power but rather the *sense of* empowerment, then the political is made personal and, ironically, the status quo may be supported.

Placing primacy on the phenomenology of the individual ignores the possibility of what Marxists deem "false consciousness." The individual's experience of power or powerlessness may be unrelated to actual ability to influence, and an increase in the sense of empowerment does not always reflect an increase in actual power. Indeed, a sense of empowerment may be an illusion when so much of life is controlled by the politics and practices at a macro level. This does not mean that individuals can have no influence or that individuals' perceptions are unimportant, but rather that to reduce power to individual psychology ignores the political and historical context in which people operate. Confusing one's actual *ability* to control resources with a *sense* of empowerment de-politicizes the latter.

Theoreticians of power distinguish *power over* ("explicit or implicit dominance") from *power to* ("the opportunity to act more freely within some realms ... through power sharing") and *power from* ("the ability to resist the power of others by effectively fending off their unwanted demands").[12] The concept of empowerment is sometimes used in a way that confounds a sense of efficacy or esteem (part of "power to") with that of actual decision-making control over resources ("power over"). Many intervention efforts aimed at empowerment increase people's "power to" act (for example, by enhancing their self-esteem), but do little to affect their "power over" resources or policies. For example, a program designed to enhance the academic success of black college students is described as "Empowerment of African-American college students." Students in the program earn higher grade point averages than comparable students not in the program, a considerable achievement.[13] Yet this program does not address control over decision-making. Although self-esteem or achievement may be related to power and control, these concepts are not the same. To consider them the same is to depoliticize the concept of empowerment.

The question arises, then, whether attempts to enhance a sense of empowerment create the illusion of power without affecting the actual distribution of power. Many interventions attempt to achieve empowerment through increasing individuals' participation in neighborhood or self-help groups. Empowerment is sometimes equated with participation, as if changing procedures will automatically lead to changes in the context or in the distribution of resources. Lewis[14] criticizes this claim in his discussion of reforms in urban education. Some changes, such as the institution of local school councils, appear to be empowering in that they give local groups more control over schools. But viewed from a larger perspective, these changes in procedure do little to affect the distribution of resources in school systems. People who participate in community organizations often feel more empowered than do nonparticipants,[15] but participation does not necessarily result in more influence or control. Chavis and Wandersman[16] found that, although people developed a greater *sense of* control through participation in a neighborhood organization, they did not perceive the group as becoming more powerful over time.

Neighborhood groups are embedded in larger forces and institutions that are nonlocal and often not susceptible to local influence.[17] For example, Brenner[18] has tracked the relationship between macro-level economic fluctuations and their micro-level impact on rates of mental hospital incarcerations. Realtors, developers, banks, mortgage institutions, and other market forces, as well as local, state, and federal governments and their agencies often affect neighborhood dynamics in ways that are difficult if not impossible for local grassroots groups to influence. Community organizing efforts have a long history in the United States, from those of Jane Addams to Saul Alinsky and contemporary attempts to change neighborhoods through group efforts. In a review of these efforts, sociologist Harvey Molotch[19] concludes that the local internal sources of change have generally been relatively unsuccessful in the light of larger, external forces of change. If interventions aimed to empower do not address these larger sociopolitical forces, they may be doomed to transitory or ineffective actions. On the other hand, attempts to address these issues may bring involvement in partisan politics that may put other constraints on psychologists' effectiveness.

A paper by Irma Serrano-Garcia[20] gives a poignant description of the inextricable relationship of empowerment and politics. Her group, affiliated with a university and a community mental health center, attempted an intervention in a poor Puerto Rican community. The intervention failed to reach many of its goals in part because it did not address the central issue in Puerto Rico, the island's political status. Members of the intervention team held a pro-independence view on this issue, yet they did not reveal their political preferences to the community. Serrano-Garcia asks:

1) If we maintain our partisan anonymity, will the community feel betrayed?
2) If a particular group of residents chooses to work with us, and their political partisanship is well known, should we refuse, or should we accept? Does

our supposed neutrality hinder our consciousness-raising efforts by forcing us to remain outside of partisan political issues?[21]

These difficult questions bring to the fore the relationship between community psychology's concept of empowerment and the larger political arena within which empowerment efforts operate.

Any serious attempt to gain power (that is, "power over") by those who are disempowered will prompt those who see themselves as losing power to fight back. Increasing control over resources may be permitted only until it becomes threatening to the dominant group. In reflecting on her intervention efforts, Serrano-Garcia concludes that:

> I am convinced that our project achieved the goals it did because its goals and strategies were and are unknown to people in power, because we are working with low-status people who are not recognized as a threat, and because we did not choose to deal with problems which directly confront governmental institutions.[22]

Gruber and Trickett[23] raise this issue in the context of organizational change efforts when they ask, "Can we empower others?" Empowerment requires a redistribution in power, but the institutional structure that puts one group in a position to empower others also works to subvert the process of empowerment. In their study of a school's attempt to share decision-making, they found that the sense of empowerment increased among students and parents, and students had greater opportunities to affect the curriculum (that is, "power to"), but few changes occurred in the distribution of "power over," that is, in the structural distribution of power in the school. The broader context of the empowerment effort, in which control rested with teachers, undermined attempts to equalize power.

Underlying empowerment ideology is a conflict model that assumes that a society consists of separate groups possessing different levels of power and control over resources.[24] "Empowerment is by definition concerned with many who are excluded by the majority society on the basis of their demographic characteristics or of their physical or emotional difficulties, experienced either in the past or the present."[25] The outsiders compete with the insiders—and with each other—for control of resources. Livert[26] raises the problem that empowerment of all underrepresented or needy groups merely increases the competition for the same resources. Empowered individuals' rational pursuit of their own best interests may end in the destruction of neighborhoods and networks of support. Livert's solution is to balance empowerment with a commitment to the community, thereby strengthening both individuals and the community as a whole. Bond and Keys[27] present a hopeful example of collaboration between two potentially conflicting groups on the board of a community agency: parents and community members. Critical to their collaboration was a culture that appreciated interdependencies and the existence of people and structures that spanned the groups' boundaries.

Empowerment of all disenfranchised groups could be dangerous. I think it is instructive that empowerment is favored not only by those who would describe themselves as politically progressive but also by those who would describe themselves as conservative—such as the Republican politician Jack Kemp, former Secretary of Housing and Urban Development, whose political group is called Empower America. There are some groups of outsiders that, one hopes, would become less empowered, rather than more powerful. For example, neo-Nazis might be considered outsiders, marginal to mainstream society, yet few community psychologists would advocate their empowerment.

Empowerment and Community

The underlying assumption of empowerment theory is that of conflict rather than cooperation among groups and individuals, control rather than communion. The image of the empowered person (or group) in research and theory reflects the belief in psychology in separation, individuation, and individual mastery.[28] Carol Gilligan[29] contrasts this view of human nature with an alternate vision that emphasizes relatedness and interdependence as central values of human experience. Although I disagree with Gilligan's assertion that these two modes are distributed along gender lines, I concur with her claim that psychology takes as its highest value the emphasis on autonomy and separation over relationality. The mature adult in psychological research is characterized by mastery, control, and separation, rather than interdependence or relatedness. Community psychology's emphasis on empowerment follows the pattern of placing primacy on agency, mastery, and control rather than connectedness.

I find this particularly ironic because one of the earliest and most influential *phenomena of interest*[30] in community psychology was the "sense of community,"[31] a concept that has been overshadowed recently by the emphasis on empowerment. My point is not that the study of community and connectedness should now supersede the study of empowerment, but rather that both are integral to human well-being and happiness and to well-functioning communities, and that both ought to be the objects of our study. However, little work has been done to integrate these two ideas.

Research on rape victims demonstrates the importance of both concepts to understanding human behavior. Contrast two victims: the first, Migael Scherer, a white middle-class woman raped and nearly strangled one morning in a laundromat by a stranger. Scherer's experience, documented in her book *Still Loved by the Sun*,[32] included encounters with sensitive police, doctors, and judges who believed her completely, skillful rape victim advocates and therapists, supportive family and friends, and so forth. She made full use of rape counseling advocates and other social services and she did not hesitate to prosecute the rapist (who was then convicted). Scherer eloquently described the feelings of smallness and vulnerability, the inability to plan more than one day at a time, and the confusion, sleeplessness, and agitation that persist long after a rape. Scherer's account is a moving description of the process by which one woman came to feel empowered and efficacious again.

Contrast her experience with that of Altavese Thomas, a poor black mother of three, gang-raped while drinking with some women friends in a poor, high-crime neighborhood. Thomas was portrayed by Michelle Fine in her critique of the view prevalent in social psychological research that "Taking-Control-Yields-Coping." Thomas refused to use the criminal justice system or to rely on kin. Fine argued that:

> . . .trusting social institutions, maximizing interpersonal supports, and engaging in self-disclosure are strategies most appropriate for middle-class and affluent individuals whose interests are served by those institutions, whose social supports can multiply available resources and contacts, and for whom self-disclosure may in fact lead not only to personal change but also to structural change.[33]

Scherer was in such a position: Her life circumstances permitted control and empowerment to be her primary goals in reestablishing her sense of trust in the world after the rape. She regained a sense of control in part through prosecution of the rapist, a strategy that might be considered to reflect empowerment or agency.

Thomas refused to prosecute the rapists. Her choice stemmed, however, not from a low "sense of empowerment" but because relatedness and connections took priority for her, given the likelihood of retaliation if she prosecuted. The circumstances of her life did not permit the actions usually considered essential for self-efficacy. Her behavior can best be understood in light of a need to protect her family. Such a need was not necessary in Scherer's case, since that protection existed already. Considering empowerment and control as the optimal goal for a rape victim denies the reality of Thomas's circumstances. Likewise, empowerment and control may not be the appropriate goal in all community situations.

According to Rachel Hare-Mustin and Jeanne Maracek,[34] autonomy and relatedness are a function not of one's gender, but rather of one's position in a social hierarchy. The highly valued attributes that our society defines as agentic are those associated with power and status because autonomy and mastery require the freedom to make choices. Those not in a position of autonomy and choice must focus on connection and communal goals to survive. Accordingly, whether individuals act in an autonomous manner or operate in a communal mode reflects their relative position in the social structure. The implication is that once those lower on the hierarchy have moved up, they may move from a relatedness mode to operate on principles of autonomy and individual agency.

The focus for community psychologists ought to be on understanding how community shapes the person—in particular, on the conditions that facilitate both efficacy or personal control and also a sense of community. Paradoxically, situations that foster community may be the opposite of those that foster empowerment. Community may exist most cohesively when people experience a shared externally generated fate such as a crisis or disaster, or a condition of poverty or oppression.[35] Alienation and a sense of separateness may result from the absence of crisis or stress, or from access to sufficient resources to cope by oneself. The psychological sense of community that is advocated as a goal by Sarason[36] and others may be a function of interdependence on a material level. Ironically, when interdependence is no longer necessary, then the psychological sense of community may disappear as well.

Carol Stack's book *All Our Kin*[37] gives a moving example of this dilemma. The poor people she interviewed participated in daily domestic exchanges of services, goods, and money that enabled them to survive fluctuations in welfare and the exigencies of living. At the same time, the rules both of the welfare system and of the exchange network prohibited them from acquiring any surplus that might enable them to improve their economic condition or life situation. A woman in the exchange network received an unexpected inheritance of $1,500 with which she and her husband hoped to make a down payment on a home. Within a month and a half, however, the money was gone, distributed to kin for compelling reasons such as a train ticket to visit a sick relative, payment for a burial, and new winter clothing for the children. Another couple had withdrawn from the network to preserve their resources when they had acquired steady jobs, and they had bought a house and furniture. Some years later, when their marriage was dissolving, the woman began giving some of her nice clothes and furniture away to her sisters and niece. She was reestablishing her place in the exchange network by obligating others to her, creating insurance against future need. The sense of community among these people was very great: they had a strong network that could be relied upon in time of trouble. It is important to note, however, that the network enabling them to survive also put constraints on their survival. Finding one's voice, controlling one's resources, and becoming empowered may reduce the interdependence that produces a strong sense of community.

There may, however, be circumstances in which the two phenomena are not contradictory. Chavis and Wandersman[38] suggest that sense of community is related to participation in a neighborhood association, similar to Maton and Rappaport's[39] finding that that development of a psychological sense of community and commitment were related to empowerment for members of a religious organization. Leavitt and Saegert's[40] research on leaders in cooperative housing projects in Harlem, New York, found that shared control was the basis for empowerment. They concluded:

> Cooperatively organized endeavors of different kinds should be explored more thoroughly as means of empowering as well as serving low-income people The real level of control a person can have over life in this society correlates highly with disposable income. The development of a co-op sector could be an alternative to the prospect that large numbers of people will be able to exert less and less control over the services and work on which they depend.

There is a danger, however, that community or empowerment can be substituted as a goal when what people actually need is better jobs and more income.

Zimmerman[41] refers to organizations such as those studied by Leavitt and Saegert as "empowered organizations (i.e., those that influence the policy process and remain viable over time)" as distinct from "empowering organizations (i.e., those that contribute to the development of psychological empowerment)." Although it is theoretically possible for organizations to do both simultaneously, there are difficult choices between these two goals that need to be made as organizations grow. Elsewhere I describe the dilemmas faced by some feminist organizations, such as rape crisis centers or battered women's centers started in the 1960s as part of the Women's Liberation Movement. These organizations began as egalitarian groups, focused not only on providing services but also on sharing leadership and developing the skills of their members. As these groups became successful, the demand for their services increased. The need for efficiency conflicted with the time-consuming process of collective decision-making, and the organizations were forced to choose between widespread participation and meeting the growing demands for services. These dilemmas, which I call the "challenges of success," highlight the contradictions between the development of community and the empowerment of individuals.[42]

If empowerment of the disenfranchised is the primary value, then what is to hold together societies made up of different groups? Competition among groups for dominance and control without the simultaneous acknowledgement of common interests can lead to conflicts like the "ethnic cleansing" that occurred in the former Yugoslavia during the 1990s. One of the primary tasks for community psychology, then, is to articulate the relationship between empowerment and community. Does empowerment of disenfranchised people and groups simultaneously bring about a greater sense of community and strengthen the ties that hold our society together, or does it promote certain individuals or groups at the expense of others, increasing competitiveness and lack of cohesion?

The empowered individual in community psychology need not be the individual in isolation or even in groups, fighting with others for power and control. Rather, we should consider connection to be as important as empowerment. This conception of community, however, challenges the belief in individual rights and freedoms which is the cornerstone of the political philosophy on which notions of empowerment rest. Pure liberalism places primacy on individual rights, not corporate or community rights. A community psychology aimed at empowerment of the individual is consistent with our dominant political philosophy.

Group or community development inevitably will, at some point, clash with that of the individual, and the empowerment of one person or group will conflict with that of another. The challenge to community psychology is to articulate a vision that encompasses not only empowerment but also community, a vision which can address the question asked by Rodney King during the Los Angeles riots of 1992: "Can't we all get along?" To answer this question, we need to consider differences, but also similarities; those things that separate, and also those we have in common—agency and communion; empowerment, and also community.

Women in Management

An Exploration of Competing Paradigms

IN RECENT YEARS, women seem to have moved successfully into the top levels of organizational management. Newspapers and magazines are filled with stories about successful women's careers, a multitude of books give advice to female managers on everything from dress to conduct in the boardroom, and companies proudly display the names of women on their boards of directors. However, statistics on women in the labor force present a stark contrast to this glowing picture. Although women make up 43 percent of the executive, administrative, and managerial occupations, they hold fewer than 3 to 5 percent of top executive positions—vice presidents and above—in Fortune 500 companies.[1] The number of female heads of Fortune 500 companies doubled by the year 2000 from a previous high of 2 to a grand total of 4.[2] The Glass Ceiling Commission, established to assess the barriers that prevent women and minorities from rising to the top levels of management, concluded that white men still fill most top managerial and executive positions.[3]

Psychological research on the experience of women in management tends to focus on personality characteristics and behavior patterns of women as explanations for their low job status. But explanations for behavior may attribute causes either to the person or to the situation.[4] Psychologists have typically paid less attention to the situational factors that may account for women's low employment status.[5] This is in line with the general tendency among psychological researchers to consider mainly person-centered variables (those that lie within the individual) as determinants of behavior, while ignoring situationally relevant factors (those external to the individual).[6] When person-centered variables become invested with causal significance, people become the targets, sometimes inappropriately, of ameliorative efforts. The disproportionate concentration on characteristics of persons as explanatory variables has serious repercussions when used as a basis for social policy because money and effort aimed at social change may be misdirected, and blame for social problems may implicitly be attributed to the victims of those problems.[7] Furthermore, the problems are not solved.

This chapter demonstrates that a situation-centered perspective can make a significant contribution to our understanding of why so few women are in top management positions.

Person-Centered Explanations

Person-centered explanations for the absence of women in top management positions suggest that women lack the characteristics necessary to lead companies and governments.[8] One reason for this alleged deficit is considered to be female socialization practices that encourage development of personality traits and/or behavior patterns that are contrary to the demands of the managerial role. Among these traits are a fear of success and an unwillingness to take risks.

A classic example of this type of explanation is the theory proposed in the late 1960s by psychologist Matina Horner as an explanation for women's lack of advancement. Put simply, she suggests that women have a fear of success because of the incompatibility between achievement and a sense of femininity. As Horner describes it:

> A bright woman is caught in a double bind. In testing and other achievement-oriented situations she worries not only about failure, but also about success. If she fails, she is not living up to her own standards of performance; if she succeeds, she is not living up to societal expectations about the female role. For women, then, the desire to achieve is often contaminated by what I call the *motive to avoid success*.[9]

Horner's methodology caught readers' imaginations and helped to popularize her research. Her subjects were asked to complete a story that began with the sentence, "After first term finals, John (Anne) finds himself (herself) at the top of his (her) medical-school class." Females wrote about Anne; males wrote about John. Horner found that more than 65 percent of the females in her study told stories that included negative imagery or concern about doing well, reflected in such themes as the social rejection accompanying success or doubts about one's femininity. The stories were often vivid and dramatic (e.g., "Anne is an acne-faced bookworm . . . "). The interpretation of these data, widely reported in the popular press at the time, was that because socialization patterns teach females to equate success with negative outcomes, women have an inner drive to avoid success.

However, a series of follow-up studies demonstrated (a) that fear of success is not necessarily an internal motivational state, but may instead be a response to situational factors, and (b) that this fear of success is not necessarily restricted to women.[10] For instance, when "medical" is changed to "nursing" in Horner's first sentence, females' stories include less negative imagery.[11] This suggests that the critical factor for understanding women's responses is recognizing the impact of the widely held belief that success in nontraditional occupations is associated with negative consequences.[12] Both women and men recognize that successful females (and perhaps successful males in a nontraditionally masculine field such as nursing) may experience obstacles and conflicts as a result of their occupational choices. Responses indicative of fear of success, therefore, may reflect expectations of "punishment" for sex role deviancy.[13] Based on the experiences of women who pioneered in nontraditional fields,[14] these fears seem to be anchored in reality. Thus researchers studying fear of success have shifted from focusing on the nature of women to emphasizing the cultural constraints on women that are mediated through sex role expectations.[15]

A second example of the women-centered type of explanation is found in Hennig and Jardim's book, *The Managerial Woman*.[16] The authors' explanation for women's lack of success assumes, first, that women lack requisite managerial skills or traits and behave in a different (and allegedly inferior) manner than men in managerial positions and, second, that these differences are the result of differential sex role socialization in childhood and adolescence. The authors argue, for example, that playing team sports teaches little boys the key elements of management—how to plan strategies, how to work with people regardless of personal feelings, how to compete, and so on. Because girls are less likely to engage in team sports, they do not learn these skills and consequently may not possess the abilities that lead to managerial success.

Hennig and Jardim[17] perceive additional differences in male and female work-related attitudes. Men see risk as an opportunity for success as well as failure, while women see it primarily as a potential loss. Men link their present work experiences to future career goals, implying progression to a reward, while women seek fulfillment in their immediate situations. Boys grow up always knowing they will have to earn a living, whereas a career is questionable in the eyes of some young girls. Hence, behavior that men may attribute to lack of motivation on the part of women is, according to these authors, actually the result of socialization experiences that put women at a disadvantage in the work world. The authors advocate that women who aspire to management should develop skills they may have missed in earlier years, such as long-range goal setting and planning.

The research literature contains mixed results on sex differences in leadership.[18] Although inconsistencies abound, leader gender has generally been shown to be an important explanatory variable in laboratory studies but not in studies conducted in field settings.[19] While people expect women to be more interpersonally oriented and men more task-oriented, these differences do not appear in studies that were carried out in organizations. Some evidence suggests, however, that women adopt a more democratic or participatory style while men adopt a more autocratic or directive style, perhaps because women who act autocratically are devalued.[20]

Researchers should use caution when interpreting the results of studies on sex differences, because findings of significant differences based on gender may be methodological artifacts.[21] The greater control possible in the laboratory not only makes differences due to gender easier to detect but also makes them more likely to occur. The artificial, short-term nature of the laboratory experiment may heighten the salience of "ascribed" or visible permanent roles, such as those related to gender, and may thus elicit responses based on role stereotyping. Subjects of research in field settings have more information available to them, particularly when the leaders and subordinates under study have been involved in actual long-term, ongoing work situations, and gender may be less salient under these conditions.[22] Also, women who rise to the top in actual organizations may be selected or trained for leadership roles in ways that minimize sex differences.[23]

In addition, findings of sex differences may reflect differences based on factors that covary with gender but that are inadequately controlled in research designs. Female supervisors tend to have less influence in organizations, and subordinates' dissatisfaction with female managers may be due to the supervisor's inability to wield influence rather than to her gender.[24] Findings of sex differences in work settings disappear when the influence of age, education, and experience of leaders and subordinates is controlled;[25] when type of occupation, level within the organization, and extent of professional training are considered;[26] and when actual rather than perceived leader behaviors are examined.[27]

Finally, although men and women may differ in their preferences for specific behaviors or leadership styles, these differences need not produce differences in overall performance. One study found that women took fewer risks in making decisions but did not differ from men in overall decision accuracy.[28] Furthermore, men and women may choose different leadership behaviors because they perceive that specific behaviors will be rewarded rather than because of their personality traits or sex role socialization. Studies indicate that the perceived effectiveness of different supervisory styles varies with the gender of the supervisor and subordinate.[29] People tend to devalue women who act autocratically relative to the evaluation of their male counterparts.[30] Women who use an authoritative leadership style violate people's belief that a woman should be interpersonally oriented and sensitive.[31] This, rather than personality characteristics, may contribute to women's greater use of a democratic style. Moreover, although men and women appear equally effective as leaders in general, the settings in which they work make a difference: women are less effective as leaders in traditionally male settings, such as the military, while men are less effective in traditionally female settings, such as education and social service organizations.[32]

Some observers, especially popular writers who claim that sex differences exist in overall performance or leadership style, tend to attribute these differences to early sex role socialization, although they do not demonstrate this causal sequence empirically.[33] The ideal way of demonstrating such causality would be through longitudinal research that first identifies early sex differences in socialization and then links these differences to behavior in later years. In the absence of such longitudinal research, we are left either with post hoc inferences about these connections without empirical bases or with successful women's retrospective accounts of their childhood experiences.

Perhaps the most influential example of these retrospective accounts has been Hennig and Jardim's description of "Twenty-Five Women Who Made It," included in *The Managerial Woman*.[34] These women, who had all reached the highest executive level in major corporations, had some striking similarities in their past experiences. All were firstborn children; most had had close relationships with their fathers, who had encouraged them to be independent, self-reliant, and risk taking; and team games had been important to them as children. Each of these women had developed a close relationship with a male boss whose encouragement and support appeared to be a critical factor in her success. Although this study provides a provocative look at women at the top, it raises as many questions as it answers. For example, although the early childhood and adolescent experiences of these women were emphasized, the actual key to their success may have been the presence of a mentor—a factor independent of their socialization. Indeed, it may be that the socialization of males which makes them willing to nurture the career of a female is the critical factor in women's success.

Situation-Centered Explanations

An alternative paradigm for explaining women's lack of success in management emphasizes the nature of the work environment faced by women who aspire to managerial careers. Characteristics of the organizational situation, rather than inner traits and skills, may shape and define women's behavior on the job.

This view is clearly expressed in Kanter's *Men and Women of the Corporation*.[35] Kanter looks at social structural factors and finds that the distribution of opportunity and power and the social composition of groups within organizations may be the critical variables for understanding women's lack of managerial success. Women's opportunities are blocked, they tend to have little power in the larger organizational hierarchy, and those who do get close to the top are often surrounded by colleagues who are predominantly male.

Kanter[36] suggests that the critical factor for women may not be their gender, but rather their number. She claimed that certain dynamics prevail when "tokens" are present in groups, regardless of whether their token status is due to gender, ethnicity, or other social characteristics. Tokens are likely to be scrutinized more closely, pressured to side with the majority against their kind, and expected to conform to stereotypes. A series of experimental laboratory studies of solo status in groups corroborates Kanter's field observations.[37] When only one black, man or woman, was in a group, he or she was perceived as disproportionately prominent, was evaluated more extremely, and was likely to be cast in special, often stereotypical, roles. Minority individuals in fully integrated groups, however, did not receive such treatment. Taylor et al. suggest a cognitive rather than motivational explanation for this phenomenon and conclude that increased attention is accorded to the solo member because of his or her uniqueness rather than because of minority group membership. But not all tokens are treated alike: the sole man in a group is likely to become its leader, while this position is rarely given to the only woman in a group.[38]

Being the only woman in a group of men may heighten attention to a woman's gender and elicit perceptions and behaviors believed to be congruent with the female role.[39] Behavior that matches sex role expectations, for example, is evaluated more positively than behavior perceived as inconsistent with expectations.[40] For women, attractiveness may further exacerbate the salience of sex role expectations. Heilman and Saruwatari[41] found that attractiveness was a disadvantage for female applicants seeking positions believed to require predominantly male skills (e.g., managerial jobs). Attractive men and unattractive women received higher ratings on traditionally masculine attributes considered essential for work success: ambition, decisiveness, and rationality.

When the findings of research emphasizing situational or structural factors are compared with those of research focusing on women's dispositions or characteristics, one finds radically different explanations for identical sorts of behavior. For example, some studies note that women tend to overemphasize the task at hand, as opposed to seeing it as a stepping-stone to further achievement. According to person-centered explanations, women do this because they have not learned to set goals and plan ahead. According to situational explanations, this behavior has a radically different cause: because women are not promoted within organizations, they overemphasize the job at hand, which becomes their major source of satisfaction and self-esteem.

As another example, women may consider the personal relationships they form with co-workers to be an important source of job satisfaction. Again, person-centered explanations see this as a reflection of women's inadequate training, which does not teach them to work with people regardless of the nature of the personal relationship involved. A situation-centered perspective, on the other hand, views women's emphasis on being well-liked by co-workers to be the result of the job situation faced by women. Since women have little chance of advancement, their sources of satisfaction do not come from the job itself, but rather from the quality of their relationships with co-workers. "Being well-liked becomes another meaning of success to people in dead-end work."[42]

Other factors in the job environment, such as the attitudes of workers toward female managers, may impede women's success.[43] Psychologist Madeline Heilman and her colleagues asked male managers to rate the characteristics of men, women, and managers and found much more overlap between descriptions of men and successful managers than between women and managers; in other words, successful managers are still seen as male.[44] Workers may be overtly hostile to women as managers, or they may discriminate in a more subtle way, for example, by attributing women's success to factors other than their ability. One study of male managers' attitudes toward working women found that negative attitudes toward women were based not on males' beliefs that women are less competent or qualified, but on the fact that having women as colleagues or bosses upsets the traditional patterns of deference between men and women.[45] In contemporary society, the distribution of power by gender favors male dominance. Women who move upward in an organizational structure upset this traditional balance of power and, in so doing, may discomfit and threaten men as well as other women. A 1965 study found that the majority of male executives in one study believed that men do not feel comfortable with a female boss, and a third of the executives felt that women in managerial positions have a bad effect on employee morale.[46] Attitudes today may be more accepting of women in leadership positions.

In field research using participant-observation methods, Mayes found that women in authority elicited hostility and/or dependence in males. She concluded that "the resistance to changing sex-role behavior on the part of men and women involves the deeply embedded fear that change means chaos and collapse in the norms and behaviors that govern the most sacred areas of everyday life—the family and sexuality."[47] Employed women may threaten men's basic concepts of masculinity.[48] Again, numbers may be critical: Lockheed[49] found that men's explanations for a woman's success emphasized her sexuality when she was in a solo status position but not when she was one among many women. Motivational dynamics need not be postulated to explain sex discrimination at work, however. Kiesler[50] identifies a cognitive basis in the process called "actuarial prejudice," the expectation of inferior performance from subgroup members based on available information about that group. Since there are fewer successful women than men, people may expect all women to be less successful and behave accordingly.

Whatever the underlying dynamics of sex role stereotyping, the effects are clear: behavior is evaluated differently according to whether it is attributed to males or to females.[51] Goldberg[52] found that professional journal articles attributed to female authors are evaluated less favorably than are the same articles attributed to male authors, although a later study failed to replicate these results.[53] Bias in evaluation may be a function of the type of work involved,[54] the demands of the job,[55] whether the job is seen as gender appropriate,[56] and whether the outcome of the work effort is clear or ambiguous. Pheterson, Kiesler, and Goldberg[57] found that entries in an art show were evaluated more favorably when attributed to males, although paintings described as prize-winning did not elicit differential ratings according to the gender of the artist.

These results suggest that when success is ambiguous, women and men evoke different evaluations; but once independent verification of success is available, the discriminations disappear. There is even some evidence that bias in evaluating successful performance works in the opposite direction. Given equally high levels of performance, women are evaluated more favorably than men.[58] When a woman outperforms competing men, however, her evaluation is commensurate with her performance; in addition, the men like her less and would exclude her from the group if it were necessary to limit group size.[59]

In a review of research on evaluation of women's competence, psychologist Virginia Valian concludes that moderate success is seen as acceptable for women. However, high success for women violates our expectations, and one way to reconcile the discrepancy is to attribute women's success to factors other than ability.[60] A review of fifty-eight experiments that focused on attribution for men's and women's success found the predicted pattern, although small in magnitude. On masculine tasks, people saw men's success as due to ability, while women's success was credited to effort.[61] If women's high performance is attributed to extra effort, it is considered deserving of higher praise than similar performance by men.[62] However, attributing women's success to effort elicits fewer and less desirable organizational rewards than those elicited by the causes typically attributed to men.[63] Pay raises were deemed appropriate when success was due to effort, but promotion was the preferred personnel action only when success was due to ability. Thus, the differential attribution of causes of success for men and women has a significant impact on the allocation of rewards in work settings.

Differential allocation of organizational rewards (such as salary and promotion) on the basis of gender lies at the heart of discriminatory employment practices. Various studies have shown that sex bias operates in selection choices,[64] promotion,[65] and determination of salary level,[66] although factors such as graduate training and field of specialization also play an influential role in personnel decisions.[67]

Discriminatory personnel practices may be a result not only of the employee's gender, but also of the perceived gender appropriateness of the occupational position. Experimental results indicate that incongruence between an applicant's sex and job role is tolerated only when the applicant is overqualified.[68] Since both males and females perceive managerial jobs as requiring typically male sex role characteristics,[69] it is likely that these jobs are seen as inappropriate for women and that women have to be more qualified than men to be accepted at this level. Even if a woman is highly qualified, factors inherent in the informal organizational structure can still impede her achievement. Organizational advancement often depends on one's ability to find suitable mentors throughout one's career,[70] but men hesitate to adopt the role of mentor to a young and aspiring female manager. Sponsoring a woman may be viewed as a risky undertaking, one in which the probability of failure is too high. Moreover, preference for males may operate independently of negative attitudes toward women. Larwood and Blackmore found that, for leadership positions, same-sex acquaintances are solicited more frequently than are cross-sex acquaintances; they concluded that "people groom for leadership those with whom they enjoy an in-group relationship."[71] Since most managers are male, they are likely to select males for advancement and promotion, regardless of their attitudes toward women.

Men's general unwillingness to be mentors to women is not balanced by a large number of women taking on this role because of the scarcity of female executives at top levels of organizations.[72] The number of potential female mentors is further reduced by the tendency of some successful female executives to suffer from the "queen bee syndrome," a set of attitudes that are anti-female. These women have succeeded both socially and professionally, but are resistant to increasing the number of female managers because they want to preserve their unique status in a man's world.[73] However, the pervasiveness of this syndrome is contradicted by research indicating that high-status women have the most favorable attitudes toward women as managers[74] and that female executives are as willing as males to be mentors.[75]

Given the dismal implications of many of these research findings, what is to be done to increase the numbers of women in management?

Implications for Research and Action

Women aspiring to management positions are bombarded with advice on how to succeed. The strategies for success tend to fall into two categories, paralleling person- versus situation-centered explanations of women's low job status. Some strategies call for personal growth by women, whereas others suggest change in the practices or social composition of organizations.

Those paths to success requiring personal growth (known today as the development of human capital, such as education, work experience, and so forth) tend to encourage either the development of skills that will help women take charge of their lives, such as assertiveness training, or the enhancement of specific management-related or technical skills, such as conducting meetings or handling finances.[76] Determining whether these strategies do in fact succeed is difficult, since assessing the validity of the underlying person-centered assumptions about women's lack of job mobility is problematic. It is possible that women's low status is due to personal attributes; however, without research that also tests and rejects rival situational or structural hypotheses, person-centered research results cannot be considered conclusive. Acquiring the requisite managerial skills may do nothing to reduce the hostility that women face on the job or to mitigate the fact that they may be in token positions. Factors such as these may interact with or even prevail over one's personal skills or dispositions.

Moreover, even the most highly skilled women may be the targets of discrimination. A study of the salaries of close to 1,500 male and female managers found that even after education, training, experience, hours worked, and numerous other similar factors were accounted for, a substantial discrepancy favoring men remained.[77] Another study of managers in twenty Fortune 500 corporations came to the same conclusion after examining women who had "all the right stuff": years of work experience equal to men, similar amounts of education, willingness to move for one's job, working in similar industries, and so forth.[78] As one writer put it, "Men have the advantage of being men."[79]

Implicit in person-centered strategies is the belief that women should adopt a model of organizational behavior that is essentially male. Women are counseled that the key to success lies in the acquisition of characteristics typically attributed to the male sex role, such as assertiveness and rationality. Yet, studies have documented the negative consequences of the traditional male role on men's physical and mental health.[80] Women who adopt characteristics of the traditional male role are likely to suffer the same negative consequences. Furthermore, the efficacy of the traditional male model for optimal organizational functioning has itself been questioned. Characteristics associated with traditional female sex roles, such as an emphasis on people as opposed to production, might actually produce better outcomes in certain work situations.[81] Approaches to leadership that emphasize personality traits without also considering situational factors have been abandoned as inconclusive after more than three decades of research on male leaders; reviving the trait approach for female managers is likely to be no more productive.

Situation-centered research also suggests strategies for increasing the upward mobility of female workers: training managers in the uniform use of objective rating scales and specific decision rules;[82] presenting affirmative action policies in a noncoercive manner;[83] changing the distribution of opportunities and power and eliminating women's token status;[84] and reducing the salience of gender and associated stereotypes by increasing the amount of information on which decisions are based.[85] Valian[86] asserts that we need to change gender schemas, the implicit hypotheses we all have about sex differences that lead us to overrate men and underrate women. Severely sanctioning those who discriminate and tangibly rewarding those who sponsor women's entry into managerial networks would also promote women's upward job mobility.

Although these situation-centered strategies may facilitate the upward mobility of women in existing organizations, they do not come any closer than person-centered strategies do to addressing fundamental questions about the impact of work on people. Simply filling slots in organizational charts with women who have adopted male work patterns ignores both the negative consequences of traditionally masculine work styles and the unique contributions that can be obtained from more traditionally feminine orientations. Furthermore, as Kanter[87] suggests, "organizational reform is not enough. It is also important to move beyond the issues of whether or not concrete individuals get their share to questions of how shares are determined in the first place— how labor is divided and how power is concentrated."

A 1999 report, "Study on the Status of Women Faculty in Science at MIT,"[88] found that junior women faculty felt well supported within their departments and did not believe that gender bias would affect their careers. In contrast, senior women, although they had tenure, felt marginalized and isolated from a significant role in their departments. Discrimination against these women took subtle forms: inequitable distribution of laboratory space, awards, and distinctions; less desirable teaching assignments; and lack of inclusion on important committees. Similarly, top female executives in one multinational corporation received the same pay and benefits as comparable men, but they managed fewer people, were given fewer stock options, and reported less satisfaction with their future career opportunities.[89] Blatant discrimination may be rare once women reach top levels of organizations, but subtle forms may persist, even in the presence of good intentions.

Contemporary organizational psychology emphasizes the interaction of employee characteristics, the nature of the job, the organizational structure, and the external environment. The complete explanation of why so few women are top-level managers will emerge only when these contingencies are reflected in research. Until psychological studies on women and management consider the interaction of both person- and situation-centered variables, researchers run the risks of ignoring factors that may explain significant proportions of variance in their findings. And programs designed to remedy women's low status may overlook key targets for change efforts.[90] Furthermore, unless the negative aspects of organizational life are examined and eliminated, women's move into top levels of management may create new problems for them while solving old ones.

Low-Paying Jobs for Women

By Discrimination or by Choice?

WOMEN'S STUDIES ENTERED THE courtroom in the 1986 case of the *Equal Employment Opportunity Commission v. Sears, Roebuck and Company*.[1] The Economic Opportunity Commission (EEOC) accused Sears of sex discrimination by channeling female workers into salaried sales jobs that paid less and were less prestigious than those that included a commission as part of compensation. Sears did not dispute the lack of women in commission sales jobs but denied that the disparity was due to discriminatory practices. Sears argued that the kinds of jobs that included commissions involved traditionally male products, such as automotive supplies, plumbing, and furnaces, and often required evening or weekend work schedules. According to Sears, women lacked interest in these kinds of jobs. To the consternation of many, scholars of women's history testified on both sides of the case, using historical information to interpret the statistical disparities in Sears's workforce in sharply contrasting ways.[2]

As an expert witness for Sears, Rosalind Rosenberg testified that commitment to the home and family, internalization of values that are predominately relationship-centered rather than work-centered, and policies and practices that make working difficult for married women and women with small children lead women to have different attitudes, goals, and expectations toward work than men. Consequently, they choose different jobs. As an expert witness for the EEOC, Alice Kessler-Harris countered that women's choices about work can be understood only within the context of opportunities available to them. Working women choose high-paying jobs if they are available to them. Furthermore, while upper-income, professional women and those who do not work for wages may hold "feminine" values of domesticity and nurturance, it is not appropriate to attribute these values to all women.[3]

Although most of the information used by Rosenberg and Kessler-Harris is historical, research on the interpersonal dynamics of the workplace is also relevant to this case. In making his decision in favor of Sears, the judge in the case was influenced not so much by historical evidence as by evidence from the immediate work environment. The judge accepted as the most credible and convincing evidence regarding women's interests the testimony of Sears managers and other store personnel who said that they had attempted unsuccessfully to recruit women to commission sales jobs. They said that women were uninterested and unwilling to take these jobs because of their highly competitive, stressful nature and unfriendly working atmosphere and because women were unfamiliar with the products involved. According to Sears's managers, women were afraid that they might not be able to compete and thus might put their jobs in jeopardy. The store witnesses' opinions were reinforced by the results of morale surveys that Sears takes of its workers every three years, asking about job satisfaction, interest in promotion, and so forth. In the surveys, noncommissioned saleswomen were more satisfied than were noncommissioned salesmen, and more men expressed interest in promotions than women. The judge concluded that women's lack of interest in commission sales was the cause of sex segregation at Sears. Responsibility for the disproportionate numbers lies with women themselves, in their own choices and behaviors. In so deciding, the judge ignored the way that the social context at Sears shapes women's attitudes and choices. That social context is not the same for women at Sears—or elsewhere—as it is for men.

Women who are pioneers in mostly male occupations have few female role models or mentors to help them in their careers. Role models of people we see as similar to ourselves can show us how things are done in unfamiliar situations and they can provide inspiration and hope: "If she can do it, then so can I." Mentors go a step further by taking a direct personal interest in our success. They introduce us to the right people, critique our work in helpful ways, and teach us what we need to know in order to succeed. The absence of female role models and mentors in commission sales at Sears was likely to have a chilling effect on women's perceptions of opportunities for success in these jobs. The impression would be that these jobs are off-limits for women,[4] and so other women would be less likely to aspire to them.[5] Perhaps women at Sears thought their chances of success were low simply because few other women had succeeded before them.[6]

The judge accepted testimony from Sears's witnesses that "women tend to be more interested than men in the social and cooperative aspects of the workplace."[7] The implication of this testimony is that this is a stable and reliable manifestation of female gender. Yet a study of men and women at work found that women's emphasis on good relationships with co-workers was not a function of their gender or personality. Rather, it was the result of the lack of advancement possibilities on the job. Little chance of advancement means that women look to their relationships with co-workers as sources of satisfaction.[8]

Other factors in the work environment also could have affected women's attitudes and job preferences. Women who were hired or promoted into commission sales were likely to be in a minority position. Certain predictable experiences happen to people who are in solo-status (token) positions.[9] They tend to be scrutinized closely, receiving more than their share of attention. The differences between them and the rest of the group are exaggerated, often in the form of jokes or teasing. Finally, they are seen by others to be acting in stereotypical ways. That is, regardless of how they actually behave, others will see them as living up to their stereotypes and will cast them in special roles. Thus, the only female in a group of male workers will become the "mother" of the group. It is she who will bring the doughnuts to meetings and remember people's birthdays. Ironically, being in a solo-status position seems to work *against* women but *for* men. The sole male member of an all-female group easily becomes its leader, a rare occurrence for solo females in all-male groups.[10] The consequence of being a woman in this solo-status position is that she is isolated. Is it any wonder, then, that when asked which jobs they prefer, women would not choose a work situation in which they would be in a minority?

Furthermore, survey findings that few women workers aspire to jobs in which few females have gone before them do not in themselves rule out discrimination by the employer. Rather, women simply could be choosing not to put themselves in a situation where they might be subject to the consequences of discrimination. The wish to minimize their own job risks does not necessarily mean that there is no discrimination at that workplace. The Sears survey asked only if women wanted commission sales jobs. It did not ask if a woman could be successful in such a job or whether she might face hostility from co-workers or customers. Thus, the conclusion follows that women's job choices are freely chosen, since an alternative explanation was never explored. To ignore the alternative explanation and to locate the cause of women's lack of success within women themselves is to blame the victim.

The second point that impressed the judge in the Sears case is that women were not deemed to be as qualified as men for commissioned sales jobs. However, the way that people were hired and promoted at Sears left considerable room for stereotypes about gender to bias the evaluation process. For instance, the most important part of the hiring process was an interview. "The interviewer would evaluate the applicant's personal characteristics, such as appearance, manner, assertiveness, and friendliness, ability to communicate, motivation, and overall potential."[11] Sears used no written guidelines for selection of commission salespersons, and the interviewers were not formally trained in what qualities to look for in commission sales candidates. In other words, the evaluation process was fairly subjective, leaving considerable room for discretion on the part of the interviewer.

A host of studies by social scientists provides clear evidence that gender has a profound effect on evaluation. In order to investigate bias in hiring decisions, researchers give people simulated job applicant folders. Half of the folders identify the applicant as Robert; the other half identify the applicant as Roberta. The rest of the information in the folders is identical. The results: women are consistently rated higher when the job involved is female-typed, while men are preferred for male-typed jobs.[12]

Once hired, women continue to face discrimination. Evaluations of women's achievement, of their potential, and of their performance on the job tend to be lower than evaluations of equivalent performance of men. This pro-male evaluation bias is more likely to operate with jobs traditionally occupied by males and with more demanding jobs. Should a woman get one of these jobs and be successful, her achievements are credited to luck rather than to ability.[13]

The more ambiguous the evaluation process, the more likely it is that gender bias will operate. The more the job involved is stereotyped as appropriate for the opposite sex, the more likely it is that gender bias will operate.[14] The Sears hiring procedure for commission sales leaves judgment up to the discretion of the interviewer for a job that is male sex-typed—the precise situation in which a pro-male bias is likely to operate. The claim that women are not as qualified as men for these jobs must be viewed in that context.

The final point on which the judge grounded his decision in the Sears case is that the claim of discrimination was based on statistical evidence rather than on the testimony of individual women who said that they had been victimized. The EEOC presented statistics demonstrating that many fewer women were hired and promoted into commission sales than could be expected, given the total pool of women potentially eligible for these jobs. The judge rejected the statistical evidence as highly misleading and instead placed great weight on the fact that no woman who worked at Sears came forth to testify that she personally had been the victim of discrimination.

However, the lack of claimants is not surprising. A study designed to explore how women feel about their jobs discovered the following paradox. When asked if women are discriminated against, a woman will say yes without hesitation. When asked if she personally is the victim of discrimination, that same woman is likely to say no. So at the same time a woman acknowledges discrimination against women in general, she will deny her own victimization. Yet the group of women who gave these responses to researchers earned $5,000–$9,000 less than men who had equivalent jobs and work backgrounds. These women were paid less than the men, and they believed that women were subject to discrimination. Yet they were unwilling or unable to acknowledge that discrimination had occurred to them.[15]

Why is this so? One possibility is that patterns of discrimination can be observed most readily only when we look at the experience of a large number of people, not just a few individuals because individual idiosyncrasies are averaged out in the group. A woman applying for a job is unlikely to know how other women have been treated in the hiring process. If she is not hired, she may look within herself for explanations for her lack of success.[16]

People tend to attribute their own success or failure to one of four factors: ability, effort, task difficulty, or luck. If I do well at something, I can credit my talent or skills, my hard work, the ease of the task, or just plain luck. But women's successes are often attributed to factors other than ability, such as luck, effort, or cheating. Women may do this to themselves as well. Ironically, women's tendency to credit their successes to luck—but to blame themselves for failures—is especially likely to occur on male sex-typed tasks.[17] An individual woman may see her failure to be hired or promoted as the result of her own inadequate abilities or efforts. Add this to women's lack of information about what has happened to other women at her work setting, and we begin to understand why so few come forward to claim discrimination. Statistical evidence may be the best way to show patterns of discrimination. Yet the judge in the Sears case was unwilling to accept statistical evidence, an action that does not bode well for those who view litigation as the means of achieving job equity.

Judicial decisions, like other decisions, do not occur in a vacuum. The climate of the times today is one in which success or failure is attributed to factors within the individual, and social context is ignored. The decision in the Sears case blames the absence of women in high-paying jobs on women themselves. This explanation can—and will—be used to justify discrimination not only in the sphere of employment, but also in virtually every area of life. Achieving equity requires not only that women and minorities change themselves to meet the demands of the work world, as we hear so often; it also requires that the work world change to eradicate the barriers that prevent women and minorities from achieving. Even if sex and race segregation in employment diminishes, some of the problems mentioned here will persist. Women may make up about half of those in managerial ranks, reflecting their numbers in the general population and reducing the impact on women of such dynamics as tokenism. But those who are minorities in the population at large, such as African Americans, are likely to remain minorities at managerial levels. The negative dynamics affecting those in "solo status" positions may still apply to them. Changing the work world has not been easy in the past. The decision in the Sears case illustrated the predominance of a worldview that will make it all the more difficult in the future.

Challenges of Success

Stages of Growth in Feminist Organizations

C REATING ORGANIZATIONS THAT SERVE and advocate for women has been an outstanding achievement of the feminist movement in the United States since the 1970s. Battered women's shelters, women's studies programs, health clinics, law firms, bookstores, theaters, art galleries, newspapers, and many other feminist organizations and enterprises have enriched women's lives and furthered the process of social change. Having been involved in several of these groups as a participant, researcher, and consultant, I have noticed that organizations with very different purposes, united only loosely by feminist ideology, confront similar issues as they grow. Some of these issues arise in any small organization as it becomes larger and more complex; others are common to social movement organizations that use a collectivist structure. But particular problems emerge when feminist values encounter the demands of life in a growing organization. This chapter explores the challenges and choices that feminist organizations face as they grow.

Feminism is not a unitary set of beliefs but rather encompasses a range of ideologies.[1] Nonetheless, two concerns are central to most variants of feminism as it developed in the United States in the 1960s: (1) opposition to the domination of men over women; and (2) a belief that women share a status as members of a subordinate group. Many of the women who started feminist organizations during this time believed that hierarchy in organizations created a system of dominance of superiors over subordinates that mirrored the dominance of men over women. In their view, the impersonal, rule-bound nature of bureaucratic interactions isolated individuals from one another, dehumanizing them and making them dependent on the organization.[2] A discussion of how to structure a rape crisis center exemplifies these claims:

> One of the goals we are working toward is an end to domination and control in relationships between people. Rape is an extreme example of this: but most of us learn to follow a similar pattern in our personal and work relationships. . . . Most traditional organizational structures are hierarchies of some kind, and as such produce competitive and domineering work relationships. In addition, such structures do not usually foster skills and leadership qualities in each person who participates in the organization, nor do they enable us to find ways of supporting those with less privilege—such as free time or financial resources—to be able to participate fully.[3]

Ending women's subordination called for social arrangements that validated individual women's feelings and experiences, embodied an ideal of "sisterhood" among women, and provided equal power and opportunity. Many feminist organizations that emerged during the 1960s and 1970s tried to manifest this vision as microcosms of a new social order. By eliminating or minimizing dominant-subordinate relationships, feminist organizations sought to enhance the development of women's skills and facilitate cooperation. Accordingly, the organizations strove to embody the values of participation and humanism, although many mixed egalitarian with hierarchical practices.

While these organizations were evolving, however, other feminists were criticizing the egalitarian model. For example, Jo Freeman's classic essay, "The Tyranny of Structurelessness," argued that collectivist structures might mask rather than eliminate hierarchies.[4] Distinguishing between power as effectiveness and power as domination, Nancy Hartsock claimed that the women's movement erred in its condemnation of leadership by confusing those who wanted to achieve with those who wanted to control others.[5] Similarly, members of the Chicago Women's Liberation Union argued that what was needed was not an absence of leadership, but rather mechanisms for keeping leadership accountable.[6] Finally, combining egalitarian social relationships and participatory democracy on the one hand, and individual freedom and development on the other, created a paradox when individuals' needs conflicted with those of the group.[7] One participant in the battered women's movement voiced this dilemma in the guilt she felt about her desire for individual recognition despite her commitment to a collectivist movement.[8]

As hundreds of women devote untold hours of effort to feminist organizations, the appropriate way to manifest feminist ideals in organizational contexts is still being contested. This debate is now complicated by the fact that a number of these organizations have grown from small, informal collectivities to large, well-established institutions. What happened when feminist beliefs and practices faced the demands of organizational growth? I looked for answers to this question in published descriptions, case studies, and surveys of feminist organizations; in research on alternative and mainstream organizations; and in my own research and observations.

My purpose is not to describe the history of particular feminist organizations, but rather to identify the general logic of their development. In doing so, I make two assumptions. First, decisions made by an organization's members, rather than predetermined factors, determine the pattern of an organization's growth. Predictably, certain issues arise as an organization increases in the size of its membership, but the outcomes lie in the interaction between the challenges of development and the choices made by members of organizations. For example, although this chapter focuses on the dynamics of growth, those participants in an organization could chose to keep it small. Second, this model is not meant to be universal but rather applies to feminist organizations that espoused an egalitarian ideology and developed in the United States during the 1970s and 1980s. The historical and political context has a powerful shaping effect on a social movement and its organizations.[9] Feminist organizations in other times and places often developed differently than those in the contemporary United States. Battered women's shelters in West Germany, for example, maintained a radical agenda, consistent with the autonomy of German feminism, in contrast to the interpenetration of liberal and radical policies in the U.S. shelter movement.[10]

In this discussion, an organization is considered feminist if it has a feminist ideology, values or goals, or if it emerged from the women's movement since the 1970s in the United States.[11] Thus, the spectrum of organizations considered here include both nonprofit and profit-making enterprises, those that are freestanding as well as those that are institutionally embedded, and those providing a service or creating a product as well as those advocating social change. Important factors differentiate these types of organizations. Nonetheless, this discussion seeks to locate common issues and choices that emerge in egalitarian feminist organizations as membership grows.

Stages in Organizational Life Cycles

Not all organizations increase in size. Those that do also change in qualitative ways as they expand, proceeding through a series of distinct developmental stages from simple to more complex structures.[12] These stages occur in a predictable order; resolution of the problems inherent in one stage facilitates successful negotiation of the next.[13] Success can propel an organization through these stages. At the same time, the ensuing transitions produce stress. Development can involve dramatic and discontinuous changes in an organization's policies and procedures, and members can disagree about the appropriate direction of growth.

Stage models of the life cycle of organizations generally begin with the newly formed organization struggling for survival and proceed to the mature organization fighting stagnation and decline. I find the model proposed by Quinn and Cameron most useful because it differentiates an initial stage of creation from a second stage in which collectivity prevails.[14] This permits close examination of the dynamics of the collectivity stage, a particularly important one for feminists because of its fit with egalitarian values. I modify this model to take into account the nature of feminist values.

The first stage in this model encompasses the birth of the organization, while the second stage contains high cohesion and commitment. In the third stage, the organization institutionalizes its policies and procedures, while it expands and decentralizes in the fourth stage. The transition from the collectivity of stage two to the formalization of stage three is the most difficult transition for any organization because it involves the most dramatic change in policies and practices.[15] Feminist organizations are especially likely to have difficulty because formalization contradicts some feminists' desire for participatory democracy and for recognition of women's individuality; therefore I consider the transition to formalization in detail here. Little information exists on the dynamics of feminist organizations in the fourth stage; consequently, my examination of this stage is brief. Because conflict can occur at any stage of organizational development, I consider it separately and focus on its organizational sources.[16]

Stages of Growth in Feminist Organizations

The Creation Stage

Innovation and creativity mark the birth of an organization.[17] The reminiscences of a feminist bookstore manager capture the spirit of participants at its inception: "Women were glowing. . . . There was a lot of excitement, a lot of hope and a belief that we were going to make a change, our lives were going to change."[18] The process of creation begins before the organization is actually established, when founders identify a problem and imagine various solutions.[19] Communication among members in a newly emerging organization is frequent, informal and face-to-face; working hours are long. The creation of an organization demands enormous amounts of effort, time, and sometimes even physical labor,[20] as a group of volunteers in Texas found when they had to spend hundreds of hours planning a battered women's shelter.[21] A physician at a women's health center told me that she was on call twenty-four hours a day, seven days a week, in the center's early days. When members of a feminist group in Minnesota decided to open an art gallery, they had to renovate a dirty and neglected building, which they did by hand to preserve the architectural details.[22] Women in Dayton held "cleaning, painting and floor-waxing parties" to prepare a two-story frame house as a women's center.[23] Although organizational demands are great, this period is exciting because the flexibility of a new and growing system permits people to grow and develop as well.[24] As women in the battered women's movement found, "no one had ever done this work before and everything had to be mastered at once, often during long work weeks of seventy hours."[25] Developing new skills and achieving new goals can reward members for long hours of hard work.

The founders of an organization usually "behave like missionaries searching for an audience to convert," selling their ideas, in part to reinforce their own beliefs.[26] Those who start social movement organizations, like those who start businesses, are often risk-takers who like to maintain personal control. They typically disdain managerial activities[27] and may institute little or no formal structure at this stage, using their personal influence when making decisions. The lack of formal mechanisms for decision-making may mean that influence is not distributed equitably among members, contradicting feminist egalitarian values.

The effort and excitement of founding an organization can mask underlying differences in members' ideologies or motivations. For example, some participants in the battered women's movement are committed to reforming the existing social system, while others seek radical transformation. Some women have been battered themselves; to others, violence is unfamiliar. Some see male domination as the cause of violence in society; others look to family pathology. The demands of creating a shelter for battered women leave little time to develop an ideological consensus. Instead, philosophy is "hammered out in between emergency phone calls or meetings with local bureaucrats offering a few thousand dollars so that a shelter might open."[28] The process of deciding how to expend resources often uncovers differences in beliefs and values that are difficult to reconcile.

Fledgling organizations typically have to acquire resources (such as money or members), obtain legitimacy, and create a niche for the organization's product or services in order to survive.[29] Acquiring resources and obtaining legitimacy may be interdependent because feminist organizations often have to prove their credibility in order to receive funds or other resources. For example, women's studies programs within universities must persuade faculty colleagues or administrators that women's studies is a legitimate academic enterprise in order to obtain funding; women's health clinics must demonstrate their professionalism to attract patients; women's bookstores must document their financial solvency to obtain a lease for store space. The need to demonstrate legitimacy may push a feminist organization in conventional directions in order to make it acceptable to other institutions and to people who can provide resources such as money or office space.

At the same time, the strength of commitment that motivates people to put time, money, and effort into the organization may lead them to adopt extreme goals or tactics. The scarcity of money in a fledging organization is likely to mean that participants are those most strongly committed to its values and mission. Few material incentives exist, so members are rewarded by furthering the cause.[30] In her study of the movement to pass the Equal Rights Amendment, for example, Jane Mansbridge identifies a tendency toward ideological purity: "mobilizing volunteers often requires an exaggerated, black or white vision of events to justify spending time and money on the cause."[31] The self-selection of activists, their sacrifices for the cause, and their frequent exposure to like-minded others propels them toward an oversimplified and unreflective stance. This may push an organization in an extreme direction, producing resistance when compromises have to be made in order to establish the organization's credibility. From its inception, tension is likely to exist between the oppositional stance of a feminist organization and its survival needs.

Accordingly, I suggest that a critical choice facing members of a newly formed feminist organization is how far to deviate from mainstream principles and practices. If an organization is too different, it may not be able to obtain enough resources to survive. Furthermore, when roles and tasks are innovative and perhaps unclear, uncertainty produces anxiety and confusion. On the other hand, if the organization is not sufficiently different, participants who are motivated by a commitment to feminism may drop out. Feminist organizations have to maintain a delicate balance between these opposing forces in order to survive.

The Collectivity Stage

It is difficult to specify precisely when one organizational stage ends and the next begins. One indicator of transition is that a concern for producing results supplants worries about survival. The success of the budding enterprise exhilarates members, producing high group morale and cohesion and individual satisfaction (as well as exhaustion). Some members feel a "sense of family" in this stage.[32] A desire to form connections and share experiences with like-minded, supportive women has motivated participants in a wide variety of women's organizations.[33] Yet bell hooks points out that many women of color whose sense of community is already strong are frustrated by the attention given to social support when they would prefer to place priority on political activity.[34]

The collectivity stage is typified by a relatively informal structure in which jobs and authority are often shared among group members. Such a structure facilitates maximum participation of members and sharing of decision-making power, dynamics valued by many feminists. Yet collectivist structures also have costs. Mansbridge summarizes the drawbacks of collectivist functioning as "time, emotion, and inequality": participatory decision-making is time-consuming, interaction can be emotionally intense, and power may be distributed unequally.[35] Differences in status, articulateness, ability to persuade, or sheer persistence enables one person's views to prevail over those of another. When the organizational decision-making structure is ambiguous, an informal hierarchy of influence develops in the absence of a formal one. Because this informal hierarchy is not a part of the formal organizational structure, there may be no way to hold it accountable; in Freeman's cautionary term, a "tyranny of structurelessness" may prevail.[36]

In a study of alternative service organizations of the 1970s, Joyce Rothschild-Whitt identified several conditions that facilitate participatory-democratic organizations.[37] Limits to size is one of these conditions, along with a transitory orientation to the organization, economic marginality, and oppositional services and values. Elsewhere I have suggested that certain conditions permit a feminist organization to maintain a collectivist structure: equal distribution of skills and knowledge among participants, dependence on members rather than on outside sources of funding, the development of procedures that permit efficient responses to external demands, an emphasis on participation rather than efficiency, the development of close personal ties among members, and dispersion of sources of power (e.g., friendship networks and expertise).[38] Organizations that lack these features are more likely to disintegrate or to move toward hierarchical forms of control; those that retain or develop these characteristics are more likely to maintain themselves as collectivities. For example, a battered women's shelter was able to maintain a counterbureaucratic organizational structure over time because of the homogeneity of its members: its staff consisted of former shelter residents rather than professional social workers. New staff recruited on the basis of similarity in beliefs got along well with existing staff, facilitating the consensual decision-making process. The drawback of such recruiting, however, was a lack of diversity among staff.[39]

A dilemma for feminist organizations is whether to encourage growth with its attendant pressures toward bureaucracy or to restrict growth in order to maintain a collectivist structure. Although a growing organization experiences pressures toward increasing hierarchy, there are other ways to resolve these pressures. Contrary to Michels's "iron law of oligarchy," which proposes that organizations invariably divide into a "minority of directors and a majority of directed,"[40] this tendency is not inevitable. For example, a group too large to function collectively can subdivide into several smaller groups.[41] Other alternatives are possible, such as spinning off small, autonomous units from a larger organization, or delegating routine decisions while deciding critical policy issues by the entire group in a modified collectivist arrangement.[42] The adoption of hierarchy is a choice made by organizational members, not inevitability.

Kathy Ferguson advocates small, face-to-face collectives as the appropriate structure for all organizations.[43] Yet small size can be problematic for a feminist organization. Limits to growth can force an organization to exclude women who want to participate, a process that seems to violate the spirit of feminism. Should a rape crisis center, for example, restrict the size of its staff in order to maintain a collectivist structure, if by doing so it will not be able to answer all of the calls for help that it receives from rape victims? Feminists' dislike of hierarchical relationships and the desire to recognize the needs of individual members may conflict with the need for efficiency, stability, and predictability. Although a collectivist structure and productivity are not always mutually exclusive, they can be antagonistic in a large organization. A focus within the organization on participation and expressiveness can impede the efficiency that is often needed for instrumental action. This dilemma emerges in different forms—for example, as a conflict between the needs of an individual compared to the needs of the organization as a whole or as a choice between participation and productivity. As members of one group asked themselves, "shall we evaluate our process tonight or get out a mailing?"[44] Differences among members in beliefs or values may crystallize when the group has to give priority to a particular goal or activity.

In commenting on Ferguson's position, Patricia Yancey Martin asks: "If . . . bureaucratic organizations really *are* the most efficient type of organizational form (other things being equal), does pursuit of more humane, democratic, responsive, non-dominating organizations require their total rejection?"[45] Perhaps collectivist forms best serve some organizational purposes while structures that are larger and more differentiated enable other goals to be reached most easily. To some extent, the question of whether or not to expand turns on the relative importance of the organization as an end in itself or as a means to an end. A feminist group whose primary aim is to foster growth and development of its members might most effectively remain small and egalitarian, while one that aspires to provide a service for others might function best with some hierarchical features. Moreover, different forms can coexist within the same organization for different functions. The subcommittees in one statewide battered women's coalition were exemplars of egalitarian functioning even though the board of the coalition was too large and unwieldy to reach decisions by consensus.[46]

The Formalization Stage

As with previous shifts to a new stage, the transition to formalization may be a gradual, uneven process. Success during the "collectivity" stage sets in motion multiple forces that press toward institutionalization of the organization's policies and practices and the development of a hierarchy of authority. Among those forces are an increase in the size of the staff, turnover in staff, and the need to obtain funding from sources outside the organization. Each of these conditions generates pressures that move the organization toward the development of positions with specialized functions, a hierarchy of titles, and more formal and impersonal communication procedures.[47]

Feminist organizations that create a product or provide a service are likely to find themselves overloaded by demand, especially if they are addressing a hitherto unmet need, such as sheltering battered women or counseling rape victims. A women's health clinic found that its small volunteer staff was unable to meet the overwhelming demand for its services in a timely fashion: "Appointments for pregnancy tests and other services often had to be scheduled at least a week after a woman's request for services."[48] Ironically, the inaccessibility of mainstream health care was a factor that prompted the founding of the clinic. As many other feminist organizations did when faced with a similar situation, they added more workers.

An increase in staff may have unanticipated consequences for the organization. New employees, hired after the excitement of creating the organization has faded, may not have the same sense of mission that the original members had; they see their employment as a job rather than a cause. Although longtime participants recognize the need for new workers, they still may resent the fact that these people were not around when employment by the organization called for sacrifice. Also, the larger number of participants permits division into factions. As a result, office politics may flourish and destroy even the illusion of unity.[49]

The greatest change associated with growth, however, is the press toward formalization of procedures and policies that accompanies an increase in the number of members. When the number of staff increases, face-to-face communication becomes too time-consuming, and more formal and impersonal means, such as memos, written guidelines, or voicemail, begin to be used. The schedules of large numbers of staff are likely to conflict, making it difficult to arrange meetings, and the heavy demand for services prohibits taking the time needed for consensual decision-making, thus encouraging stratification of authority. The specialization of job functions that often accompanies organizational expansion usually is more efficient, reducing the need for every person to master every task, allowing members to focus on their areas of interest and to develop sophisticated skills. However, specialization also may prevent everyone from having an overview of the whole organization, thus requiring central coordination and control.[50]

Increased numbers of staff make it difficult to manage an organization by means of personal influence. Rather, the need for efficient operating systems in order to coordinate the activities of large numbers of people requires institutionalized decision-making procedures.[51] Goal-setting and formally adopted plans and policies typify the tendency toward formalization of operations. In these ways, the organization becomes less dependent on the personal qualities or charisma of its leaders.

The pattern of development that has occurred in many rape crisis centers exemplifies this process of change. Many of these centers, begun in the 1960s as collectives, first developed standing committees in order to enable members to pursue specialized interests. Steering committees were created as nonhierarchical vehicles for coordination and control. As the centers became more formalized, they added boards of directors to their governance structure. Most centers came to resemble traditional bureaucratic organizations in form.[52]

The centralization of authority in the position of a leader that occurs as part of the formalization process can create tensions in feminist organizations. Judy Remington argues that the women's movement accepts powerful women only in a kind of maternal role, as nurturers, rather than as leaders strong in other ways.[53] Indeed, the role of mother has been proposed as a model of feminist leadership.[54] Members' desire for nurturance from female leaders may not be unique to feminist groups. Studies comparing female and male leaders find only a few differences between them, but people perceive and react to female versus male leaders very differently.[55] Teresa Bernardez hypothesizes that a female leader unwittingly arouses expectations that she will be the perfect mother who provides selflessness, total acceptance, self-abnegation, lack of aggression and criticism, and nurturance.[56] When she does not live up to this ideal, irrational and intense anger and criticism may befall her. Furthermore, female leaders are not seen as legitimate holders of positions of authority in our society.[57] Accordingly, they may be caught between organization members' unrealistically high expectations of what leaders can provide and a paradoxical lack of belief in the legitimacy of their position.

Centralization of authority and formalization of procedures may reduce the opportunity of some members to exert influence. Founders who are used to controlling their organizations may find a more rule-bound, less subjective style of management anathema. They may be unwilling to step aside because of a proprietary interest in the organization. The reluctance of founders to institutionalize leadership by establishing procedures and policies that do not require their personal judgment has been labeled the "founder's trap."[58] Ironically, just as the organization attracts more clients or external funding, the founder's personal style of management may become inappropriate because of the expansion in organizational size. Especially when they have taken risks or made sacrifices to get the organization off the ground, founders may resent their sudden obsolescence and may resist change. A critical challenge in this situation is to loosen the founders' control of the organization. In some cases, this means the founders will depart; Suzanne Staggenborg identifies a long list of social movement founders, feminist and otherwise, who chose to leave or were ejected from organizations that they had begun.[59]

Founders may leave an organization when the process of formalization diminishes their influence. Many reasons prompt others to leave. Long-term participants become frustrated and bored by the time-consuming nature of participatory processes, yet participation requires that an organization respond to a newcomer's concern with more than the assurance that her suggestions have already been tried or the discussion held many times. When hierarchy emerges, those with a strong commitment to collectivist process may depart. Some find distasteful the accommodations that may be necessary to obtain funding. As time passes, the work to be done and the processes by which to do it may become routine, providing workers little opportunity for new learning and thus decreasing their job satisfaction.[60] In addition, if professionalization of the organization requires advanced credentials of members, those without such credentials may be unwilling to accept low status positions and leave.

Others may leave simply because of their own developmental needs. An organization and its founding members age simultaneously. Many contemporary feminist organizations were started in the 1970s by women who were then in their twenties. These women are now much older. Some longtime participants may be entering a stage in their own lives when the organization is less central to them. Those with competing commitments may be unwilling or unable to devote long hours and enormous amounts of energy as they once did.

High turnover can necessitate the development of formal mechanisms so that new members can be incorporated quickly. Written job descriptions, employee handbooks, and orientation and training procedures integrate new members more easily into an organization. Although these practices clarify job expectations, they also can reduce the opportunity for individual variability in the execution of a job. In this way, turnover moves an organization toward institutionalization.

One advantage of turnover is that it provides the opportunity to move beyond the homogeneity of membership typical of organizations in their early stages. Turnover also revivified the political agenda of a feminist health clinic when a woman with political experience and commitment was hired as director.[61] Nonetheless, the departure of valued members can be painful, especially if the exit of women of color, lesbians, or working-class women leaves the organization open to charges, even if unwarranted, of racism, heterosexism, or elitism. Turnover may also be difficult if newer members do not have the same commitment to feminism as those who joined earlier, making them less willing to sacrifice for the organization.

The values of newcomers to the organization may conflict with those of long-term members. In a parallel fashion, those outside the organization may not agree with or understand a feminist organization's emphasis on participation and shared power, and they may press the organization to become more bureaucratic and formalized. The necessity to obtain resources from outside exacerbates this pressure. A rape crisis center, for example, may find that it needs donations and grants from local community members and government sources to sustain itself. To get these funds, it must adopt conventional bureaucratic practices in order to convince outsiders that it is both successful at its mission and fiscally responsible. Traditional forms demonstrate the legitimacy of an organization to external institutions.[62] Outside institutions that control access to resources can require elements of bureaucracy in a feminist organization.[63] One battered women's shelter adopted two bureaucratic features—extensive record-keeping and detailed job descriptions—to satisfy its funding sources.[64] Such procedures, while necessary to attract funding, tend to have the effect of specializing job functions and formalizing an organization's operations.

Obtaining funds may lead to salary discrepancies among staff or the distinction between salaried staff and volunteers, generating differentiation of interests since salaried and volunteer staff experience different risks and advantages. Salaried staff are more vulnerable to the outcome of decisions, because volunteers may leave if they become unhappy while salaried staff depend on the organization for an income. But salaried staff typically have more information about the organization than volunteers, in part because they spend more time there, allowing them to know more and thus exert more influence on decisions.[65]

The need for money from outside sources can shape not only the structure but also the goals of an organization. Piven and Cloward argue that social movements that become institutionalized lose their advocacy thrust because concern for organizational maintenance replaces the focus on social protest.[66] For example, at a women's health clinic, the fact that funds were available for direct services but not for community education or patient advocacy meant that funding priorities became organizational priorities. Some members of the clinic hesitated to oppose a government bill restricting abortions because such a public stance might jeopardize their funding.[67] As one feminist stated: "Who controls the women's organizations in town? It's largely men. We still get our funding through being good girls."[68] Since few funders give money for oppositional programs, the need for outside funding can influence an organization to avoid a controversial stance. But the impact of outside funding may not always be conservatizing. In Los Angeles, state funding enabled the creation of two black-rape crisis centers, expanding racial and ethnic diversity in the anti-rape movement.[69]

Formalization in an organization can clarify responsibilities and relationships, yet formalization is not without drawbacks. Feminists groups may resist the pressures on a growing organization to develop hierarchy because they abhor the inequality inherent in bureaucracy. Although not all feminists claim that a collective structure is mandatory in a feminist organization, most agree that hierarchy should be minimal and broad participation should prevail. This conviction leads to tension when organizations become more differentiated. Staggenborg compared the more formalized Chicago chapter of the National Organization for Women (NOW) with the relatively more informal, decentralized Chicago Women's Liberation Union (CWLU); she found that NOW survived while the CWLU died because NOW's structure permitted it to solve problems of organizational maintenance and internal dissent. NOW experienced problems of formalization, however, as fewer people could participate in decision-making, fewer projects were adopted, and more attention was devoted to organizational maintenance.[70]

Most growing organizations experience "the tension between innovation and institutionalization, and the transition from personal to impersonal and from collective to instrumental points of view."[71] Bureaucracy, with its specification of job functions, can eliminate idiosyncratic job performance in order to permit the coordination of the work of many people.[72] The need for predictability, however, can come at a cost to the individuals involved. "The uniformity, the routinization, and the fragmentation of behavior run counter not only to the factor of individual differences but to the needs of people for self-determination, spontaneity, accomplishment, and the expression of individual skills and talents."[73] In bureaucratic organizations, an informal social system meets people's social and emotional needs, resolving some of the frustration caused by the repression of individuality. Feminist organizations have tried to minimize this frustration by incorporating the recognition of individual needs into the formal practices of the organization; yet, inevitably, individual needs will conflict with organizational demands.

Ferguson contends that an organization that becomes bureaucratic ceases to be truly feminist. In her opinion, appeals to the greater efficiency of bureaucracy overlook factors that dehumanize and disempower people. But the need to compete with other organizations for scarce resources such as volunteers or foundation funds (or customers or students) means that inefficiency can cause an organization's demise.[74] Ferguson contrasts bureaucracy, which sees people as objects to be manipulated, with egalitarian structures, which permit individual autonomy and self-development.[75] But implying that bureaucracy is masculine and dominating, while collectivity is feminine and humanizing, stereotypes not only gender but also organizational structures. This dichotomy glosses over the multidimensionality of both types of structural arrangements and the advantages and disadvantages of each. It leaves no room to consider "the oppressive, unresponsive elements in collective practices or the democratic impulses in hierarchical practices."[76] Indeed, the accountability permitted by bureaucracy can provide a check on abuses of power that may not be possible in a nonbureaucratic organization. Bureaucracy also can enable the organization to have an impact beyond the range of particular individuals.[77] Nonetheless, Ferguson's powerful description of the pernicious effects of bureaucracy cautions against extreme specialization and hierarchy. Hence, one challenge facing feminist organizations is to adopt the minimal degree of hierarchy that is necessary to achieve particular goals. The press for a more differentiated structure in feminist organizations may stem from a desire for greater clarity about the division of labor rather than a need for many levels of authority.

The formalization of policies and procedures in a feminist organization may result in an organizational structure that no longer resembles the founders' conception. This process is not unique to feminist organizations. Labeled the "paradox of success," those things that make an organization innovative and desirable are the very things that may have to change to ensure its success in the long run.[78] Ironically, although formalizing procedures reduces uncertainty and lends stability to an organization, formalization removes the flexibility that permitted innovation to occur in the first place. An organization ought to undergo periodic self-scrutiny to ensure that the features that made it innovative are not lost. In doing so, it is important to remember that the emphasis on rationality in the descriptions of formal organizations may belie how things actually work. As Meyer and Rowan state:

> Prevailing theories assume that the coordination and control of activity are the critical dimensions on which formal organizations have succeeded in the modern world. . . . But much of the empirical research on organizations casts doubt on this assumption . . . : structural elements are only loosely linked to each other and to activities, rules are often violated, decisions are often unimplemented, or if implemented have uncertain consequences, technologies are of problematic efficiency, and evaluation and inspection systems are subverted or rendered so vague as to provide little coordination.[79]

Meyer and Rowan suggest that some elements of organizational structure are adopted primarily to give legitimacy to the organization, having symbolic significance rather than being functional in other ways.

Feminist organizations must balance a quest for effective functioning with an emphasis on feminist goals and values. Vision and direction may fade while the organization gains efficiency from professional management. Because some feminists believe that bureaucratic-hierarchical organizations inevitably oppress workers, they may see the formalization of a feminist organization as a moral failure. In contrast, others view bureaucratic structures as benefiting feminist organizations by facilitating the accomplishment of certain goals and ensuring fairness and accountability. In Martin's words, "How power is actually used, and for what purposes, may be more important than its hierarchical or collectivist arrangement."[80] The challenge to feminist organizations is to adhere to an alternative vision even while adopting some bureaucratic forms.

Elaboration of Structure

The fourth stage of organizational development, elaboration of structure, is characterized by expansion, delegation, and coordination as well as renewal and generativity.[81] Typical of this stage is a large, multiunit organization, with a central headquarters and decentralized divisions.[82] When organizations reach this fourth stage, they typically need to decentralize and give more authority to those lower in the hierarchy. For example, a women's health center I consulted with in a large Midwestern city opened a second facility because of high demand. The second facility needed a degree of autonomy rather than centralized control of its operations in order to function effectively. Other feminist organizations have national offices and branch chapters in many cities. Because conditions in those cities vary, the branch offices require some autonomy.

Decentralization offers the opportunity for the subunits of the organization to return to the participatory practices of earlier stages, and it permits the flexibility an organization needs in order to respond to pressures to change. Decentralization runs the risk, however, of competition and conflict among the subparts of the organization. Personal ties among members, and among leaders, form cross-group linkages that can hold the larger organization together. A common ideology is particularly important as a unifying force. The many hours spent in fractious discussion at national or regional meetings and conferences can be seen positively as attempts to communicate and solidify that common ideology.[83]

State coalitions of battered women's shelters have some features of elaborated structures. These coalitions, which often receive and distribute funds for their shelter members, typically are governed by delegates representing individual shelters. A coalition can be politically active in ways that individual shelters cannot due to the heavy demands on each shelter for services or fundraising. In this case, large size of the organization (albeit through confederation) permits political activity that is difficult to accomplish in a smaller organization. Claire Reinelt labels as an "inside-outside" strategy the aim of many battered women's coalitions to build a political movement while struggling with mainstream institutions. Feminists in a Texas coalition developed a feeling of collective power as they successfully engaged state agencies. Rather than co-opting the shelters as earlier feminists feared, contact with mainstream institutions enabled this coalition to influence government funding agencies and changed laws. This changed the attitude of feminists. As Reinelt explains, "No longer was the state conceived as a unified agent of patriarchy. Instead, the state came to be viewed as a terrain of political activism."[84]

Formalization initiated during the previous stage of development enables expansion to occur. At the same time, it reduces the organization's ability to innovate. A stultifying emphasis on rules and procedures can result in organizational decline.[85] Flexibility and adaptation to societal changes are critical if the organization is to renew itself. For feminist organizations, flexibility includes the recognition of the diversity of beliefs and needs among women of different generations and life situations. Those growing up in the 1990s are likely to have different needs and interests than those who came to feminism in earlier times. Large, well-established membership organizations must recognize generational differences if they are to attract young participants. Accepting that feminist agendas will differ as generations change—or as membership expands to include women different from the original founders— is critical. Decentralization can permit the flexibility needed for change and thus facilitate that process of renewal.

Conflict in Feminist Organizations

Movement through each of the stages outlined here can generate painful conflict in feminist organizations. The principle of "sisterhood"—unity among women—occupied a central place in the feminist ideology of the 1960s. Indeed, one of the memorable slogans of that time was that "sisterhood is powerful." Adherence to an ideal, perhaps sentimentalized, vision of sisterhood was often interpreted to mean that conflict among women was antithetical to feminism. Yet those of us who grew up with sisters as siblings know that competition and conflict are inherent in the sisterly relationship. Like real sisters, feminists disagree about substantive matters; they feel envy, jealousy, and resentment toward each other; and they compete with each other.[86] The echoes in contemporary relationships of unresolved familial conflicts among mothers, daughters, and sisters can make disagreements among women hurtful and threatening.[87]

Conflict within feminist groups differs from that within other organizations, in part because of the importance of the feminist group to its members: "That involvement may represent the single social structure in women's lives where, at least ideologically if not functionally, the status of women is likely to be treated as greater than second class."[88] Conflict also threatens the sense of community that motivates many women to join feminist organizations. The social and psychological importance of the feminist organization to its members heightens the danger of ostracism that some fear accompanies disagreement. For example, Jane Mansbridge describes the nervousness she felt because of fear of rejection in presenting a position that deviated from the "party line" in a pro-ERA group.[89] In her case, the fears were unwarranted. In other situations, however, such fears have been grounded in reality. A feminist historian became the target of public attacks not only on her position but also on her motives and scholarly integrity when she testified in court against another feminist historian in defense of Sears, Roebuck, charged with sex discrimination.[90] Those on both sides of the feminist debate about pornography have been publicly accused of antifeminism.[91] It is not the existence of disagreement among feminists that is of concern here, but rather the attempts "in the classic manner of sectarians, . . . to read one another out of the feminist movement."[92]

Unresolved interpersonal conflicts may hinder effective organizational functioning and make development more difficult. When differences in a group become so extensive that it is impossible to retain an illusion of unity and group harmony, then conflict may surface with a vengeance. For example, angered by a member's tardiness and arrogance, other staff at a women's health center rejected a suggestion that they confront her with criticisms, opting instead to take her out for a pizza dinner to show support for her. Some time later, however, she was ousted from the collective.[93]

Some conflicts among women are grounded in individual differences in personality, beliefs, abilities, or ambitions. As material rewards become more available within organizations, conflict and competition can increase. The emphasis on cooperation in feminist philosophy may have been a product of feminists' marginality rather than their beliefs or values. "It is not so much poverty that creates the breeding ground for competition as it is the possibility of wealth."[94]

Conflicts stemming from differences that are delineated by group identity pose particularly difficult problems for feminist organizations that hope to forge bonds among women. As early as 1970, the black feminist lawyer Florynce Kennedy rejected what she called the "sisterhood mystique" because it masked the fact that some women oppress other women.[95] Tensions between black and white women have deep roots in U.S. history. As bell hooks points out, "Historically many black women experienced white women as the white supremacist group who most directly exercised power over them, often in a manner far more brutal and dehumanizing than that of racist white men."[96] Feminists' beliefs in social equality do not automatically exempt them from deeply ingrained attitudes of the dominant culture. Differences in social class also divide women. Working-class women have been baffled by some middle-class feminists' rejection of "professionalism" as a means to social equality; to them, professional skills are a way to escape dead-end, dehumanizing jobs. The feminist goal of empowerment also affronts many working-class women (and others) who do not see themselves as passive and dependent.[97]

A fundamental paradox exists in the idea of empowering others: the institutional structure that puts some people in the position to empower undermines the act of empowerment:

> Virtually all empowerment efforts involve a grant of power by a favored group to others in the organization. Unless the favored group changes the very circumstances that have given it power in the first place, the grant of power is always partial. Unfortunately, the limited nature of the grant works to undercut the effectiveness of the group that has been empowered. This ineffectiveness, in turn, discourages the original power holders from working to expand the grant.[98]

For example, at one battered women's shelter, the staff's power to decide whether residents might remain in the shelter illuminated the contradiction between an ideology of equality and actual practice. Staff determined that recognition by residents of the psychological dynamics of the battering cycle (which they defined as "empowerment") should be the priority, and they encouraged residents to discuss their experiences and feelings in order to understand this process. Yet the economic needs of many residents were more urgent to them than psychological development. "The staff aren't realistic enough about your situation," one resident complained. "I am a woman with four kids and I'm basically out on the street. They come in here all dressed up and smelling of perfume and ask me, 'How are you feeling today?'"[99] "Empowerment" is an ambiguous term. It can refer to an increase in an individual's sense of self and capacity for assertion, or to an increase in her formal participation in decision-making. At times, feminists endorse the latter in theory but the former in practice.

Differences in roles among organization members may also produce conflict. For example, the fiscal responsibility assumed by a board of directors might cause the board members to hesitate in committing funds to a risky project, while staff members' daily exposure to women's needs might make that same project seem mandatory to them. A dispute developed in a Texas battered women's shelter between those who managed and obtained funds and those who provided services; the dispute was resolved by firing the service providers, a painful irony since they had founded the shelter.[100] The interests of different constituencies (or "stakeholders") within an organization inevitably will clash, in some cases reflecting inequalities in the larger society. The creation of mechanisms or decision-rules for mediating these conflicts furthers the process of formalization.

Another source of conflict within feminist organizations is the groups' adoption of multiple broad, ambitious goals that deny the scarcity of resources available. I have seen some feminist organizations experience chronic turmoil because members are reluctant to set priorities among goals. Taking on the mission to achieve multiple purposes while having the ability to meet only a few can generate resentment and hostility among those who feel ignored or betrayed by the organization. Setting priorities among goals can force painful choices on an organization. Not making explicit decisions about which goals to emphasize, however, can leave organization's members in a continuing state of dissatisfaction and distrust.

To women for whom confrontation is a new, unpracticed way of acting, expressing differences can feel "raw and searing."[101] Cultural differences in communication styles also contribute to the difficulty of dealing with conflict. In bell hooks's college classes, white women students interpreted loud confrontations among black women as anger and hostility, while black women defined the same behavior as playful teasing.[102] The disappointment of finding differences among women when the desire for solidarity, both emotional and political, is so strong exacerbates the pain of conflict in feminist organizations. Public conflict among feminists also buoys those who deride feminist beliefs and practices and thus harms the credibility of the feminist movement as a whole.

The idea that women should operate only in a cooperative mode denies reality and clouds the process of conflict management. Conflict is an inevitable part of organizational life. "Its presence should not surprise us. It is the absence of ways of negotiating competing demands that we should worry about."[103] Jean Baker Miller suggests that women should reclaim conflict but reject models based on domination and subordination, basing our actions instead on the way that women have tried, in families and other relationships, to handle conflict in a manner that fosters everyone's development.[104] Conflict resolution techniques have been developed that permit opposing parties to articulate their differences and seek common ground.[105] Feminists at the 1983 Seneca Falls Women's Peace Encampment, torn about whether to display the American flag, set up a committee made up of "five women in strong opposition, five women in determined support, and five easygoing intermediate mediators." After seven hours of deliberation, they decided to include the American flag in a panoply of flags, many of them handmade by camp residents.[106] Yet some differences may be irreconcilable, or simply not amenable to collaborative solutions. Developing, in Miller's words, an "etiquette of conflict" that permits differences to be negotiated while retaining connections among women is a formidable task facing women's organizations today.

Conclusion

Feminist ideals of the 1960s inspired the creation of women's movement organizations. Many of these organizations began with a preference for collective structures and a desire for unity among women. The experience of recent years has tested those values against the realities of organizational growth and has deepened our understanding of organizational dynamics.

Hierarchy in organizations creates inequalities in relationships, but because inequality exists within collective structures also, hierarchy has some advantages. Egalitarian structures with a humanistic emphasis permit participation and individuality, but they fail to foster efficiency and predictability. This tension makes it necessary at times to choose between productivity and equality or to develop strategies, such as limiting the size of the organization, to enable egalitarian arrangements. Both bureaucratic and collectivist structures are multidimensional, each with advantages and disadvantages. Instead of asking whether certain organizational structures are "more" or "less" feminist, the critical question is whether they are useful for reaching particular goals.

The press toward bureaucracy that accompanies growth suggests that feminist organizations will become similar in form to mainstream organizations if they expand. However, alternatives to expansion, such as dividing into small groups, can preserve egalitarian relations, and feminism's democratic ideology mitigates against extreme centralization of control. A feminist organization can adopt some bureaucratic features without becoming a bureaucratic behemoth.

As a consultant, I have often heard members blame organizational problems on other individuals' deficient motives, abilities, or commitment to feminism. Yet organizational growing pains, not personal deficits, generate many of the tensions in feminist organizations. Individual differences are highly visible, whereas the shaping power of organizational arrangements is less transparent. Psychologists label as the "fundamental attribution error" the tendency of people to attribute other people's behavior to intrapsychic factors while considering situational factors to be the cause of their own actions.[107] Recognition that tensions can stem from systemic factors rather than members' lack of commitment to feminism reduces the guilt and blame that confound the already difficult process of conflict management. Moving from individualistic to organizational explanations permits consideration of new solutions other than simply ousting people from the organization.

The assumption in American culture that bigger is better leads to the equation of growth with success. Nonetheless, growth may lead feminist organizations in directions that are antithetical to some of the beliefs and values that originally inspired their creation. Tension exists between organizational survival and growth on the one hand, and some aspects of feminist ideology on the other. Yet survival and perhaps growth may be necessary to achieve feminist goals.

Feminist organizations have played a critical role in bringing both women and women's issues to the public agenda. Moreover, organizational memories are conduits for the wisdom gained from feminism's history. To condemn organizations as nonfeminist because they adopt bureaucratic features is to deny some of the realities of life in a growing organization. To adopt bureaucracy without recognizing its tension with feminist values, however, is to reduce the potential of these organizations to act as vehicles for social change. The transformative power of feminism is mediated in part through feminist organizations. Understanding the choices that face feminist organizations as they grow will better enable us to create strategies to address both organizational needs and feminist values.

13

The Impact of Welfare Reform on Men's Violence against Women

WELFARE "REFORM" (or "recision," as some critics call it) is perhaps the most important social policy change in our lifetimes, reversing more than sixty years of government support for the poor. The federal Personal Responsibility and Work Opportunity Act of 1996 includes strict time limits on receiving public aid and rigid requirements for moving from welfare to work. These changes are likely to have a powerful impact on women who are battered by intimate partners. Advocates of battered women argue that welfare helps women escape violent relationships; consequently, restricting access to public aid may add to the difficulties of leaving abusers.[1] New child support enforcement provisions that pressure men to acknowledge paternity may provoke them to retaliate against the mothers of their children.[2] In addition, many abusive partners do not want women to become independent and will sabotage their employment or participation in job training programs.[3] Accordingly, work participation requirements may inadvertently increase violence.

Acknowledging the possibility of increased violence, Senators Paul Wellstone of Minnesota and Patty Murray of Washington state sponsored the Family Violence Option (FVO) to the federal welfare reform legislation.[4] The FVO offers states the opportunity to provide counseling and other services to women with abusive partners and temporarily to waive work and other requirements for them. Thirty-one states have officially chosen the FVO and nine more are planning to adopt it, while ten others have taken domestic violence into account in their state welfare plans.[5]

Despite widespread support among those in the battered women's movement for the FVO, little systematic research has examined whether changes in welfare status provoke violence. Research on welfare reform is hindered by the absence of a theoretical understanding of the relationship of economic status to violence. Without such a theoretical perspective, we are left with a collection of scattered research findings but no systematic way to comprehend how changes in welfare status affect violence. Traditional theories of violence, in particular exchange theory, have limits as frameworks for examining the impact of welfare reform. Here we illustrate how feminist contributions to theories of intimate violence extend our thinking and provide a useful perspective for research on the impact of welfare reform.

Social science theories of men's violence against women attribute it to a wide range of causes, such as men's pathology (e.g., abnormal personality traits or alcoholism), inner tension, an instrumental power strategy, a reflection of cultural norms and institutional practices, or learned behavior.[6] Economic factors such as welfare receipt may not be the only, or even the most important, contributors to intimate violence,[7] yet the likely broad impact of welfare reform compels consideration of this issue. Here we focus on change in women's financial status, although other noncash aspects of welfare receipt, such as paternity identification, may be important as well.

The Role of Economic Factors in Intimate Violence

Making the link between battering and poverty has been problematic because of ideological conflict between advocates for the poor and for women with abusive partners.[8] Many feminists attribute intimate violence to men's desire to control women that it is supported by deeply held and widely shared norms condoning male dominance.[9] The battered women's movement has aimed to change these norms and to hold men accountable for their violence (in addition to providing protective and supportive services for women). Moreover, in order to focus public attention on the issue of battering, many in the battered women's movement have emphasized that battering is not "merely" a problem of poverty but rather is embedded in all levels of society.[10] In contrast, advocates for the poor are likely to see intimate violence as a product of poverty; they may view attempts to attribute moral guilt and criminal liability to batterers who are poor (and/or of minority status) as a form of blaming the victim.

However, disagreement exists among advocates for battered women. Crenshaw,[11] for example, has criticized the emphasis on the universality of intimate violence as an attempt to move attention away from poor and/or minority women and focus instead on white middle-class victims. Most challenging to the belief in the classless nature of intimate violence, however, is empirical evidence that, although violence crosses socioeconomic lines, it is much more frequent among those with low incomes.[12] Data from several years of the National Crime Victimization Survey consistently indicate that victimization from intimate violence increases as women's family income decreases. Women in families with incomes under $10,000 are victimized at a rate of 19.9 per thousand, roughly four times the rate of women with incomes of $50,000 or more.[13]

Rates of violence against women on welfare are strikingly high.[14] Among a representative sample of welfare recipients in Massachusetts, 65 percent were victims of violence by a current or former boyfriend or husband; one-fifth had been victimized in the past twelve months.[15] Similarly, 55 percent of a sample of welfare recipients in Washington state reported being physically or sexually abused by a spouse or boyfriend.[16] More than 60 percent of homeless and low-income housed mothers in a Massachusetts study, most of whom were receiving welfare, reported assaults by intimate male partners.[17]

Multiple factors may account for the connection between poverty and intimate violence. Just as child abuse, elder abuse, and other forms of family violence are more common among those who are poor, so too is wife abuse. When resources are scarce due to poverty, the stresses that all families face may be compounded. Gelles claims that "the family, with the exception of the military in times of war and the police, is society's most violent social institution."[18] Some structural factors that may account for the frequency of violence within families include the greater amount of time spent interacting with family members compared with others, the intensity of involvement with family members, and the privacy accorded families, which lessens social control. Furthermore, the family is constantly undergoing changes and transitions, which may increase tensions.[19] Although all families may face stress, the lower level of resources among those who are poor may make them more vulnerable to its effects. Moreover, poor women may have few options that would enable them to escape an abusive relationship.

However, evidence indicates that some abuse is deliberately intended to prevent women from becoming economically self-sufficient. About 47 percent of abused women in a welfare-to-work program reported that their intimate partner tried to prevent them from obtaining education or training. Both abused and nonabused women in this sample were discouraged from working by their partners, but women with abusive partners faced active interference.[20] Among women in three urban battered women's shelters, 46 percent of their male partners forbade women from getting a job and 25 percent forbade them from going to school. Of those who worked or went to school anyway, 85 percent missed work because of abuse while 56 percent missed school; 52 percent were fired or quit because of abuse.[21] Eight percent of randomly selected women in a low-income neighborhood in Chicago reported that their boyfriend or husband prevented them from going to school or work in the past twelve months.[22] Psychological symptoms associated with abuse victimization, such as depression, insomnia, nightmares, and flashbacks, also may interfere with employment or education.[23]

Anecdotal evidence from job training providers also supports the claim that disruptive and threatening actions by women's intimate partners are intended to sabotage women's efforts at financial independence, perhaps out of the partner's fear that women will leave the relationship or form other relationships at work.[24] Abusive partners engage in a variety of tactics from turning off alarm clocks, failing to fulfill childcare responsibilities, and destroying textbooks before an exam to administering beatings and highly visible bruises so that women cannot go to job interviews or to work, and harassing women and their co-workers on the job.[25]

The assumption of many who advocate welfare reform is that stringent restrictions on public aid will prompt an increase in women's employment and economic self-sufficiency. Although it is beyond the scope of this chapter to address this assumption,[26] it seems likely that women who leave welfare will experience a change in their economic resources. The impact of this change on levels of violence might depend on whether a woman simply loses welfare, resulting in a decline in her resources, or manages to find employment that pays her the same or more than she previously received in welfare.

Intimate violence is a complex phenomenon, likely due to multiple causes. Yet to understand the impact of welfare reform on violence, we need to view battering through an economic lens. Of the many theories of violence,[27] exchange theory seems most useful for such an analysis because it permits consideration of partners' financial resources. Exchange theory would predict that violence would decrease when women's economic resources increase because, in gaining greater resources, women have also gained power. However, as we will illustrate, the lack of consideration to the dynamics of male dominance limits the usefulness of exchange theory. In contrast to exchange theory's predictions, the desire for male dominance might result in a "backlash" should women gain resources.[28] From this perspective, battering would increase as violence-prone men attempt to compensate for their relative loss of dominance. Here we show how the feminist "backlash hypothesis" extends our thinking on intimate violence and provides a framework for research on the impact of welfare reform on women with abusive partners. In doing so, we demonstrate how policy analysis benefits from the incorporation of feminist thinking.

The Resource Exchange Approach to Understanding Intimate Violence

Exchange theory proposes that behavior is a product of a calculus of costs and benefits.[29] Participants in intimate relationships expect a fair exchange of rights and obligations from one another. The rewards a person receives in a relationship must somehow balance the investments put into it. Rewards may be in the form of financial and material goods, social approval, compliance, and so forth, while investments include such factors as social status and job security. An imbalance of investments and rewards may cause the individual who contributes less in terms of income or status to be at a disadvantage; it may also threaten the overall status position of the family.[30]

According to exchange theory, therefore, the relative amount of resources of each partner determines the degree of power each person holds in the relationship. The "principle of least interest" suggests that the person with the most resources is least dependent on the relationship.[31] Given the principle of least interest, violence should be associated with an imbalance in marital power, that is, husbands with more marital power than their wives can afford to be abusive.

Straus and his colleagues at the University of New Hampshire's Family Violence Research Center have applied exchange theory to family violence, emphasizing the role of inequality and the balance of power in the family.[32] Indeed, in a nationally representative sample of American couples, husband-dominated marriages had the highest rate of abuse, while egalitarian marriages had the lowest.[33] Marital dependency of the wife is also associated with higher levels of violence.[34]

This approach to understanding intimate violence is based on the assumption that men use violence as a means of control because they can get away with it; women have too few resources to affect the balance of power in the relationship. Gelles combined exchange theory with social control theory to suggest that men batter because they are not punished for doing so.[35] As he put it, "People will use violence in the family if the costs of being violent do not outweigh the rewards."[36] Loss of status was one of the costs of violence, according to Gelles, in addition to other costs such as retaliation by the victim, arrest, or imprisonment. Hence women's lack of economic self-sufficiency creates dependence on men, which enables men to batter without fearing the loss of the relationship. If women's resources increased, however, the balance of power within the relationship would change.

Resources other than money may contribute to the balance of power between partners. In a materialistic society such as the United States, however, the amount of money each partner contributes may be an important factor in determining relative power in relationships.[37] If welfare reform results in a woman's loss of economic resources and a consequent reduction in her power within the family, exchange theory suggests that the level of violence against her would increase. However, should a woman gain employment that provides more resources (and therefore more power) than previously, she should be less likely to be beaten, or the violence should be less severe, because she would have more power in the relationship.

Thus we would predict, based on exchange theory, that when economic resources are relatively equal between partners, or the woman has more resources than her partner, violence should be less severe than when the women has fewer resources than her partner. But examining relationships simply on the basis of resources within the couple may overlook important contextual factors. Structural factors, such as discrimination against women in the workplace, may limit women's resources. Nonetheless, in contrast to poor men, especially those who suffer discrimination in employment because of race or ethnicity, poor women's access to welfare or job training may be a means of gaining relative power.

Kalmuss and Straus[38] used data from a nationally representative sample to examine the relationship of violence and wives' economic dependence on their marital partner, as indicated by whether or not she worked, whether there were children age five or younger at home, and whether the husband earned 75 percent or more of the couple's income. Women who were highly economically dependent on their marriage experienced more physical abuse from their husbands than women whose dependency was low. Aguire[39] found that the fewer the wife's resources, the more likely it was that she would return to the abuser. Aguire concludes that, in addition to obtaining shelter, women with abusive partners need programs that will insure their economic independence.

But increasing women's economic resources may not reduce violence against them. Some evidence, such as the higher victimization rates of women who are separated compared to women who are divorced or married, suggests that it is the very process of moving toward independence that may exacerbate or even cause violence against women. Women who are separated have an average annual rate of violent victimization from intimates that is three times greater than women who are divorced and thirty times greater than those who are married.[40] Consequently, an increase in economic resources, if it increases women's independence, may provoke violence from abusive partners. The key factor here is a desire on the part of men to maintain dominance over women, a factor that exchange theory does not take into account.[41]

Feminist Approaches to Understanding Intimate Violence

Feminists see violence as the product of men's desire to dominate and control women.[42] More than twenty years ago, in one of the earliest feminist works on wife abuse, Del Martin[43] described violence as the husband's means of maintaining dominance. Martin emphasized the importance of the economic dependence of women on men and the way in which social institutions, including economic, legal, and religion systems, relegate women to subordinate positions.

Men use violence as an influence tactic, enabling them to have greater decision-making power in a relationship.[44] As Schechter put it, "Violence is only one of the many ways in which men express their socially structured right to control and chastise."[45] According to Dobash and Dobash,[46] men benefit in several ways from violence against women: "to silence them, to 'win' arguments, to express dissatisfaction, to deter future behavior and to merely demonstrate dominance." Russell[47] asserts that male violence against women is a reaction to the erosion of their power relative to that of women, a backlash against a loss of control. However, not all men use force to dominate women, and battering occurs in lesbian relationships as well.[48] Nonetheless, the feminist emphasis on violence against women as coercive control could hold for homosexual as well as heterosexual couples.[49]

The emphasis on control suggests that when women gain economic resources, men will attempt to compensate in order to maintain dominance. Thus increased violence against women may be one form of men's backlash against women's move toward independence.[50] The feminist "backlash hypothesis" rests on cultural norms that advocate male dominance in society. Indeed, wife-beating rarely occurs in cultures that do not support male dominance.[51] The Violence against Women Survey conducted by Statistics Canada found that men who adhere to an ideology of family patriarchy (i.e., who believed in male power and authority over women in marriage) are more likely to abuse their wives, although not all men who believe in patriarchal values are abusers.[52] In a telephone survey of 604 women randomly selected in metropolitan Toronto, women reported that men who adhered to an ideology of patriarchy were the most likely to abuse their wives.[53]

Given feminists' typical opposition to evolutionary theory, it is ironic that feminist theories of male dominance overlap to some extent with evolutionary psychologists' theories of social dominance orientation, that is, a favoring of one's own group to dominate other groups. Pratto[54] and her colleagues postulate that social dominance orientation, higher in males than in females, accounts for the gender differences in a wide variety of policy-related attitudes, such as conservatism, racism, and sexism. Evolutionary psychologists trace gender differences in social dominance orientation to reproductive aspects of behavior (that is, male competition for selection as mates of reproductively attractive females), while feminists typically attribute male dominance to other factors. Yet differences among men in social dominance orientation may help explain why some men are willing to use violence while others are not. For example, wives may come to prefer egalitarian authority structures in relationships if working enables them to become economically independent; those husbands who retain a belief in male dominance may react with violence to a challenge to their power.[55] Violence becomes the "ultimate resource" that backs up feelings of entitlement to dominance if superiority in other resources is absent.[56]

Considerable research on intimate violence has looked separately at the characteristics of men who batter or at the characteristics of victimized women.[57] However, it is important to consider the combination of characteristics of both parties in the relationship in order to understand violence. With respect to economic factors, the discrepancy between a woman's employment/income and that of her partner may be a critical contributor to violence rather than the absolute status of either partner. For example, McCloskey[58] found that income disparities favoring women, rather than overall family resources, predicted men's violence toward their wives. Consequently, considering women or abusive men separately overlooks critical factors because it may be the gap between their resources, rather than the absolute level of her (or his) resources, that is important. Hence, welfare recipients may be differentially affected by reform depending on the resources of their partners.

Most of the social science research on violence, with a few exceptions,[59] is cross-sectional rather than longitudinal. Because the backlash hypothesis assumes change occurs over time, the absence of longitudinal research makes it impossible to assess its usefulness definitively. Nevertheless, we can examine whether existing cross-sectional studies support the proposition that violence is greater when women are closer to economic equality than when the gap between women's and men's resources is large. Given the backlash hypothesis, we might expect that violence becomes a means of coercive control by men when partners' resources are relatively equal. If women have the same (or even more) resources than men, then dominance-prone men may use violence as a means of maintaining control.[60]

In a review examining risk factors for violence, Hotaling and Sugarman[61] found that the likelihood of husband-to-wife violence increases if the wife has more education or higher income than the husband. Three studies that have considered partners' ratio of resources also provide some support for the backlash hypothesis. Dugan, Nagin, and Rosenfeld[62] found that declining rates of intimate partner homicide were partially explained by the changing economic status of women. As women's economic status improves, the rate at which women kill their intimate partners declines (perhaps because increased income enables them to leave the relationship), but not the rate at which women are killed by their partners. Instead, there was some (albeit weak) evidence that women's improved economic status increases rather than decrease women's chances of being victimized.

A second study comes to a similar conclusion. McCloskey found that violence against women increased as income differences lessened: "The less disparity in income, or the more resources the woman has relative to her husband, the more frequent and escalated the violence."[63] In this study, disparities in income and occupational prestige were measured; disparities in other resources, such as education or investment in the relationship, may also be relevant.

Finally, Babcock and her colleagues[64] assessed several dimensions of marital power, including communication skill, income, occupational status, education, and decision-making power, as well as marital violence. Husbands who battered their wives were more likely than nonviolent men to report an interactional pattern in which the husband makes demands and the wife withdraws, a pattern that typically gives the withdrawer the more powerful position. Thus the findings of this study also provide some evidence that abusive men compensate with physical aggression for their lack of power in a relationship.

Both exchange theory and the backlash hypothesis may correctly predict male violence, the former when a woman's resources are low, and the latter when her resources begin to increase. When a woman has few resources and is dependent on a relationship for economic or emotional sustenance, a male partner may feel free to use violence without fear of retaliation or loss of the relationship. Yet, contrary to exchange theory, should that woman gain resources, her male partner may continue to use violence or even escalate that violence to maintain his control. A nationwide survey of violence in families provides support for this claim. In an examination of the relationship between gender inequality and violence in the United States, wife beating was most common in states where institutions support male dominance within the family, that is, in the least egalitarian states (based on the economic, educational, political, and legal status of women in those states). However, it was next highest in the most egalitarian states. One interpretation of these seemingly contradictory findings is that violence in egalitarian states was men's response to women's relative independence.[65] A subsequent analysis of data from those states in which women enjoyed high status found that wife abuse was highest in husband-dominant families.[66]

Using data collected from a cross-sectional national sample of 2,143 American couples in 1976,[67] Smith[68] found that the wife's occupational prestige level affected the relationship between status and husbands' violence. Wives with low-prestige jobs have a relatively high probability of being assaulted regardless of husbands' prestige. Wives with high occupational prestige have a lower risk of abuse overall, but high-status wives' chances of being assaulted increase as their husbands' status decreases.

Methodological and Conceptual Limitations of Current Research

The feminist backlash hypothesis has extended our thinking about violence against women. Yet it is difficult to assess the backlash hypothesis because few studies of violence against women take a longitudinal perspective, considering how relationships change over time.[69] Although studies have documented the significant drop in welfare rolls in many states, little research has followed those who have left welfare in order to monitor the impact of their change in status. And many studies of the impact of welfare reform do not include violence as a variable of interest.

Power in relationships is a difficult construct to measure.[70] Researchers tend to infer power from such variables as occupational prestige and income. Such factors may not always translate into interpersonal power, and other resources not often considered (such as verbal ability) may be relevant. Researchers who study power directly typically have measured the extent of each partners' decision-making power by using some variant of Blood and Wolfe's Decision Power Index[71] which asks who has the "final say" in decisions regarding such domains as what type of car to buy, and whether to have children. Renzetti[72] summarizes the drawbacks of this method: "It treats all decisions as if they are of equal weight, it fails to account for the authority to delegate decision-making responsibilities and it overlooks the everyday division of labor within an intimate relationship." Furthermore, resources that give one power (i.e., power bases) may be distinct from power processes (i.e., techniques to gain power) and power outcomes (i.e., who makes the final decision).[73]

Some critics argue that theories of intimate violence implicate women in the causation of their own abuse. Exchange theory could be interpreted to attribute a causal role to women whose resources are low, while the backlash hypothesis could be seen as placing similar blame on women whose resources increase. In both cases, by focusing on the level of women's resources relative to men's, women seem to be in some way responsible for the abuse.[74] Only recently has the focus shifted from studying victims of male violence to studying perpetrators, from asking why she stays to examining why he batters. Yet the most useful research may be that which considers both parties in the relationship simultaneously.

Research on this topic suffers from other limitations. Few studies consider the possibility of learning or development, that is, that women (and men) may change their behavior as the result of the outcomes of previous behavior. Ferraro and Johnson[75] found that women with abusive partners used several rationalizations to justify being battered, including viewing the spouse as a deeply troubled person whom women can "save"; blaming the abuse on some external force, such as pressures at work; or blaming themselves for the violence. In this study, only after women stopped rationalizing violence did they begin to seek alternatives.

But the greatest difficulty in applying theories to predict the impact of welfare reform on violence is the multifactorial nature of causes of violence.[76]

Although violence against women is a complex phenomenon with multiple precipitating factors on the personal, situational, and societal levels, the contemporary battered women's movement has emphasized a conceptualization of violence as a form of male power and control over women.[77] Economic variables are not in themselves likely to be the only cause or contributor to violence. Other factors, such as cultural norms approving the use of violence, the lack of empathy on the part of batterers, past experience of abuse, or drug or alcohol abuse may also play a part. Moreover, distinctions among types of batterers suggest that income disparities may not have the same effect in all cases.[78]

In addition, when considering women's economic resources, it is necessary to include possible sources of income in addition to welfare. Contrary to popular belief, many women who receive welfare also work.[79] The average amount of welfare a woman receives each month is small. In New York City, for example, a mother with one child receives a maximum monthly cash benefit of $468, which totals only $5,616 a year.[80] In Illinois, such a family would receive only $278 per month.[81] Furthermore, unskilled work typically is unstable; such jobs receive low wages and few job-related benefits such as health care; and these jobs may incur costs in child care, transportation, and clothing. Moving from welfare to work may not always lift welfare recipients out of poverty or even give them more resources than they had received on welfare.

Implications for Social Policy

Welfare policies that do not consider the impact of violence in women's lives are not likely to insure economic independence.[82] The previous analysis cautions that women may be vulnerable to abuse not only when they lose resources, but also when they gain them. Although social and economic equality of women has long been a goal of feminist advocacy, the process of achieving equality may inadvertently put some women at greater risk of violence. The response to this dilemma is not to reduce the press for equality or pay equity, but rather to take into account the unintended consequences of change. The possibility of increases in battering redoubles the need for efforts to reduce violence and to provide more protective resources or services (such as shelters) for women likely to suffer abuse. Moreover, the link between violence and poverty suggests that antipoverty efforts may have an ameliorative effect on violence.[83] Job training and placement may be useful not only for women leaving welfare, but also for unemployed men who batter, reducing some of the pressures of poverty that may contribute to abuse.

As described earlier, the Family Violence Option (FVO) to the federal welfare legislation offers states the opportunity to screen and identify women with abusive partners, to refer those women to counseling and supportive services, and to temporarily waive some welfare requirements for them. These provisions recognize the negative impact of abuse on obtaining and holding a job. Yet implementing the FVO may be difficult.[84] Women may be reluctant to identify themselves as abused; few supportive services may be available for them; and states may be unwilling to waive work requirements if that threatens their ability to meet mandated "work participation" percentages. Vigorous execution of the FVO provisions seems to be one effective strategy for keeping women from further harm (although it risks pathologizing and stigmatizing women with abusive partners).[85] But once women have obtained employment, the backlash hypothesis suggests that the need for protective and supportive services does not end. The "male model" of work is competitive and isolating. Women in transition from welfare to work, especially those who have been abused, may be in need of special supports and tangible aid, such as legal services to help them end a violent relationship.

Welfare reform only went into effect in the United States in the late 1990s, and we are beginning to see women leaving public aid in large numbers. Glowing accounts of the decrease in welfare rolls and stories about heroic women who have successfully navigated their way out of welfare have appeared frequently in media accounts of welfare reform, heralding the success of this policy. But the success of welfare reform should not be measured solely by the decline in caseloads. The central question is the degree of well-being of those who no longer receive public aid. Only by taking into account some of the unintended consequences of welfare reform, such as the possibility of escalated violence against women, will we know the full impact of changes in policies.

Feminists have underscored the importance of understanding the life experiences of people who traditionally have been left out of our research programs—not only women, but also people of color, those from working-class backgrounds, and so forth. The need for diversity in our research samples has been acknowledged by many. Yet feminist concerns with dominance and power relationships have not received equal consideration. Bertrand Russell claimed that "the fundamental concept in social science is Power, in the same sense in which Energy is the fundamental concept in Physics. Like Energy, Power has many forms."[86] To understand women's lives, it is critical to consider factors, such as a belief in the acceptability of male dominance, that permeate the environment in which many women live. By incorporating an awareness of the dynamics of power and control, social policy analyses and recommendations will be better able to examine and ameliorate vexing social problems.

Notes

CHAPTER 1

1. Richardson, L. (1994). "Writing: A method of inquiry." In N. Denzin & Y. Lincoln (Eds.), *Handbook of qualitative research* (pp. 516–529). Thousand Oaks, CA: Sage.

CHAPTER 2

1. Grant, J. (1987). I feel therefore I am: A critique of female experience as the basis for a feminist epistemology. *Feminism and epistemology: Approaches to research in women and politics.* Binghamton, New York: Haworth Press.

2. Sherif, C. W. (1979). Bias in psychology. In J. A. Sherman & E. T. Beck (Eds.), *A Prism of Sex: Essays in the sociology of knowledge* (pp. 93–133). Madison: University of Wisconsin Press.

3. Sewart, J. J. (1979). Critical theory and the critique of conservative method, p. 311. In S. G. McNall (Ed.), *Theoretical perspectives in sociology* (pp. 310–322). New York: St. Martin's.

4. Cook, T. D. (1985). Postpositivist critical multiplism. In L. Shotland & M. M. Mark (Eds.), *Social science and social policy* (pp. 21–62). Beverly Hills, CA: Sage; Prilleltensky, I. (1989). Psychology and the status quo. *American Psychologist, 44,* 795–802; Rabinow, P., & Sullivan, W. M. (1979). The interpretive turn: Emergence of an approach. In Rabinow, P., & Sullivan, W. M. (Eds.), *Interpretive social science: A reader* (pp. 1–21). Berkeley: University of California Press; Sampson, E. E. (1985). The decentralization of identity: Toward a revised concept of personal and social order. *American Psychologist, 40,* 1203–1211; Shields, S. (1975). Functionalism, Darwinism, and the psychology of women: A study in social myth. *American Psychologist, 30,* 739–754.

5. Gergen, K. J. (1973). Social psychology as history. *Journal of Personality and Social Psychology, 26,* 309–320; Manicas, P. T., & Secord, P. F. (1983). Implications for psychology of the new philosophy of science. *American Psychologist, 38,* 399–413; Sampson, E. E. (1978). Scientific paradigms and social values: Wanted—A scientific revolution. *Journal of Personality and Social Psychology, 36,* 1332–1343.

6. Foucault, M. (1980). In C. Gordon (Ed.), *Power/Knowledge: Selected interviews and other writings.* New York: Pantheon; Foucault, M. (1981). *The history of sexuality, Vol. 1. An introduction.* Harmondsworth, England: Viking.

7. Degler, C. (1991). *In search of human nature.* New York: Oxford University Press; Shields, S., Functionalism, Darwinism, and the psychology of women: A

study in social myth; Wittig, M. A. (1985). Metatheoretical dilemmas in the psychology of gender. *American Psychologist, 40*, 800–811.

8. Keller, E. F. (1985). *Reflections on gender and science*. New Haven, CT: Yale University Press; Merchant, C. (1980). *The death of nature: Women, ecology, and the scientific revolution*. New York: Harper & Row.

9. Farrington, B. (1951). Temporis partus masculus: An untranslated writing of Francis Bacon (p. 197). *Centaurus*, 1; quoted in E. F. Keller, *Reflections on gender and science*, p. 36.

10. Harding, S. (1986). *The science question in feminism*. Ithaca, NY: Cornell University Press, p. 125.

11. Hubbard, R. (1988). Some thoughts about the masculinity of the natural sciences. In M. M. Gergen, *Feminist thought and the structure of knowledge* (pp. 1–15). New York: New York University Press; Reinharz, S. (1985). Feminist distrust: Problems of context and context in sociological work. In D. N. Berg & K. K. Smith (Eds.), *The self in social inquiry: Researching methods* (pp. 153–172). Beverly Hills, CA: Sage.

12. Gergen, M. (1988). Building a feminist methodology. *Contemporary Social Psychology, 13*, 47–53.

13. Epstein, C. F. (1988). *Deceptive distinctions: Sex, gender, and the social order*. New Haven, CT: Yale University Press.

14. Weisstein, N. (1971). *Psychology constructs the female or, the fantasy life of the male psychologist*. Boston: New England Free Press.

15. Epstein, C. F., *Deceptive distinctions: Sex, gender, and the social order*, pp. 17–45; Frieze, I. H., Parsons, J. E., Johnson, P. B., Ruble, D. N., & Zellman, G. L. (1978). *Women and sex roles: A social psychological perspective*, New York: W. W. Norton, pp.11–27; Hyde, J. (1985). *Half the human experience: The psychology of women* (3rd ed., pp. 7–15). Lexington, MA: D. C. Heath; Lips, H. (1988). *Sex and gender: An introduction* (pp. 64–75). Mountain View, CA: Mayfield; Millman, M. & Kanter, R. (eds.) (1975). *Another voice: Feminist perspectives on social life and social sciences*. Garden City, NY: Anchor Books; Wilkinson, S. (1986). Sighting possibilities: Diversity and commonality in feminist research. *Feminist social psychology: Developing theory and practice* (pp. 7–24). Milton Keynes, England: Open University Press.

16. Epstein, C. F., *Deceptive distinctions: Sex, gender, and the social order;* Farberow, N. L. (1963). *Taboo topics*. New York: Atherton; McHugh, M., Koeske, R., & Frieze, I. (1986). Issues to consider in conducting nonsexist psychological research: A guide for researchers. *American Psychologist, 41*, 879–890; Smith, D. (1987). *The everyday world as problematic*. Boston: Northeastern University Press.

17. Rix, S. E. (Ed.). *The American Woman 1990–1991*. New York: W. W. Norton.

18. Wicherski, M., Guerrero, R., & Kohout, J. (1999). 1998–1999 Faculty salaries in graduate departments of psychology. Washington, DC: American Psychological Association; 1997–98 Faculty Salaries Survey. Washington, DC: American Psychological Association Research Office.

19. Wisnieski, L. A., Personal communication with author, 4 February 2000. Women's Programs Office, American Psychological Association, Washington, DC.

20. Gilligan, C. (1982). *In a different voice: Psychological theory and women's development*. Cambridge: Harvard University Press.

21. Freud, S. (1961). Some psychical consequences of the anatomical distinctions between the sexes. In J. Strachey (Ed. and Trans.), *The standard edition of the complete psychological works of Sigmund Freud*, (Vol. 19, pp. 248–258). London: Hogarth Press. (Original work published 1925.)

22. Jacklin, C. N. (1981). Methodological issues in the study of sex-related differences. *Developmental Review*, *1*, 266–273.

23. Meyer, J. (1988). Feminist thought and social psychology. In M. Gergen (Ed.), *Feminist thought and the structure of knowledge* (pp. 105–123). New York: New York University Press.

24. Lips, H., *Sex and gender: An introduction*.

25. Unger, R. K. (1981). Sex as a social reality: Field and laboratory research. *Psychology of Women Quarterly*, *5*, 645–653.

26. Unger, R. K. (1979). Toward a redefinition of sex and gender. *American Psychologist*, 1979, *34*, 1085–1094; McHugh, M., Koeske, R., & Frieze, I., Issues to consider in conducting nonsexist psychological research: A guide for researchers.

27. Unger, R. K., Toward a redefinition of sex and gender.

28. Epstein, C. F., *Deceptive distinctions: Sex, gender, and the social order*.

29. Unger, R. K., Toward a redefinition of sex and gender.

30. Fine, M. & Gordon, S. M. (1989). Feminist transformations of/despite psychology. In M. Crawford & M. Gentry (Eds.), *Gender and thought: Psychological perspectives* (pp. 146–174). New York: Springer-Verlag.

31. Hyde, J. (1990). Meta-analysis and the psychology of gender differences. *Signs: Journal of Women in Culture and Society*, *16*, 55–73.

32. Feingold, A. (1988). Cognitive gender differences are disappearing. *American Psychologist*, *43*, 95–103.

33. Eagly, A. H. (1978) Sex differences in influenceability. *Psychological Bulletin*, 1978, *85*, 86–116.

34. Jacklin, C. N., Methodological issues in the study of sex-related differences, p. 271.

35. Gergen, K. J., Social psychology as history.

36. Connell, R. W. (1987). *Gender and power: Society, the person, and sexual politics*. Stanford, CA: Stanford University Press.

37. Fine, M., & Gordon, S. M., Feminist transformations of/despite psychology; Parlee, M. (1979). Psychology and women. *Signs: Journal of Women in Culture and Society*, *5*, 121–133; Sherif, C. W., Bias in psychology.

38. Fine, M. (1984). Coping with rape: Critical perspectives on consciousness. *Imagination, Cognition, and Personality: The Scientific Study of Consciousness, 3*, 249–267.

39. Kitzinger, C. (1987). *The social construction of lesbianism*. London: Sage.

40. Lips, H., *Sex and gender: An introduction*.

41. Connell, R. W., *Gender and power: Society, the person, and sexual politics*.

42. Rossi, A. (1979). Reply by Alice Rossi. *Signs: Journal of Women in Culture and Society*, *4*, 712–717.

43. Eagly, A. H. (1987). *Sex differences in social behavior: A social-role interpretation*. Hillsdale, NJ: Lawrence Erlbaum.

44. Epstein, C. F., *Deceptive distinctions: Sex, gender, and the social order*, p. 44.

45. Kahn, A. S., & Yoder, J. D. (1989). The psychology of women and conservatism: Rediscovering social change. *Psychology of Women Quarterly*, *13*, 417–432; Prilleltensky, I., Psychology and the status quo.

46. Kitzinger, C., *The social construction of lesbianism;* Sampson, E. E. (1985). The decentralization of identity: Toward a revised concept of personal and social order.

47. Kahn, A. S. & Yoder, J. D., The psychology of women and conservatism: Rediscovering social change.

48. Reinharz, S., Feminist distrust: Problems of context and context in sociological work.

49. McHugh, M., Koeske, R., & Frieze, I., Issues to consider in conducting nonsexist psychological research: A guide for researchers.

50. Harding, S., *The science question in feminism*.

51. Epstein, C. F., *Deceptive distinctions: Sex, gender, and the social order*; McHugh, M., Koeske, R., & Frieze, I., Issues to consider in conducting nonsexist psychological research: A guide for researchers.

52. Belenky, M. F., Clinchy, B. M., Goldberger, N. R., & Tarule, J. M. (1986). *Women's ways of knowing: The development of self, voice, and mind*. New York: Basic Books; Gilligan, C. (1991), *In a different voice: Psychological theory and women's development*. Smith, D., *The everyday world as problematic*.

53. Hare-Mustin, R. T. (1991). Sex, lies, and headaches: The problem is power. In T. J. Goodrich (Ed.), *Women and power: Perspectives for family therapy*. New York: W. W. Norton.

54. Harding, S, *The science question in feminism*.

55. Morgan, G. (1983). Toward a more reflective social science. In G. Morgan (Ed.). *Beyond method: Strategies for social research* (pp. 368–376). Beverly Hills: Sage.

56. Rosenthal, R. (1966). *Experimenter effects in behavioral research*. New York: Appleton-Century-Crofts.

57. Harding, S., *The science question in feminism*.

58. McHugh, M., Koeske, R., & Frieze, I., Issues to consider in conducting nonsexist psychological research: A guide for researchers.

59. Deaux, K. (1984). From individual differences to social categories. *American Psychologist*, *39*, 105–116.

60. Maccoby, E. E. (1990). Gender and relationships: A developmental account. *American Psychologist*, *43*, 513–520.

61. Morawski, J. G. (1990). Toward the unimagined: Feminism and epistemol-

ogy in psychology. In R. L. Hare-Muston & J. Maracek (Eds.), *Making a difference: Psychology and the construction of gender* (pp. 150–183). New Haven, CT: Yale University Press.

62. Hare-Mustin, R. T., & Maracek, J. (1990). *Making a difference: Psychology and the construction of gender*. New Haven, CT: Yale University Press.

63. Harding, S. (1991). *Whose science? Whose knowledge?* Ithaca, NY: Cornell University Press; Harding, Sandra., *The science question in feminism*.

64. Maracek, J. (1989). Introduction. (Special issue on theory and method in feminist psychology). *Psychology of Women Quarterly, 13*, 367–377; p. 372.

65. Harding, S., *The science question in feminism*.

66. Carlson, R. (1972). Understanding women: Implications for personality theory and research. *Journal of Social Issues, 28*, 17–32; Peplau, L. A., & Conrad, E. (1989). Feminist methods in psychology. *Psychology of Women Quarterly, 13*, 379–400.

67. Keller, E. F., *Reflections on gender and science*.

68. Chodorow, N. (1978). *The reproduction of mothering*. Berkeley: University of California Press.

69. Stack, C. (1986). The culture of gender: Women and men of color. *Signs: Journal of Women in Culture and Society, 11*, 321–324.

70. Markus, H., & Oyserman, D. (1989). Gender and thought: The role of the self-concept. In M. Crawford & M. Gentry (Eds.), *Gender and thought: Psychological perspectives* (pp. 100–127).

71. Harding, S., *The science question in feminism*.

72. Sherif, C. W., Bias in psychology.

73. Epstein, C. F., *Deceptive distinctions: Sex, gender, and the social order*.

74. Acker, J., "Issues in the sociological study of women's work." In A. Stromberg & S. Harkness (Eds.), *Women Working* (pp. 134–161). Palo Alto, CA: Mayfield, 1978.

75. Smith, D., *The everyday world as problematic*.

76. Miller, J. B. (1986). *Toward a new psychology of women (2nd ed.)*. Boston: Beacon.

77. Code, L. B. (1981). Is the sex of the knower epistemologically significant? *Metaphilosophy, 12*, 267–276.

78. Cherryholmes, C. H. (1988). Construct validity and the discourses of research. *American Journal of Education, 96*, 421–457.

79. Reinharz, S. (1992). *Social research methods, feminist perspectives*. New York: Oxford University Press.

80. Morawski, J. G. (1988). Impasse in feminist thought? In M. M. Gergen (Ed.), *Feminist thought and the structure of knowledge* (pp. 182–194). New York: New York University Press.

81. Gilligan, C., *In a different voice: Psychological theory and women's development*.

82. Greeno, C. G., & Maccoby, E. E. (1986). How different is the "different voice"? *Signs: Journal of Women in Culture and Society, 11*, 1986, 310–316; Mednick

M. T. (1989). On the politics of psychological constructs: Stop the bandwagon, I want to get off. *American Psychologist*, *44*, 1118–1123.

83. Gilligan, C. (1986). Reply by Carol Gilligan. *Signs: Journal of Women in Culture and Society*, *11*, 328.

84. Crawford, M. (1989). Agreeing to differ: Feminist epistemologies and women's ways of knowing. In M. Crawford & M. Gentry (Eds.), *Gender and thought: Psychological perspectives*, pp. 128–145; Epstein, C. F., *Deceptive distinctions: Sex, gender, and the social order*, pp. 81–83.

85. Becker, H. S. (1967). Whose side are we on? *Social Problems*, *14*, 239–247; p. 241.

86. Riger, S. (1990). Ways of knowing and organizational approaches to community research. In P. Tolan, C. Keys, F. Chertok & Jason, L., *Researching community psychology* (pp. 42–50). Washington, DC: American Psychological Association.

87. Foucault, M., *Power/Knowledge: Selected interviews and other writings*, p. 81.

88. Merton, R. (1972). Insiders and outsiders: A chapter in the sociology of knowledge. *American Journal of Sociology*, *78*, 9–47.

89. hooks, b. (1984). *Feminist theory: From margin to center*. Boston: South End Press.

90. Gorelick, S. (1991). Contradictions of feminist methodology. *Gender & Society*, 5, 459–477; Spelman, E. V. (1988). *Inessential woman: Problems of exclusion in feminist thought*. Boston: Beacon Press.

91. Merton, R., Insiders and outsiders: A chapter in the sociology of knowledge.

92. Lorde, A. (1984). *Sister outsider: Essays and speeches* (p. 114). New York: The Crossing Press.

93. Harding, S. (1987). Introduction: Is there a feminist method? *Feminism and methodology: Social science issues*. Bloomington: Indiana University Press.

94. Haraway, D. (1988). Situated knowledges: *The science question in feminism* and the privilege of partial perspective. *Feminist Studies*, *14*, 575–599.

95. Hare-Mustin, R. T. & Maracek, J., *Making a difference: Psychology and the construction of gender*; Wilkinson, S., Sighting possibilities: Diversity and commonality in feminist research.

96. Howard, G. S. (1991). Culture tales: Narrative approach to thinking, cross-cultural psychology, and psychotherapy. *American Psychologist*, *46*, 187–197.

97. Cherryholmes, C. H., Construct validity and the discourses of research, p. 436.

98. Carroll, L. (1923). *Alice's adventures in wonderland and through the looking glass*. Philadelphia: Winston. (Original work published 1872.)

99. Weedon, C. (1987) *Feminist practice and poststructuralist theory*. New York: Basil Blackwell.

100. Gavey, N. (1989). Feminist poststructuralism and discourse analysis: Contributions to a feminist psychology. *Psychology of Women Quarterly*, *13*, 459–476.

101. MacKinnon, C. A. (1987). Feminism, Marxism, method, and the state:

Toward feminist jurisprudence. In S. Harding (Ed.), *Feminism and methodology: Social science issues* (p. 136). Bloomington: Indiana University Press.

102. MacKinnon, C. A., Feminism, Marxism, method, and the state: Toward feminist jurisprudence, p. 140.

103. Gergen, K. J. (1985). The social constructionist movement in modern psychology. *American Psychologist, 40,* 255–265.

104. Hare-Mustin, R. T., & Maracek, J., *Making a difference: Psychology and the construction of gender.*

105. Luria, Z. (1986). A methodological critique. *Signs: Journal of Women in Culture and Society,* 1986, *11,* 316–320.

106. Unger, R. K., Toward a redefinition of sex and gender.

107. Scott, J. W. (1988). Deconstructing equality-versus-difference: Or, the uses of poststructuralist theory for feminism. *Feminist Studies, 14,* 33–50.

108. Hare-Mustin, R. T., & Maracek, J., *Making a difference: Psychology and the construction of gender,* pp. 1–2.

109. Gavey, N., Feminist poststructuralism and discourse analysis: Contributions to a feminist psychology, p. 462.

110. Hare-Mustin, R. T., & Maracek, J. (1988). The meaning of difference: Gender theory, postmodernism, and psychology. *American Psychologist, 43,* 355–464.

111. Riger, S. (1991). Gender dilemmas in sexual harassment policies and procedures. *American Psychologist, 46,* 497–505.

112. Gergen, K. J., The social constructionist movement in modern psychology.

113. Kitzinger, C. (1986). Introducing and developing Q as a feminist methodology: A study of accounts of lesbianism. In S. Wilkinson (Ed.), *Feminist social psychology: Developing theory and practice* (pp. 151–172). Milton Keynes, England: Open University Press; Kitzinger, C (1987). *The social construction of lesbianism.*

114. Unger, R. K., Draper, R. D., & Pendergrass, M. L. (1986) Personal epistemology and personal experience. *Journal of Social Issues, 42,* 67–79.

115. Cherryholmes, C. H., Construct validity and the discourses of research; Gavey, N., Feminist poststructuralism and discourse analysis: Contributions to a feminist psychology.

116. Gavey, N., Feminist poststructuralism and discourse analysis: Contributions to a feminist psychology.

117. Hare-Mustin, R. T. (in press). Sex, lies, and headaches: The problem is power; Walkerdine, V. (1986). Post-structuralist theory and everyday social practices: The family and the school. In Wilkinson, S. (Ed.), *Feminist social psychology: Developing theory and practice.*

118. Martin, J. (1990). Deconstructing organizational taboos: The suppression of gender conflict in organizations. *Organizational Science, 5,* 339–359.

119. Martin, J., Deconstructing organizational taboos: The suppression of gender conflict in organizations.

120. Gergen, K. J., The social constructionist movement in modern psychology, p. 272.

121. Grant, J., I feel therefore I am: A critique of female experience as the basis for a feminist epistemology, p. 113.

122. Gergen, K. J., The social constructionist movement in modern psychology; Unger, R. K. (1983). Through the looking glass: No Wonderland yet! (The reciprocal relationship between methdlogy and models of reality.) *Psychology of Women Quarterly*, 8, 9–32.

123. Gavey, N., Feminist poststructuralism and discourse analysis: Contributions to a feminist psychology.

124. Snitow, A. (1990). A gender diary. In M. Hirsch & E. F. Keller (Eds.), *Conflicts in feminism* (pp. 9–43). New York: Routledge.

125. Weedon, C., *Feminist practice and poststructuralist theory*.

126. Hartsock, N. (1987). Epistemology and politics: Minority vs. majority theories. *Cultural Critique*, 7, 187–206.

127. Segal, L. (1986). *Is the future female? Troubled thoughts on contemporary feminism*. London: Virago.

128. Unger, R. K. (1988). Psychological, feminist, and personal epistemology: Transcending contradiction. In M. M. Gergen (Ed.), *Feminist thought and the structure of knowledge* (p. 137). New York: New York University Press.

129. Reinharz, S., *Social research methods, feminist perspectives*; Rosenberg, R. (1982). *Beyond separate spheres*. New Haven, CT: Yale University Press.

130. A. L. Peplau & E. Conrad, Feminist methods in psychology.

131. Acker, J., Barry, K., & Esseveld, J. (1983). Objectivity and truth: Problems in doing feminist research. *Women's Studies International Forum*, 6, 423–435; Wittig, M. A., Metatheoretical dilemmas in the psychology of gender.

132. Wilkinson, S., Sighting possibilities: Diversity and commonality in feminist research.

133. Gergen, M., Building a feminist methodology, p. 47.

134. Acker, J., Barry, K., & Esseveld, J., "Objectivity and truth: Problems in doing feminist research."

135. Lather, P. (1988). Feminist perspectives on empowering research methodologies. *Women's Studies International Forum*, 11, 569–581.

136. Stacey, J. (1988). Can there be a feminist ethnography? *Women's Studies International Forum*, 11, 21–27.

137. Wilkinson, S., Sighting possibilities: Diversity and commonality in feminist research.

138. Gavey, N., Feminist poststructuralism and discourse analysis: Contributions to a feminist psychology; Weedon, C., *Feminist practice and poststructuralist theory*.

139. Andersen, M. (1981), "Corporate wives: Longing for liberation or satisfied with the status quo?" *Urban Life*, 10, 311–327.

140. Lather, P. (1986). Research as praxis. *Harvard Educational Review*, 56, 257–277.

141. Kidder, L. (1982). Face validity from multiple perspectives. In D. Brinberg & L. Kidder (Eds.), *Forms of validity in research* (pp. 41–58). San Francisco: Jossey-Bass.

142. Reinharz, S., *Social research methods, feminist perspectives*.

143. Jaggar, A., & Struhl, P. R. (1978). *Feminist frameworks: Alternative theoretical accounts of the relations between women and men*. New York: McGraw-Hill, 1978.

144. Star, S. L. (1979, January). Strategic heresy as scientific method: feminism and the psychology of consciousness. Paper presented to the American Association for the Advancement of Science. Quoted in Reinharz, S., *Social research methods, feminist perspectives*, p. 769.

145. Lorber, J. (1988). From the Editor. *Gender & Society, 1*, 5–8; p. 8.

146. Buss, A. R. (1976). Galton and sex differences: An historical note. *Journal of the History of the Behavioral Sciences, 12*, 283–285.

147. Feingold, A., Cognitive gender differences are disappearing; Hyde, J., Meta-analysis and the psychology of gender differences.

148. Maccoby, E. E., Gender and relationships: A developmental account.

149. Deaux, K., & Major, B. (1987). Putting gender into context: An interactive model of gender-related behavior. *Psychological Review, 94*, 369–389.

150. West, C., & Zimmerman, D. H. (1987). Doing gender. *Gender & Society, 1*, 125–151.

151. Connell, R. W. (1985). Theorizing gender. *Sociology, 19*, 260–272; Connell, R. W., *Gender and power: Society, the person and sexual politics*; Crawford, M. & Maracek, J. (1989). Psychology reconstructs the female 1968–1988. *Psychology of Women Quarterly, 13*, 147–165.

152. West, C., & Zimmerman, D. H., Doing gender, p. 146.

153. Morris, J. (1974). *Conundrum*. New York: Harcourt, Brace, Jovanovich.

154. Manicas, P. T., & Secord, P. F., Impliciations for psychology of the new philosophy of science, p. 408.

155. Unger, R. K. (1989). Sex, gender, and epistemology. In M. Crawford & M. Gentry (Eds.), *Gender and thought: Psychological perspectives*, pp. 17–35.

156. Buss, A. R. (1978). The structure of psychological revolutions. *Journal of the History of the Behavioral Sciences, 14*, 57–64; Reigel, K. F. (1979). *Foundations of dialectical psychology*. New York: Academic Press; Sampson, E. E. (1978). Scientific paradigms and social values: Wanted—A scientific revolution; Unger, R. K., Through the looking glass: No Wonderland yet!

157. Reinharz, S., *Social research methods, feminist perspectives*.

158. Unger, R. K., Through the looking glass: No Wonderland yet!

159. Harding, S., *Whose science? Whose knowledge?*

CHAPTER 3

1. Rosenberg, R. L. (1982). *Beyond separate spheres: Intellectual origins of modern feminism*. New Haven, CT: Yale University Press.

2. Morawski, J. (1985). The measurement of masculinity and femininity: Engendering categorical realities. *Journal of Personality, 53*, 196–223.

3. Constantinople, A. (1973). Masculinity-femininity. An exception to a famous dictum. *Psychological Bulletin, 80*, 389–407.

4. Bem, S. (1974). The measurement of psychological androgyny. *Journal of Consulting and Clinical Psychology*, 42, 155–162.

5. Unger, R. K., & Crawford, M. (1992). *Women and gender: A feminist psychology*. New York: McGraw-Hill.

6. Conway, J., Borque, S. C., & Scott, J. W. (1987). Introduction: The concept of gender. *Daedalus, 116*, xxi–xxix; MacKinnon, C. A. (1990) Legal perspectives on sexual difference. In D. L. Rhode (Ed.), *Theoretical perspectives on sexual difference* (pp. 213–215). New Haven, CT: Yale University Press; Unger, R. K. (1979) Toward a redefinition of sex and gender. *American Psychologist, 34*, 1085–1094; Yanagisako, S., & Collier, J. F. (1990). The mode of reproduction in anthropology. In D. L. Rhode (Ed.), *Theoretical perspectives on sexual difference*, pp. 131–141.

7. Money, J., Hampson, J., & Hampson, J. (1955). An examination of some basic sexual concepts: The evidence of human hermaphroditism. *Bulletin of the Johns Hopkins Hospital*, 97, 301–319.

8. Deaux, K. (1985). Sex and gender. *Annual Review of Psychology, 36*, 49–81; Deaux, K. (1993). Commentary: Sorry, wrong number—A reply to gentile's call. *Psychological Science*, 4, 125–126; Unger, R. K., & Crawford, M., *Women and gender: A feminist psychology*.

9. Unger, R. K., Toward a redefinition of sex and gender.

10. Deaux, K. (1985). Sex and gender. *Annual Review of Psychology, 36*; Deaux, K., & Major, B. (1987). Putting gender into context: An interactive model of gender-related behavior. *Psychological Review*, 94, 369–389; Unger, R. K. & Crawford, M., *Women and gender: A feminist psychology*.

11. Yanagisako, S., & Collier, J. F., The mode of reproduction in anthropology.

12. Offen, K. (1990). Feminism and sexual difference in historical perspective. In D. L. Rhode (Ed.), *Theoretical perspectives on sexual difference*, pp. 13–20.

13. Unger, R. K., Toward a redefinition of sex and gender.

14. Fausto-Sterling, A. (1993). The five sexes: Why male and female are not enough. *The Sciences*, March/April, 21–25.

15. Fausto-Sterling, A., The five sexes: Why male and female are not enough.

16. Herdt, G. (1990). Mistaken gender: 5-alpha reductase hermaphroditism and biological reductionism in sexual identity reconsidered. *American Anthropologist*, 92, 433–446; Hinde, R. A. (1991). A biologist looks at anthropology. *Man*, 26, 538–608.

17. Foucault, M. (1980). Introduction. In Richard Dougall (trans.), *Herculine Barbin: Being the recently discovered memoirs of a nineteenth-century French hermaphrodite* (p. viii). New York: Pantheon Books.

18. Kessler, S. (1990). The medical construction of gender: Case management of intersexed infants. *Signs: Journal of Women in Culture and Society*, 16, 3–26.

19. Foucault, M. (1980). Introduction. In *Herculine Barbin: Being the recently discovered memoirs of a nineteenth-century French hermaphrodite*, p. xi.

20. Dewhurst, J., & Gordon, R. R. (1969). *The intersexual disorders*. London: Bailliere, Tindall & Cassell.

21. Kessler, S., The medical construction of gender: Case management of intersexed infants.

22. Fausto-Sterling, A., The five sexes: Why male and female are not enough.

23. Hoyenga, K. B., & Hoyenga, K. T. (1993). *Gender-related differences: Origins and outcomes*. Boston: Allyn & Bacon.

24. Fausto-Sterling, A., The five sexes: Why male and female are not enough.

25. Barnes, W. S. (1984). Sibling influences within family and school contexts. Unpublished doctoral dissertation, Harvard Graduate School of Education, Cambridge, MA, cited in Belle, D. (1985). Ironies in the contemporary study of gender. *Journal of Personality, 53*, 400–405.

26. Roscoe, W. (1991). *The Zuni man-woman*. Albuquerque: University of New Mexico Press; Williams, W. L. (1987). Women, men, and others. *American Behavioral Scientist, 31*, 135–141.

27. Unger, R. K., & Crawford, M., *Women and gender: A feminist psychology*.

28. Herdt, G. (1990). Mistaken gender: 5-alpha reductase hermaphroditism and biological reductionism in sexual identity reconsidered; Williams, W. L. (1987). Women, men, and others.

29. Thorne, B. (1990). Children and gender: Constructions of difference. In D. L. Rhode (Ed.), *Theoretical perspectives on sexual difference*, pp. 100–113.

30. Harding, S. (1987). The instability of the analytical categories of feminist theory. In S. Harding & J. F. O'Barr (Eds.), *Sex and scientific inquiry* (pp. 283–302). Chicago: University of Chicago Press.

31. Lott, B. (1990). Dual natures or learned behavior: The challenge to feminist psychology. In R. T. Hare-Mustin & J. Maracek (Eds.), *Making a difference: Psychology and the construction of gender* (pp. 65–101). New Haven, CT: Yale University Press.

32. Gilligan, C. (1982). *In a different voice: Psychological theory and women's development*. Cambridge, MA: Harvard University Press.

33. Hare-Mustin, R., & Maracek, J. (1988). The meaning of difference: Gender theory, postmodernism, and psychology. *American Psychologist, 43*, 455–464.

34. Harding, S., The instability of the analytical categories of feminist theory, p. 300.

35. Yanagisako, S., & Collier, J. F., The mode of reproduction in anthropology.

36. Gould, S. J. (1981). *The mismeasure of man*. New York: W. W. Norton; Keller, E. F. (1985). *Reflections on gender and science*. New Haven, CT: Yale University Press; Tavris, C. (1992). *The mismeasure of woman*. New York: Simon and Schuster.

37. Hubbard, R. (1979). Have only men evolved? In S. Harding and M. A. Hintikka (Eds.), *Discovering reality* (p. 45). Dordrecht, Holland: Rediel.

38. Shields, S. (1975). Functionalism, Darwinism, and the psychology of women: A study in social myth. *American Psychologist, 30*, 739–754.

39. Martin, E. (1991). The egg and the sperm: How science has constructed a romance based on stereotypical male-female roles. *Signs: Journal of Women in Culture and Society, 16*, 485–501.

40. Rossi, A. (1977). A biosocial perspective on parenting. *Daedalus, 106*, 120.

41. Martin, E., The egg and the sperm: How science has constructed a romance based on stereotypical male-female roles, p. 489.

42. Martin, E., The egg and the sperm: How science has constructed a romance based on stereotypical male-female roles.

43. Keller, E. F. (1987). On the need to count past two in our thinking about gender and science. *New Ideas in Psychology, 5*, 275–287.

44. Fausto-Sterling, A. (1987). Society writes biology/biology constructs gender. *Daedalus, 116*, 74–75.

45. Hubbard, R. (1990). *The politics of women's biology*. New Brunswick, NJ: Rutgers University Press.

46. Harding, S. (1991). *Whose science? Whose knowledge? Thinking from women's lives* (p. 45). Ithaca, NY: Cornell University Press.

47. Money, J. (1987). Sin, sickness, or status? Homosexual gender identity and sychoneuroendocrinology. *American Psychologist, 42*, 384–399.

48. Dawkins, R. (1976). *The selfish gene* (p. ix). Oxford: Oxford University Press; Archer, J. (1991). Human sociobiology: Basic concepts and limitations. *Journal of Social Issues, 47*, 11–26; Oyama, S. (1991). Bodies and minds: Dualism in evolutionary theory. *Journal of Social Issues, 47*, 27–42.

49. Shields, W. M., & Shields, L. M. (1983). Forcible rape: An evolutionary perspective. *Ethology and Sociobiology, 4*, 115–136.

50. Baron, L. (1985). Does rape contribute to reproductive success? Evaluation of sociobiological views of rape. *International Journal of Women's Studies, 8*, 266–277; for a general discussion of sexism in sociobiology, see Travis, C. B. & Yeager, C. P (1991). Sexual selection, parental investment, and sexism. *Journal of Social Issues, 47*, 117–129.

51. Fausto-Sterling, A. (1985). *Myths of gender: Biological theories about women and men*. New York: Basic Books.

52. LeVine, R. A. (1991). Gender differences: Interpreting anthropological data. In M. T. Notman & C. C. Nadelson (Eds.), *Women and men: new perspectives on gender differences* (pp.1–8). Washington, DC: American Psychiatric Press.

53. Sidanius, J., Cling, B. J., & Pratto, F. (1991). Ranking and linking as a function of sex and gender role attitudes. *Journal of Social Issues, 47*, 131–149.

54. Feingold, A. (1988). Cognitive gender differences are disappearing. *American Psychologist, 43*, 95–103.

55. Hyde, J. S. (1990). Gender differences in mathematics performance: a meta-analysis. *Psychological Bulletin, 107*, 139–155.

56. Feingold, A. (1994). Gender differences in variability in intellectual abilities: a cross-cultural perspective. *Sex Roles.* 30, 91–92.

57. Maccoby, E. E., & Jacklin, C. N. (1974). *The psychology of sex differences*. Stanford, CA: Stanford University Press.

58. Feingold, A., Cognitive gender differences are disappearing; Hyde, J. S. & Linn, M. C. (Eds.) (1986). *The psychology of gender: Advances through meta-analysis*. Baltimore, MD: Johns Hopkins University Press.

59. Gilligan, C., *In a different voice: Psychological theory and women's development*.

60. Rossi, A. (1977). A biosocial perspective on parenting.

61. Gross, H. E. (1979). Considering "A biosocial perspective on parenting." *Signs: Journal of women in culture and society*, 4, 695–697.

62. Weedon, C. (1987). *Feminist practice and poststructuralist theory*. New York: Basil Blackwell.

63. Segal, L. (1988). *Is the future female? Troubled thoughts on contemporary feminism*. New York: P. Bedrick.

64. Fausto-Sterling, A., *Myths of gender: Biological theories about women and men*, p. 221.

65. Moir, A., & Jessel, D. (1991). *Brain sex: The real difference between men and women* (p. 36). Secaucus, NJ: Carol Publishing Group.

66. Geertz, C. (1973). *The interpretation of cultures* (p. 37). New York: Basic Books.

67. Geertz, C., *The interpretation of cultures*.

68. Keller, E. F., On the need to count past two in our thinking about gender and science, p. 279.

69. Hinde, R. A., A biologist looks at anthropology.

70. Samaroff, A. J., & Chandler, M. J. (1975). Reproductive risk and the continuum of caretaking causality. In F. D. Horowitz (Ed.), *Review of child development research* (vol. 4, pp. 187–244). Chicago: The University of Chicago Press.

71. Ehrhardt, A. A. (1985). The psychobiology of gender. In A. S. Rossi (Ed.), *Gender and the life course* (pp. 81–96). New York: Aldine.

72. Plomin, R. (1989). Environment and genes: Determinants of behavior. *American Psychologist*, 44, 105–111.

73. Plomin, R., Environment and genes: Determinants of behavior.

74. Hoyenga, K. B., & Hoyenga, K. T., *Gender-related differences: Origins and outcomes*, p. 20.

75. Yanagisako, S. & Collier, J. F., The mode of reproduction in anthropology.

76. Hinde, R. A., A biologist looks at anthropology.

77. Buss, A. R. (1978). The structure of psychological revolutions. *Journal of the History of the Behavioral Sciences*, 14, 57–64.

78. Hinde, R. A. (1991). A biologist looks at anthropology.

79. McClintock, M. (1971). Menstrual synchrony and suppression. *Nature*, 229, 244–245.

80. Goldman, S. D., & Schneider, H. G. (1987) Menstrual synchrony: social and personality factors. *Journal of Social Behavior & Personality* 2, 243–250; Graham, C. A. (1991). Menstrual synchrony: an update and review. *Human Nature*, 2, 293–311; Weller, L., & Weller, A. (1995). Menstrual synchrony: Agenda for future research; *Psychoneuroendocrinology*. 20,(4), 377–383; Weller, L., & Weller, A. (1993, Winter). Human menstrual synchrony: A critical assessment. *Neuroscience & Biobehavioral Reviews*, 17, 427–439.

81. Cacioppo, J. T., & Berntson, G. G. (1992). Social psychological contributions to the decade of the brain: Doctrine of multilevel analysis. *American Psychologist*,

47, 1019–1028; Madsen, D. (1985). A biochemical property relating power seeking in humans. *American Political Science Review*, 79, 448–457.

82. Jeffcoate, W. J., Lincoln, N. B., Selby, C., & Herbert, M. (1986). Correlation between anxiety and serum prolactin in humans. *Journal of Psychosomatic Research*, 30, 217–222.

83. Jacklin, C. N. (1989). Female and male: Issues of gender. *American Psychologist*, 44, 127–133.

84. Hinde, R. A., A biologist looks at anthropology; Hyde, J. S., Gender differences in mathematics performance: a meta-analysis.

85. Ehrhardt, A. A., The psychobiology of gender.

86. Bem, S. L. (1987). Masculinity and femininity exist only in the mind of the perceiver. In J. M. Reinisch, L. A. Rosenblum, & S. A. Sanders (Eds.), *Masculinity/femininity: Basic perspectives* (p. 305). New York: Oxford University Press.

87. Deaux, K. (1987). Psychological constructions of masculinity and femininity. In J. M. Reinisch, L. A. Rosenblum, & S. A. Sanders (Eds.), *Masculinity/feminity: Basic perspectives* (pp. 289–303). New York: Oxford University Press; Lott, B., Dual natures or learned behavior: The challenge to feminist psychology; Unger, R. K., & Crawford, M., *Women and gender: A feminist psychology*.

88. Gallagher, W. (1993). *The power of place: How our surroundings shape our thoughts, emotions, and actions*. New York: Poseidon.

89. Samaroff, A. J., & Chandler, M. J., Reproductive risk and the continuum of caretaking causality.

90. Samaroff, A. J., & Chandler, M. J., Reproductive risk and the continuum of caretaking causality.

91. Hinde, R. A., A biologist looks at anthropology, p. 586.

92. Maccoby, E. E. (1987). The varied meanings of "masculine" and "feminine." In J. M. Reinisch, L. A. Rosenblum, & S. A. Sanders (Eds.), *Masculinity/femininity: Basic perspectives* (pp. 304–311). New York: Oxford University Press.

93. Hinde, R. A., A biologist looks at anthropology, p. 587.

94. Ehrhardt, A. A. (1987). A transactional perspective on the development of gender differences. In J. M. Reinisch, L. A. Rosenblum, & S. A. Sanders (Eds.), *Masculinity/feminity: Basic perspectives* (pp. 281–285). New York: Oxford University Press.

95. Rossi, A., A biosocial perspective on parenting; Gross, H. E., Considering "A biosocial perspective on parenting."

96. Maccoby, E. E., The varied meanings of "masculine" and "feminine."

97. Conner, J. M., Schackman, M., & Serbin, L. A. (1978). Sex-related differences in response to practice on a visual-spatial test and generalization to a related test. *Child Development*, 49, 24–29.

98. Maccoby, E. E., The varied meanings of "masculine" and "feminine."

99. Maccoby, E. E. (1990). Gender and relationships: A developmental account. *American Psychologist*, 45, 513–520.

100. Snyder, M. Tanke, E. D., & Berscheid, E. (1977). Social perception and interpersonal behavior: On the self-fulfilling nature of social stereotypes. *Journal of*

Personality and Social Psychology, 35, 656–666; Zanna, M. P., & Pack, S. J. (1975). On the self-fulfilling nature of apparent sex differences in behavior. *Journal of Experimental Social Psychology, 11,* 583–591.

101. Jacklin, C. N., Female and male: Issues of gender, p. 131.

102. Purifoy, F. E., & Koopmans, L. H. (1980). Androstenedione, T and free T concentrations in women of various occupations. *Social Biology, 26,* 179–188.

103. Ehrhardt, A. A., A transactional perspective on the development of gender differences.

104. Hinde, R. A., A biologist looks at anthropology.

105. Ehrhardt, A. A., A transactional perspective on the development of gender differences.

106. Madsen, D., A biochemical property relating power seeking in humans.

107. Unger, R. K. (1992). Will the real sex difference please stand up? *Feminism and Psychology, 2,* 231–238.

108. Parlee, M. B. (1981). Appropriate control groups in feminist research. *Psychology of Women Quarterly, 5,* 637–644.

109. Fine, M., & Gordon, S. M. (1989). Feminist transformations of/despite psychology. In M. Crawford & M. Gentry (Eds.), *Gender and thought: Psychological Persepctives* (pp. 146–174). New York: Springer-Verlag.

110. Jacklin, C. N. (1987). Feminist research and psychology. In C. Farnham (Ed.), *The impact of feminist research in the academy* (pp. 95–107). Bloomington: Indiana University Press.

111. Levine, M., & Levine, A. (1970). *A social history of helping services: Clinic, court, school, and community.* New York: Appleton-Century-Crofts.

112. Degler, C. (1991). *In search of human nature: The decline and revival of Darwinism in American social thought.* New York: Oxford University Press.

113. Shweder, R. (1991, March 17). Dangerous thoughts. . . . *The New York Times Book Review,* pp. 30–31, 35.

114. Caplan, P., McCurdy-Myers, J., & Gans, M. (1992). Should "premenstrual syndrome" be called a psychiatric abnormality? *Feminism and Psychology, 2,* 27–44; Tavris, C., *The mismeasure of woman.*

115. Plomin, R., Environment and genes: Determinants of behavior.

116. LeVay, S. (1991). A difference in hypothalamic structure between heterosexual and homosexual men. *Science, 253,* 1034–1037.

117. Keller, E. F., On the need to count past two in our thinking about gender and science.

118. Cacioppo, J. T., & Berntson, G. G. (1992). Social psychological contributions to the decade of the brain: Doctrine of multilevel analysis.

119. Hyde, J. S., & Linn, M. C. (Eds.) (1986). *The psychology of gender: Advances through meta-analysis.*

CHAPTER 4

1. Buss, D. M. (1995). Psychological sex differences: Origins through sexual selection. *American Psychologist, 50,* 153–168.

2. Buss, D. M., Psychological sex differences: Origins through sexual selection.

3. Fausto-Sterling, A. (1997). Gender and biology. *Journal of Social Issues*, *53*, 233–258.

4. Eagly, A. H (1987). *Sex differences in social behavior: A social-role interpretation*. Hillsdale, NJ: Erlbaum.

5. Miller, J. B. (1986). *Toward a new psychology of women*. Boston: Beacon Press. (Originally published 1976.)

6. Lott, B. (1997). The personal and social correlates of a gender difference ideology. *Journal of Social Issues*, *53*, 279–297.

7. Feingold, A. (1988). Cognitive gender differences are disappearing. *American Psychologist*, 43, 95–103.

8. Brody, L. (1997). Gender and emotion: Beyond stereotype. *Journal of Social Issues*, *53*, 369–393.

9. Epstein, C. F. (1997). The multiple realities of sameness and difference: Ideology and practice in the workplace. *Journal of Social Issues*, *53*, 259–278; p. 266.

10. Markus, H., & Oyserman, D. (1989). Gender and thought: The role of the self-concept. In M. Crawford & M. Gentry (Eds.), *Gender and thought: Psychological perspectives* (pp. 100–127). New York: Springer-Verlag.

11. Wink, P. (1997). Beyond ethnic differences: Contextualizing the influence of ethnicity on individualism and collectivism. *Journal of Social Issues*, *53*, 329–349.

12. Unger, R. (1992). Will the real sex differences please stand up? *Feminism & Psychology*, 2, 231–238; p. 236.

13. Hurtado, A. (1997). Understanding multiple group identities: Inserting women into cultural transformation. *Journal of Social Issues*, *53*, 299–328.

14. Tavris, C. (1992). *The mismeasure of woman* (p. 92). New York: Simon & Schuster.

15. Hyde, J. S. (1994). Should psychologists study gender differences? Yes, with some guidelines. *Feminism and Psychology*, *4*, 507–512.

16. Barnett, R. C. (1997). How our paradigms shape the stories we tell: Paradigm shifts in the study of gender and health. *Journal of Social Issues*.

17. Bem, S. L. (1993). *The lenses of gender: Transforming the debate on sexual inequality*. New Haven, CT: Yale University Press; Mansbridge, J. (1993). Feminism and democratic community. In J. W. Chapman & I. Shapir (Eds.), *Democratic Community: Nomos XXXV* (New York: New York University Press).

18. Rhode, D. (1990). Theoretical perspectives on sexual difference. In D. Rhode, *Theoretical perspectives on sexual difference* (pp. 1–9). New Haven, CT: Yale University Press.

19. James, J. B. (1997). Beyond difference as a model for studying gender: In search of new stories to tell. *Journal of Social Issues*, *53*, 213–232, p. 223.

20. Hare-Mustin, R. T., & Maracek, J. (1988). The meaning of difference: Gender theory, postmodernism, and psychology. *American Psychologist*, *43*, 455–464; p. 456.

21. Jacklin, C N. (1987). Feminist research and psychology. In C. Farnham

(Ed.), *The impact of feminist research in the academy* (pp. 95–107). Bloomington: Indiana University Press.

22. Danziger, K. (1990). *Constructing the subject: Historical origins of psychological research*. New York: Cambridge University Press.

23. Rosenberg, R. (1982). *Beyond separate spheres: Intellectual roots of modern feminism*. New Haven, CT: Yale University Press.

24. Halpern, D. F. (1986). *Sex differences in cognitive abilities*. Hillsdale, NJ: Lawrence Erlbaum.

25. Halpern, D. F., *Sex differences in cognitive abilities*.

26. Sherif, C. (1979). *Bias in psychology*. In J. A. Sherman & E. T. Beck (Eds.), *The prism of sex: Essays in the sociology of knowledge* (pp. 93–133). Madison: University of Wisconsin Press.

27. Goldfoot, D. A., & Neff, D. A. (1987). Assessment of behavioral sex differences in social contexts: Perspectives from primatology. In J. M. Reinisch et al. (Eds.), *Masculinity/femininity: Basic perspectives* (pp. 179–195). New York: Oxford University Press.

28. Maccoby, E. E. (1990). Gender and relationships: A developmental account. *American Psychologist, 45*, 513–520; p. 514.

29. Danziger, K., *Constructing the subject: Historical origins of psychological research*.

30. Epstein, C. F. (1988). *Deceptive distinctions: Sex, gender, and the social order*. New Haven, CT: Yale University Press.

31. Dovidio, J. F., Ellyson, S. L., Keating, C. F., Heltman, K., & Brown, C. E. (1988). The relationship of social power to visual displays of dominance between men and women. *Journal of Personality and Social Psychology, 54*, 233–242.

32. Gergen, K. (1973). Social psychology as history. *Journal of Personality and Social Psychology, 26*, 309–320.

33. Rosenberg, R., *Beyond separate spheres: Intellectual roots of modern feminism*.

34. Mednick, M. T. (1989). On the politics of psychological constructs: Stop the bandwagon, I want to get off. *American Psychologist, 44*, 1118–1123.

35. Scott, J. (1988). Deconstructing equality-versus-difference: or, the uses of poststructuralist theory for feminism. *Feminist Studies, 14*, 33–50; p. 44.

36. Epstein, C. F., *Deceptive distinctions: Sex, gender, and the social order*, p. 232.

37. Morris, J. (1974). *Conundrum* (pp. 148–149). New York: Harcourt, Brace, Jovanovich.

38. Thorne, B. *Gender play*. (1993). New Brunswick, NJ: Rutgers University Press.

39. Shinn, M. (1990). Mixing and matching: Levels of conceptualization, measurement, and statistical analysis in community research. In P. Tolan, C. Keys, F. Chertok, & L. Jason. (Eds.), *Researching community psychology: Issues of theory and methods*. (pp. 111–126). Washington, DC: American Psychological Association.

40. Fine, M. (1984). Coping with rape: Critical perspectives on consciousness. *Imagination, cognition, and personality, 3*, 249–267.

41. Wittner, J. (1995). *Personal talk and sexual politics in Domestic Violence*

Court. Paper presented at the annual meeting of the Midwestern Psychological Association.

42. Mark, M. M., & Shotland, R. L. (1985) Stakeholder-based evaluation and value judgments. *Evaluation Review, 9*, 605–626.

43. Bolman, L. G., & Deal, T. E. (1984). *Modern approaches to understanding and managing organizations*. San Francisco: Jossey-Bass.

44. Cacioppo, J. T., & Berntson, G. G. (1992). Social psychological contributions to the decade of the brain: Doctrine of multilevel analysis. *American Psychologist, 47*, 1019–1028.

CHAPTER 5

1. Reinharz, S. (1984). Women as competent community builders. In A. U. Rickel, M. Gerrard, & I. Iscoe (Eds.), *Social and psychological problems of women: Prevention and crisis intervention*. Washington, DC: Hemisphere Publishing Corporation.

2. Lewin, K. (1951). *Field theory in social science*. New York: Harper.

3. Bakan, D. (1966). *The duality of human existence* Chicago: Rand McNally.

4. Parsons, T., *The social system*. Glencoe, IL: Free Press, 1951; Parsons, T., & Shils, E., *Toward a general theory of action*. Cambridge, MA: Harvard University Press, 1952.

5. Miller, J. B. (1976). *Toward a new psychology of women*. Boston: Beacon Press, 1976.

6. Gilligan, C. (1982). *In a different voice: Psychological theory and women's development*. Cambridge, MA: Harvard University Press.

7. Kerber, L. (1986). Some Cautionary Words for Historians. *Signs: Journal of Women in Culture and Society, 11*, 304–310.

8. Baruch, G., Barnett, R. & Rivers, C. (1983). *Lifeprints* (p. 22). New York: McGraw-Hill.

9. Johnson, M. (1988) *Strong mothers, weak wives: The search for gender equality*. Berkeley, CA: University of California Press.

10. Lott, B. (1990) Dual natures or learned behavior: the challenge to feminist psychology. In R. T. Hare-Mustin & J. Maracek (Eds.) *Making a difference: Psychology and the construction of gender* (pp. 71). New Haven, CT: Yale University Press.

11. Unger, R. (1990). Imperfect reflections of reality: Psychology constructs gender. In R. T. Hare-Mustin & J. Maracek (Eds.) *Making a difference: Psychology and the construction of gender*, pp. 116.

12. Stewart, A., & Malley, J. (1989). Case studies of agency and communion in women's lives (pp. 61–76). In R. K. Unger (Ed.), *Representations: Social Constructions of Gender*. Amityville, NY: Baywood Publishing.

13. Hare-Mustin, R. T., and Maracek, J. (1986). Autonomy and gender: Some questions for therapists. *Psychotherapy, 23*, 205–212.

14. Lott, B., Dual natures or learned behavior: the challenge to feminist psychology. pp. 65–101.

15. Snodgrass, S. E. (1985). Women's intuition: The effects of subordinate role on interpersonal sensitivity. *Journal of Personality and Social Psychology, 49,* 146–155.

16. Buss, A. R. (1978). The structure of psychological revolutions. *Journal of the History of the Behavioral Sciences 14,* 57–64.

17. Deaux, K., and Major, B. (1987). Putting gender into context: An interactive model of gender-related behavior. *Psychological Review, 94,* 369–389.

18. Bandura, A. (1989). Human agency in social cognitive theory. *American Psychologist, 44,* 1175.

19. Parsons, J. E., Ruble, D. N. Hodges, K. L., and Small, A. W. (1976). Cognitive-developmental factors in emerging sex differences in achievement-related expectancies, *Journal of Social Issues, 32,* 47–62.

20. Meece, J. L., Eccles-Parsons, J., Kaczala, C. M., Goff, S. B, and Futterman, R. (1982). Sex differences in math achievement: Toward a model of academic choice, *Psychological Bulletin, 91,* 324–348.

21. Dweck, C. S., and Goetz, T. E. (1981). Attributions and learned helplessness. In J. H. Harvey, W. Ickes, and R. F. Kidd (Eds)., *New directions in attribution theory* (vol. 2). Hillsdale, NJ: Lawrence Erlbaum.

22. Ozer, E. M. and Bandura, A. (1990). Mechanisms governing empowerment effects: A self-efficacy analysis. *Journal of Personality and Social Psychology, 58,* 472–486.

CHAPTER 6

1. Chavis, D., Stucky, P., & Wandersman, A. (1983). Returning basic research to the community: A relationship between scientist and citizen. *American Psychologist, 38,* 424–434; Nyden, P., & Wiewel, W. (1992). Collaborative research: Harnessing the tensions between researcher and practitioner. *American Sociologist, 23,* 43–55.

2. Gondolf, E., Yllo, K., & Campbell, J. (1997). Collaboration between researchers and advocates. In G. K. Kantor & J. Jasinski (Eds.), *Out of darkness: Contemporary research perspectives on family violence* (pp. 255–267). Thousand Oaks, CA: Sage; Jacobson, N. S. (1994). Rewards and dangers in researching domestic violence. *Family Process, 33,* 81–85.

3. Renzetti, C. (1997). Confessions of a reformed positivist: Feminist participatory research as good social science. In M. D. Schwartz (Ed.), *Researching sexual violence against women: Methodological and personal perspectives* (pp. 131–143). Thousand Oaks, CA: Sage.

4. Cancian, F. M. (1993). Conflicts between activist research and academic success: Participatory research and alternative strategies. *American Sociologist, 24,* 92–106; Hall, B. L. (1992). From margins to center? The development and purpose of participatory research. *American Sociologist, 23,* 14–28; Petras, E. M., & Porpora, D. V. (1993). Participatory research: Three models and an analysis. *American Sociologist, 24,* 107–1225; Stoecker, R., & Bonacich, E. (1992). Why participatory research? Guest editors' introduction. *American Sociologist, 23,* 5–14.

5. Renzetti, C., Confessions of a reformed positivist: Feminist participatory research as good social science.

6. Levin, R. (1999). Participatory evaluation: Bringing researchers and service providers together as collaborators rather than adversaries. *Violence against Women*, 5, 1213–1227.

7. Lundy, M., Massat, C. R., Smith, J., & Bhasin, S. (1996). Constructing the research enterprise: Building research bridges between private agencies, public agencies and universities. *Journal of Applied Social Sciences*, 20, 169–176.

8. Gondolf, E., Yllo, K., & Campbell, J., Collaboration between researchers and advocates.

9. Lundy, M., Massat, C. R., Smith, J., & Bhasin, S., Constructing the research enterprise: Building research bridges between private agencies, public agencies and universities.

10. Lennett, J. & Colten, M. E. (1999). A winning alliance: Collaboration of advocates and researchers on the Massachusetts Mothers Survey. *Violence against Women*, 5, 1118–1139.

11. Gondolf, E., Yllo, K., & Campbell, J., Collaboration between researchers and advocates.

12. Fine, M. (1989). The politics of research and activism: Violence against women. *Gender & Society*, 3, 549–558.

13. Gelles, R. J. (1994). Research and advocacy: Can one wear two hats? *Family Process*, 33, 93–95; Jacobson, N. S., Rewards and dangers in researching domestic violence.

14. Lykes, M. B. (1989). Dialogue with Guatemalan Indian women: Critical perspectives on constructing collaborative research. In R. K. Unger (Ed.), *Representations: Social constructions of gender*, pp. 167–185.

15. Altman, D. G. (1995). Sustaining interventions in community systems: On the relationship between researchers and communities. *Health Psychology*, 14, 526–536.

16. Altman, D. G., Sustaining interventions in community systems: On the relationship between researchers and communities.

17. Gordon, M. T., & Riger, S. (1989). *The female fear*. New York: Free Press.

18. Gondolf, E., Yllo, K., & Campbell, J., Collaboration between researchers and advocates.

19. Urban, B. Y., & Bennett, L. (1999). When the community punches a timeclock: Evaluating a domestic abuse prevention program in a garment factory. *Violence against Women*, 5, 1178–1193.

20. Urban, B. Y., & Bennett, L., When the community punches a timeclock: Evaluating a domestic abuse prevention program in a garment factory.

21. Campbell, J., Dienemann, J., Kub, J., Wurmser, T., and Loy, E. (1999). Collaboration as partnership between a school of nursing and a domestic violence agency. *Violence against Women*, 5, 1140–1157.

22. Gondolf, E., Yllo, K., & Campbell, J., Collaboration between researchers and advocates.

23. Altman, D. G., Sustaining interventions in community systems: On the relationship between researchers and communities.

24. Lennett, J. & Colten, M. E., A winning alliance: Collaboration of advocates and researchers on the Massachusetts Mothers Survey.

25. Andersen, M. (1981). Corporate wives: Longing for liberation or satisfied with the status quo? *Urban Life, 10,* 311–327.

26. Lather, P. (1986). Research as praxis. *Harvard Educational Review, 56,* 257–277.

27. Gorelick, S. (1991). Contradictions of feminist methodology. *Gender & Society, 5,* 459–477.

28. Gondolf, E., Yllo, K., & Campbell, J., Collaboration between researchers and advocates.

29. Riger, S. (1994). Challenges of success: Stages of growth in feminist organizations. *Feminist Studies, 20,* 275–300.

30. Levin, R., Participatory evaluation: Bringing researchers and service providers together as collaborators rather than adversaries.

31. Levin, R., Participatory evaluation: Bringing researchers and service providers together as collaborators rather than adversaries.

32. Altman, D. G., Sustaining interventions in community systems: On the relationship between researchers and communities.

33. Sherman, L. W. (1992). *Policing domestic violence: Experiments and dilemmas.* New York: Free Press.

34. Schmidt, J. D., & Sherman, L. W. (1993). Does arrest deter domestic violence? Special issue: The impact of arrest on domestic assault. *American Behavioral Scientist, 36,* 601–609.

35. Edleson, J. (1998, July 28). Forced bonding or community collaboration? Partnerships between science and practice in research on woman battering (p. 3). Paper presented at the National Institute of Justice Annual Conference on Criminal Justice Research and Evaluation: Viewing Crime and Justice from a Collaborative Perspective. Washington, DC.

36. Lundy, M., Massat, C. R., Smith, J., & Bhasin, S., Constructing the research enterprise: Building research bridges between private agencies, public agencies and universities.

37. Campbell, J., Dienemann, J., Kub, J., & Wurmser, T. Collaboration as partnership between a school of nursing and a domestic violence agency.

38. Block, C. R., Engel, B., Naureckas, S. M., & Riordan, K. A. (1999). Chicago Women's Health Risk Study: Lessons in collaboration. *Violence against Women, 5,* 1158–1177.

39. Wiewel, W., & Lieber, M. (1998). Goal achievement, relationship building, and incrementalism: The challenges of university-community partnerships. *Journal of Planning Education and Research, 17,* 291–301.

40. Cancian, F. M., Conflicts between activist research and academic success: Participatory research and alternative strategies; Israel, B. A., Schurman, S. J., & Hugentobler, M. K. (1992). Conducting action research: Relationships between

organization members and researchers. *Journal of Applied Behavioral Science, 28,* 74–101.

41. Block, C. R., Engel, B., Naureckas, S. M., & Riordan, K. A., Chicago Women's Health Risk Study: Lessons in collaboration.

42. Gondolf, E., Yllo, K., & Campbell, J., Collaboration between researchers and advocates.

43. Gilfus, M., Fineran, S., Jensen, S., Cohan, D., & Hartwick, L. (1999). Researchers and advocates in dialogue. *Violence against Women, 5,* 1194–1212.

44. Brown, P. (1995). The role of the evaluator in comprehensive community initiatives. In J. Connell, A. Kubisch, L. Schorr, & C. H. Weiss (Eds.), *New approaches to evaluating community initiatives* (pp. 201–225). Washington, DC: Aspen Institute; Israel, B. A., Schurman, S. J., & Hugentobler, M. K., Conducting action research: Relationships between organization members and researchers; Renzetti, C., Confessions of a reformed positivist: Feminist participatory research as good social science.

45. Levin, R., Participatory evaluation: Bringing researchers and service providers together as collaborators rather than adversaries.

46. Campbell, J., Dienemann, J., Kub, J., & Wurmser, T., Collaboration as partnership between a school of nursing and a domestic violence agency; Gondolf, E., Yllo, K., & Campbell, J., Collaboration between researchers and advocates.

47. Gordon, M. T. & Riger, S., *The female fear.*

48. Stanko, E. (1997). "I second that emotion": Reflections on feminism, emotionality, and research on sexual violence. In M. D. Schwartz (Ed.), *Researching sexual violence against women: Methodological and personal perspectives,* p. 75.

49. Moran-Ellis, J. (1996). Close to home: The experience of researching child sexual abuse. In M. Hester, L. Kelly, & J. Radford (Eds.), *Women, violence, and male power* (p. 181). Buckingham, England: Open University Press.

50. Lennett, J. & Colten, M. E., A winning alliance: Collaboration of advocates and researchers on the Massachusetts Mothers Survey.

51. Gilfus, M., Fineran, S., Jensen, S., Cohan, D., & Hartwick, L., Researchers and advocates in dialogue.

52. Saegert, S. (1993). Charged contexts: Difference, emotion and power in environmental design research. *Architecture & Comportement/Architecture & Behavior, 9,* 69–84.

53. Park, P. (1992). The discovery of participatory research as a new scientific paradigm: Personal and intellectual accounts. *American Sociologist, 23,* 29–42.

54. Reason, P. (1993). Sitting between appreciation and disappointment: A critique of the Special Edition of *Human Relations* on action research. *Human Relations, 46,* 1253–1270.

55. Nyden, P., & Wiewel, W., Collaborative research: Harnessing the tensions between researcher and practitioner.

56. Gondolf, E., Yllo, K., & Campbell, J., Collaboration between researchers and advocates.

57. Gelles, R. J., Research and advocacy: Can one wear two hats?, p. 95.

58. Riger, S. (1992). Epistemological debates, feminist voices: Science, social values, and the study of women. *American Psychologist*, 47, 730–740.

59. Levin, R., Participatory evaluation: Bringing researchers and service providers together as collaborators rather than adversaries.

60. Koss, M. (1998, August). *Does feminist rape research stand up to attack?* Paper presented at the annual meeting of the American Psychological Association, San Francisco.

61. Renzetti, C., Confessions of a reformed positivist: Feminist participatory research as good social science.

62. Jacobson, N. S., Rewards and dangers in researching domestic violence, p. 81.

63. Edleson, J., Forced bonding or community collaboration? Partnerships between science and practice in research on woman battering.

64. Mangham, I. L. (1993). Conspiracies of silence? Some critical comments on the action research Special Issue. *Human Relations*, 46, 1243–1251; Reason, P., Sitting between appreciation and disappointment: A critique of the Special Edition of *Human Relations* on action research; Wiewel, W., & Lieber, M., Goal achievement, relationship building, and incrementalism: The challenges of university-community partnerships.

65. Lennett, J. & Colten, M. E., A winning alliance: Collaboration of advocates and researchers on the Massachusetts Mothers Survey.

66. Levin, R., Participatory evaluation: Bringing researchers and service providers together as collaborators rather than adversaries.

67. Urban, B., Y., & Bennett, L., When the community punches a timeclock: Evaluating a domestic abuse prevention program in a garment factory.

68. Gondolf, E., Yllo, K., & Campbell, J., Collaboration between researchers and advocates.

69. Renzetti, C., Confessions of a reformed positivist: Feminist participatory research as good social science.

70. Fine, M. (1992). Passions, politics, and power: Feminist research possibilities. In M. Fine, *Disruptive voices: The possibilities of feminist research* (p. 220). Ann Arbor: The University of Michigan Press.

71. Gilfus, M., Fineran, S., Jensen, S., Cohan, D., & Hartwick, L., Researchers and advocates in dialogue.

72. Block, C. R., Engel, B., Naureckas, S. M., & Riordan, K. A., Chicago Women's Health Risk Study: Lessons in collaboration.

73. Block, C. R., Engel, B., Naureckas, S. M., & Riordan, K. A., Chicago Women's Health Risk Study: Lessons in collaboration.

CHAPTER 7

1. Bolman, L. G., & Deal, T. E. (1984). *Modern approaches to understanding organizations*. San Francisco: Jossey-Bass.

2. Riger, S., & Keys, C. (1987). Feminist organizations as organized anarchies: A portrait of consensus decision making in action. Paper presented at the First Biennial Community Psychology conference, Charleston, SC.

3. Wandersman, A., Florin, P., Friedmann, R., & Meier, R. (1987). Who participates, who does not, and why? An analysis of voluntary neighborhood organizations in the United States and Israel. *Sociological Forum, 2*, 534–555.

4. Cherniss, D. (1980). *Professional burnout in human services organizations*. New York: Praeger; Shinn, M., Rosario, M., Morch, H., & Chestnut, D. E. (1984). Coping with job stress and burnout in the human services. *Journal of Personality and Social Psychology, 46*, 864–876.

5. Keys, C. B., & Frank, S. (1987). Community psychology and the study of organizations: A reciprocal relationship. *American Journal of Community Psychology, 15*, 239–251.

6. Mulvey, E. P., Linney, J. A., & Rosenberg, M. (1987). Organizational control and treatment program design as dimensions of institutionalization in settings of juvenile offenders. *American Journal of Community Psychology, 15*, 321–335.

7. Tannenbaum, A. S. (1974). *Hierarchy in organizations*. San Francisco: Jossey-Bass.

8. Gruber, J., & Trickett, E. J. (1987). Can we empower others? The paradox of empowerment in the governing of an alternative public school. *American Journal of Community Psychology, 15*, 353–371.

9. Keys, C. B., & Frank, S. (1987). Community psychology and the study of organizations: A reciprocal relationship; Shinn, M., & Perkins, D. (2000). Contributions from organizational psychology. In J. Rappaport & E. Seidman (Eds.), *The handbook of community psychology* (pp. 615–641). New York: Kluwer Academic/Plenum.

10. Nord, W. R. (1974). The failure of current applied behavioral science—A Marxian approach. *Journal of Applied Behavioral Science, 10*, 557–569.

11. Keys, C. B. (1988). Personal communication.

12. Shinn, M., & Perkins, D., Contributions from organizational psychology.

13. Lewis, D., Riger, S., Wagenaar, H., Rosenberg, H., Reed, S., & Lurigio, A. (1988). *Worlds of the mentally ill: How deinstitutionalization works in the city*. Carbondale, IL: Southern Illinois University Press; Lewis, D. A., Lurigio, A., Riger, S., Rosenberg, H., Pavkov, T., & Reed, S. (1994). *The state mental patient and urban life*. Springfield, IL: Charles C. Thomas.

14. Shadish, W. R. (1984). Policy research: Lessons from the implementation of deinstitutionalization, *American Psychology, 39*, 725–738.

15. Rodriguez, R. (1982). *Hunger of memory: The education of Richard Rodriguez*. New York: Bantam.

16. Sennet, R., & Cobb, J. (1973). *The hidden injuries of class*. New York: Vintage.

17. Becker, H. (1967, Winter). Whose side are we on? *Social Problems, 14*, 239–247; Miller, J. B. (1986). *Toward a new psychology of women* (2nd ed.). Boston: Beacon Press.

18. Kalifon, Z. (1985). *Recidivism and community mental health care: A review*

of the literature. Unpublished manuscript, Department of Anthropology, Northwestern University, Evanston, IL.

19. For more extensive discussions of these issues, see: Becker, H., Whose side are we on?; Bleir, R. (1984). *Science and gender: A critique of biology and its theories on women*. Elmsford, NY: Pergamon; Keller, E. F. (1985). *Reflections on gender and science*. New Haven, CT: Yale University Press; Mischler, E. G. (1979). Meaning in context: Is there any other kind? *Harvard Educational Review, 49* (1), 1–19; Oakley, A. (1981). Interviewing women: A contradiction in terms. In H. Roberts (Ed.), *Doing feminist research*. London: Routledge & Kegan Paul; Reinharz, S. (1979); *On becoming a social scientist: From survey research and participant observation to experiential analysis*. San Francisco: Jossey-Bass.

20. Belenky, M. F., Clinchy, B. M., Goldberger, N. R., & Tarule, J. M. (1986). *Women's ways of knowing: The development of self, voice, and mind*. New York: Basic Books.

21. Belenky, M. F., Clinchy, B. M., Goldberger, N. R., & Tarule, J. M., *Women's ways of knowing: The Development of self, voice and mind*, p. 18.

22. Belenky, M. F., Clinchy, B. M., Goldberger, N. R., & Tarule, J. M., *Women's ways of knowing: The development of self, voice, and mind*, p. 216.

23. Belenky, M. F., Clinchy, B. M., Goldberger, N. R., & Tarule, J. M., *Women's ways of knowing: The development of self, voice, and mind*, p. 139.

24. Belenky, M. F., Clinchy, B. M., Goldberger, N. R., & Tarule, J. M., *Women's ways of knowing: The development of self, voice, and mind*, p. 183.

25. Reinharz, S., *On becoming a social scientist: From survey research and participant observation to experiential analysis*.

26. Westkott, M. (1979). Feminist criticism of the social sciences. *Harvard Educational Reviews, 49* (4), 422–430; p. 426.

27. Gilligan, C. (1982). *In a different voice: Psychological theory and women's development*. Cambridge, MA: Harvard University Press.

28. Reinharz, S. (1984). Women as competent community builders: The other side of the coin. In A. U. Rickel, M. Gerrard, & I. Iscoe (Eds.), *Social and psychological problems of women*. New York: Hemisphere.

29. Chicago Foundation for Women. (1988, March 30). Women's leadership development & initiative (Minutes of advisory committee).

30. Leavitt, J., & Saegert, S. (1984). Women and abandoned buildings. *Social Policy, 15*, 32–39.

31. Leavitt, J., & Saegert, S. (1990). *From abandonment to hope: Community households in Harlem* (p. 205). New York: Columbia University Press.

32. Reinharz, S., Women as competent community builders: The other side of the coin.

33. Leavitt, J., & Saegert, S., Women and abandoned buildings, p. 38.

34. Sherif, C. (1987). Bias in psychology. In S. Harding (Ed.), *Feminism and methodology: Social science issues* (pp. 37–56). Bloomington: Indiana University Press.

35. Shadish, W. R., Policy research: Lessons from the implementation of deinstitutionalization.

36. Mitroff, I. (1983). Beyond experimentation: New methods for a new age. In E. Seidman (Ed.), *Handbook of social interventions* (pp. 163–177). Beverly Hills, CA.: Sage.

37. Bryk, A. S. (1983). *Stakeholder-based evaluation*. San Francisco: Jossey-Bass.

38. Mark, M. M., & Shortland, R. L. (1985). Stakeholder-based evaluation and value judgments. *Evaluation Review, 9,* 605–626.

39. Bolman, L. G., & Deal, T. E., *Modern approaches to understanding organizations.*

40. Mark, M. M., & Shortland, R. L., Stakeholder-based evaluation and value judgments.

41. Cook, T. D., & Shadish, W. R., Jr. (1986). Program evaluation: The worldly science. *Annual Review of Psychology, 37,* 193–232.

42. Shinn, M. (1990). Mixing and matching: Levels of conceptualization, measurement, and statistical analysis in community research. In P. Tolan, C. Keys, F. Chertok, & L. Jason (Eds.), *Researching community psychology* (pp. 111–126). Washington, DC: American Psychological Association.

43. Mark, M. M., & Shortland, R. L., Stakeholder-based evaluation and value judgments.

44. Bolman, L. G., & Deal, T. E., *Modern approaches to understanding organizations.*

45. Seidman, E. (1983). Unexamined premises of social problem solving. In E. Seidman (Ed.), *Handbook of social intervention* (p. 66). Beverly Hills, CA: Sage.

46. Loo, C., Fong, K., & Iwamasa, G. (1988). Ethnicity and cultural diversity: An analysis of work published in community psychology journals, 1965–1985; *Journal of Community Psychology, 16,* 332–349; Lounsbury, J., Leader, D., Meares, E., & Cook, M. (1980). An analytic review of research in community psychology. *American Journal of Community Psychology, 8,* 415–441; McClure, L., Cannon, D., Belton, E., D'Ascoli, C., Sullivan, B., Allen, S., Connor, P., Stone, P., & McClure, G. (1980). Community psychology concepts and research base: Promise and product. *American Psychologist, 35,* 1000–1011; Novaco, R., & Monahan, J. (1980). Research in community psychology: An analysis of work published in the first six years of the *American Journal of Community Psychology: American Journal of Community Psychology, 8,* 131–146.

47. Keller, E. F. (1985). *Reflections on gender and science.* New Haven, CT: Yale University Press.

CHAPTER 8

1. U.S. Merit Systems Protection Board. (1981). *Sexual harassment in the federal workplace: Is it a problem?* Washington, DC: Government Printing Office; U.S. Merit Systems Protection Board. (1988). *Sexual harassment in the federal government: An update.* Washington, DC: Government Printing Office. U.S. Merit Systems Protection Board (1995). *Sexual harassment in the federal workplace: Trends, progress, continuing challenges.* Washington, DC: Government Printing Office.

2. LaFontaine, E., & Tredeau, L. (1986). The frequency, sources, and correlates

of sexual harassment among women in traditional male occupations. *Sex Roles, 15*, 433–442; Maypole, D. E., & Skaine, R. (1982). Sexual harassment of blue-collar workers. *Journal of Sociology and Social Welfare, 9*, 682–695.

3. Burleigh, N., & Goldberg, S. (1989). Breaking the silence: Sexual harassment in law firms. *ABA Journal, 75*, 46–52.

4. Littler-Bishop, S. Seidler-Feller, D., & Opaluch, R. E. (1982). Sexual harassment in the workplace as a function of initiator's status: The case of airline personnel. *Journal of Social Issues, 38*, 137–148.

5. Gutek, B. A. (1985). *Sex and the workplace*. San Francisco: Jossey-Bass.

6. Kenig, S., & Ryan, J. (1986). Sex differences in levels of tolerance and attribution of blame for sexual harassment on a university campus. *Sex Roles, 15*, 535–549.

7. Garvey, M. S. (1986). The high cost of sexual harassment suits. *Labor Relations, 65*, 75–79; p. 75.

8. U.S. Merit Systems Protection Board, *Sexual harassment in the federal workplace: Is it a problem?*

9. Konrad, A. M. & Gutek, B. A. (1986). Impact of work experiences on attitudes toward sexual harassment. *Administrative Science Quarterly, 31*, 422–438.

10. Fain, T. C. & Anderton, D. L. (1987). Sexual harassment: Organizational context and diffuse status. *Sex Roles, 5–6*, 291–311; LaFontaine, E., & Tredeau, L., The frequency, sources, and correlates of sexual harassment among women in traditional male occupations; Robinson, W. L., & Reid, P. T. (1985). Sexual intimacy in psychology revisited. *Professional Psychology: Research and Practice, 16*, 512–520.

11. Fitzgerald, L. F., Schullman, S. L., Bailey, N., Richards, M., Swecker, J., Gold, Y., Ormerod, M., & Weitzman, L. (1988). The incidence and dimensions of sexual harassment in academia and the workplace. *Journal of Vocational Behavior, 32*, 152–175.

12. Lott, B., Reilly, M. E., and Howard, D. R. (1982) Sexual assault and harassment: A campus community case study. *Signs: Journal of Women in Culture and Society, 8*, 309.

13. Maypole, D. E. (1986). Sexual harassment of social workers at work: Injustice within? *Social Work, 31*, 1, 29–34.

14. Dziech, B., & Weiner, L. (1984). *The lecherous professor*. Boston: Beacon Press.

15. Robertson, C., Dyer, C. E., & Campbell, D. (1988). Campus harassment: Sexual harassment policies and procedures at institutions of higher learning. *Signs: Journal of Women in Culture and Society, 13*, 792–812.

16. Reilly, M. E., Lott, B., & Gallogly, S. (1986). Sexual harassment of university students. *Sex Roles, 15*, 333–358.

17. Adams, J. W., Kottke, J. L., & Padgitt, J. S. (1983). Sexual harassment of university students. *Journal of College Student Personnel, 23*, 484–490; Benson, D. J., & Thomson, G. (1982). Sexual harassment on a university campus: The confluence of authority relations, sexual interest, and gender stratification. *Social Problems, 29*, 236–251; Brandenburg, J. B. (1982). Sexual harassment in the university:

Guidelines for establishing a grievance procedure. *Signs: Journal of Women in Culture and Society*, 8, 320–336; Cammaert, L. P. (1985). How widespread is sexual harassment on campus? *International Journal of Women's Studies*, 8, 388–397; Meek, P. M., & Lynch, A. Q. (1983). Establishing an informal grievance procedure for cases of sexual harassment of students. *Journal of NAWDAC*, 46, 31; Schneider, B. E. (1987). Graduate women, sexual harassment, and university policy. *Journal of Higher Education*, 58, 46–65.

18. Livingston, J. A. (1982). Responses to sexual harassment on the job: Legal, organizational, and individual actions. *Journal of Social Issues, 38*, (4), 5–22.

19. Maypole, D. E., Sexual harassment of social workers at work: Injustice within?

20. Morgenson, G. (1989, May 15). Watch that leer, stifle that joke. *Forbes*, 69–72.

21. U.S. Merit Systems Protection Board, *Sexual harassment in the federal workplace: Is it a problem?*; U.S. Merit Systems Protection Board, *Sexual harassment in the federal government: An update.*

22. Bumiller, K. (1987). Victims in the shadow of the law: A critique of the model of legal protection. *Signs: Journal of Women in Culture and Society*, 12, 421–439.

23. For a discussion of this distinction in legal cases, see: Cohen, C. F. (1987, November). Legal dilemmas in sexual harassment cases. *Labor Law Journal, 38* 681–689.

24. Equal Employment Opportunity Commission. (1980). Guidelines on Sexual Harassment, 29 C. F. R. Sec. 1604.11.

25. Terpstra, D. E., & Baker, D. D. (1988). Outcomes of sexual harassment charges. *Academy of Management Journal, 31*, 185–194.

26. Trager, T. B. (1988). Legal considerations in drafting sexual harassment policies. In J. Van Tol (Ed.), Sexual harassment on campus: A legal compendium, (pp. 181–190). Washington, DC: National Association of College and University Attorneys.

27. Gutek, B., & O'Connor, M. (1995). The empirical basis for the reasonable work standard. *Journal of Social Issues, 51*, 151–166.

28. Gutek, B. A., Morasch, B., & Cohen (1983). Interpreting social-sexual behavior in a work setting. *Journal of Vocational Behavior, 22*, 30–48; Lester, D., Banta, B., Barton, J., Elian, N., Mackiewicz, L., & Winkelried, J. (1986). Judgments about sexual harassment: Effects of the power of the harasser. *Perceptual and Motor Skills, 63*, 990; Popovich, P. M., Licata, B. J., Nokovich, D., Martelli, T., & Zoloty, S. (1987). Assessing the incidence and perceptions of sexual harassment behaviors among American undergraduates. *Journal of Psychology, 120*, 387–396.

29. Rossi, P. H. & Weber-Burdin, E. (1983). Sexual harassment on the campus. *Social Science Research, 12*, 131–158.

30. Jones, T. S., Remland, M. S. & Brunner, C. C. (1987) Effects of employment relationship, response of recipient, and sex of rater on perceptions of sexual harassment. *Perceptual and Motor Skills, 65*, 55–63.

31. Pryor, J. B. & Day, J. D. (1988). Interpretations of sexual harassment: An attributional analysis. *Sex Roles, 18*, 405–417.

32. Pryor, J. B. (1985). The lay person's understanding of sexual harassment. *Sex Roles, 13*, 273–286.

33. Thomann, D. A., & Wiener, R. L. (1987). Physical and psychological causality as determinants of culpability in sexual harassment cases. *Sex Roles, 17*, 573–591.

34. McIntyre, D. I., & Renick, J. C. (1982). Protecting public employees and employers from sexual harassment. *Public Personnel Management Journal, 11*, 282–292.

35. Kenig, S., & Ryan, J., Sex differences in levels of tolerance and attribution of blame for sexual harassment on a university campus; Konrad, A. M., & Gutek, B. A., Impact of work experiences on attitudes toward sexual harassment; Lester, D., Banta, B., Barton, J., Elian, N., Mackiewicz, L., & Winkelried, J., Judgments about sexual harassment: Effects of the power of the harasser; Powell, G. N. (1986). Effects of sex role identity and sex on definitions of sexual harassment. *Sex Roles, 14*, 9–19; Rossi, P. H., & Weber-Burdin, E., Sexual harassment on the campus.

36. Gutek, B. A., *Sex and the workplace*.

37. Adams, J. W., Kottke, J. L., & Padgitt, J. S., Sexual harassment of university students; Collins, E. G. C., & Blodgett, T. B. (1981). Some see it . . . some won't. *Harvard Business Review, 59*, 76–95; Kenig, S., & Ryan, J. (1986). Sex differences in levels of tolerance and attribution of blame for sexual harassment on a university campus; U.S. Merit Systems Protection Board, *Sexual harassment in the federal workplace: Is it a problem?*

38. Kirk, D. (1988, August). *Gender differences in the perception of sexual harassment*. Paper presented at the Academy of Management National Meeting, Anaheim, CA.

39. Jensen, I. W., & Gutek, B. A. (1982). Attributions and assignment of responsibility in sexual harassment. *Journal of Social Issues, 38*, 121–136; Kenig, S., & Ryan, J., Sex differences in levels of tolerance and attribution of blame for sexual harassment on a university campus.

40. Linenberger, P. (1983). What behavior constitutes sexual harassment? *Labor Law Journal* (April), 238–247.

41. Becker, H. S. (1967). Whose side are we on? *Social Problems, 14*, 241.

42. Kanter, R. M. (1977) *Men and women of the corporation*. New York: Basic Books; Kenig, S., & Ryan, J., Sex differences in levels of tolerance and attribution of blame for sexual harassment on a university campus.

43. MacKinnon, C. A. (1987). Feminism, Marxism, method, and the state: Toward feminist jurisprudence. In Harding, S. (Ed.), *Feminism and methodology: Social science issues*. Bloomington: Indiana University Press, pp. 136, 140.

44. Kenig, S., & Ryan, J., Sex differences in levels of tolerance and attribution of blame for sexual harassment on a university campus; Pryor, J. B., The lay per-

son's understanding of sexual harassment; Pryor, J. B., & Day, J. D., Interpretations of sexual harassment: An attributional analysis.

45. Jones, E. E. & Nisbett, R. E. (1971). *The actor and the observer: Divergent perceptions of the causes of behavior*. Morristown, NJ: General Learning Press.

46. Pryor, J. B., & Day, J. D., Interpretations of sexual harassment: An attributional analysis.

47. Jensen, I. W., & Gutek, B. A., Attributions and assignment of responsibility in sexual harassment.

48. Kenig, S., & Ryan, J., Sex differences in levels of tolerance and attribution of blame for sexual harassment on a university campus.

49. Abbey, A. (1982). Sex differences in attributions for friendly behavior: Do males misperceive females' friendliness? *Journal of Personality and Social Psychology*, 42, 830–838; Abbey, A., & Melby, C. (1986). The effects of nonverbal cues on gender differences in perceptions of sexual intent. *Sex Roles*, 15, 283–298; Saal, F. E., Johnson, C. B., & Weber, N. (1989) Friendly or sexy? It may depend on whom you ask. *Psychology of Women Quarterly*, 13, 263–276; Shotland, R. L., & Craig, J. M. (1988). Can men and women differentiate between friendly and sexually interested behavior? *Social Psychology Quarterly*, 51, 66–73.

50. Tangri, S. S., Burt, M. R., & Johnson, L. B. (1982). Sexual harassment at work: Three explanatory models. *Journal of Social Issues*, 38, 52.

51. Dziech, B., & Weiner, L., *The lecherous professor*.

52. Benson, D. J., & Thomson, G., Sexual harassment on a university campus: The confluence of authority relations, sexual interest and gender stratification; Fitzgerald, L. F., Schullman, S. L., Bailey, N., Richards, M., Swecker, J., Gold, Y., Ormerod, M., & Weitzman, L., The incidence and dimensions of sexual harassment in academia and the workplace; Glaser, R. D., & Thorpe, J. S. (1986). Unethical intimacy: A survey of sexual contact and advances between psychology educators and female graduate students. *American Psychologist, 41*, 43–51; Kenig, S., & Ryan, J., Sex differences in levels of tolerance and attribution of blame for sexual harassment on a university campus; Maihoff, N., & Forrest, L. (1983). Sexual harassment in higher education: An assessment study. *Journal of NAWDEC* (Winter), 3–38; Robinson, W. L., & Reid, P. T. (1985). Sexual intimacy in psychology revisited; Wilson, K. R. & Krause, L. A. (1983). Sexual harassment in the university. *Journal of College Student Personnel*, 24, 219–224.

53. Wilson, M. (1988). Sexual harassment and the law. *The community psychologist*, 21, 16–17.

54. Robertson, C., Dyer, C. E., & Campbell, D., Campus harassment: Sexual harassment policies and procedures at institutions of higher learning.

55. American Association of University Professors. (1983). Sexual harassment: Suggested policy and procedures for handling complaints. *Academe*, 69, 15a–16a; American Council on Education. (1986). Sexual harassment on campus: Suggestions for reviewing campus policy and educational programs. Washington, DC: The Council.

56. Brandenburg, J. B., Sexual harassment in the university: Guidelines for

establishing a grievance procedure; Meek, P. M., & Lynch, A. Q., Establishing an informal grievance procedure for cases of sexual harassment of students.

57. Brett, J. M., Golding, S. B., & Ury, W. L. (1990). Designing systems for resolving disputes in organizations. *American Psychologist, 45*, 162–170.

58. Rowe, M. P. (1981, May–June). Dealing with sexual harassment. *Harvard Business Review, 59*, 42–46.

59. Kanter, R. M., *Men and women of the corporation*, p. 127.

60. Miller, J. B. (1976). *Toward a new psychology of women* (p. 127). Boston: Beacon Press.

61. Merry, S. E., & Silbey, S. S. (1984). What do plaintiffs want? Reexamining the concept of dispute. *Justice System Journal, 9*, 151–178.

62. Metha, J., & Nigg, A. (1983). Sexual harassment on campus: An institutional response. *Journal of NAWDAC, 46*, 9–15; Gilligan, C. (1982). *In a different voice: Psychological theory and women's development.* Cambridge, MA: Harvard University Press.

63. Kolb, D. M. & Coolidge, G. G. (1988). *Her place at the table: A consideration of gender issues in negotiation* (Working paper series 88–5.) Harvard Law School, Program on Negotiation.

64. See, e.g., for a summary of criticisms: Menkel-Meadow, C. (1985). Portia in a different voice: Speculating on a woman's lawyering process. *Berkeley Women's Law Journal, 1*, 39–63.

65. Robertson, C., Dyer, C. E., & Campbell, D., Campus harassment: Sexual harassment policies and procedures at institutions of higher learning.

66. Robinson, W. L. & Reid, P. T., Sexual intimacy in psychology revisited.

67. Rifkin, J. (1984). Mediation from a feminist perspective: Promise and problems. *Mediation, 2*, 21–31.

68. Robertson, C., Dyer, C. E., & Campbell, D., Campus harassment: Sexual harassment policies and procedures at institutions of higher learning.

69. Fain, T. C. & Anderton, D. L., Sexual harassment: Organizational context and diffuse status.

70. Robertson, C., Dyer, C. E., & Campbell, D., Campus harassment: Sexual harassment policies and procedures at institutions of higher learning, p. 801.

71. Robinson, W. L., & Reid, P. T., Sexual intimacy in psychology revisited.

72. Sandler, B. (1988). Personal communication.

73. Fain, T. C. & Anderton, D. L., Sexual harassment: Organizational context and diffuse status; LaFontaine, E., & Tredeau, L., The frequency, sources, and correlates of sexual harassment among women in traditional male occupations; McIntyre, D. I. & Renick, J. C., Protecting public employees and employers from sexual harassment.

74. Lott, B., Reilly, M. E., & Howard, D. R., Sexual assault and harassment: A campus community case study; Reilly, M. E., Lott, B., & Gallogly, S., Sexual harassment of university students.

75. Lott, B., Reilly, M. E., & Howard, D. R., Sexual assault and harassment: A campus community case study, p. 318.

76. Fitzgerald, L. F., Schullman, S. L., Bailey, N., Richards, M., Swecker, J., Gold, Y., Ormerod, M., & Weitzman, L., The incidence and dimensions of sexual harassment in academia and the workplace.

77. Brewer, M. (1982). Further beyond nine to five: An integration and future directions. *Journal of Social Issues, 38,* 149–157.

78. Robertson, C., Dyer, C. E., & Campbell, D., Campus harassment: Sexual harassment policies and procedures at institutions of higher learning.

79. Livingston, J. A., Responses to sexual harassment on the job: Legal, organizational, and individual actions.

80. Terpstra, D. E., & Cook, S. E. (1985). Complainant characteristics and reported behaviors and consequences associated with formal sexual harassment charges. *Personnel Psychology, 38,* 559–574.

81. Terpstra, D. E., & Baker, D. D., Outcomes of sexual harassment charges.

82. Coles, F. S. (1986) Forced to quit: Sexual harassment complaints and agency response. *Sex Roles, 14,* 81–95.

83. Garvey, M. S., The high cost of sexual harassment suits.

84. Livingston, J. A., Responses to sexual harassment on the job: Legal, organizational, and individual actions.

85. Brewer, M. B., & Berk, R. A. (1982). Beyond nine to five: Introduction. *Journal of Social Issues, 38,* 1–4.

86. Adams, J. W., Kottke, J. L., & Padgitt, J. S., Sexual harassment of university students; Lott, B., Reilly, M. E., and Howard, D. R., Sexual assault and harassment: A campus community case study.

87. McCormack, A. (1985). The sexual harassment of students by teachers: The case of students in science. *Sex Roles, 13,* 21–32.

88. Cammaert, L. P., How widespread is sexual harassment on campus?; Crull, P. (1982). The stress effects of sexual harassment on the job. *American Journal of Orthopsychiatry, 52,* 539–543; Hamilton, J. A., Alagna, S. W., King, L. S., & Lloyd, C. (1987). The emotional consequences of gender-based abuse in the workplace: New counseling programs for sex discrimination. *Women and Therapy, 6,* 155–182; Livingston, J. A., Responses to sexual harassment on the job: Legal, organizational, and individual actions; Schneider, B. E., Graduate women, sexual harassment, and university policy.

89. Coles, F. S., Forced to quit: Sexual harassment complaints and agency response.

90. Meek, P. M., & Lynch, A. Q., Establishing an informal grievance procedure for cases of sexual harassment of students.

91. Jensen, I. W., & Gutek, B. A., Attributions and assignment of responsibility in sexual harassment.

92. Morgenson, G., Watch that leer, stifle that joke.

93. MacKinnon, C. A. (1979) *Sexual harassment of working women: A case of sex discrimination.* New Haven, CT: Yale University Press.

94. Brewer, M., Further beyond nine to five: An integration and future directions.

95. Beauvais, K., Workshops to combat sexual harassment: A case study of changing attitudes. *Signs: Journal of women in culture and society*, *12*, 130–145.

96. Dziech, B., & Weiner, L., *The lecherous professor*.

97. Gutek, B. A., *Sex and the workplace*.

98. LaFontaine, E., & Tredeau, L., The frequency, sources, and correlates of sexual harassment among women in traditional male occupations.

99. Hoffman, F. L. (1986). Sexual harassment in academia: Feminist theory and institutional practice. *Harvard Educational Review*, *56* (2), 107–121.

100. Schneider, B. E., Graduate women, sexual harassment, and university policy.

101. Kirp, D. L., Yudof, M. G., & Franks, M. S. (1986). *Gender justice*. Chicago: University of Chicago Press.

102. Project on the Status and Education of Women. (1982). The campus climate: A chilly one for women? Washington, DC: Association of American Colleges.

103. Fuehrer, A., & Schilling, K. M. (1985). The values of academe: Sexism as a natural consequence. *Journal of Social Issues*, *41*, 29–42.

CHAPTER 9

1. Sampson, E. E. (1983). *Justice and the critique of pure psychology* (p. 46). New York: Plenum.

2. Quoted in Sampson, E. E., *Justice and the critique of pure psychology*, p. 137.

3. Rappaport, J. (1987). Terms of empowerment/exemplars of prevention: Toward a theory for community psychology. *American Journal of Community Psychology*, *16*, 121–144; p. 122.

4. Zimmerman, M. A. (2000). Empowerment theory: Psychological, organizational, and community levels of analysis. In J. Rappaport & E. Seidman (Eds.), *Handbook of community psychology* (pp. 43–63). New York: Kluwer Academic/ Plenum.

5. Kieffer, C. (1984). Citizen empowerment: A developmental perspective. *Prevention in Human Services*, *3*, 9–36; p. 32.

6. Ozer, E. M., & Bandura, A. (1990). Mechanisms governing empowerment effects: A self-efficacy analysis. *Journal of Personality and Social Psychology*, *58*, 472–486.

7. Sampson, E. E., *Justice and the critique of pure psychology*, p. 12.

8. Buss, A. R. (1978). The structure of psychological revolutions. *Journal of the History of the Behavioral Sciences*, *14*, 57–64; Sampson, E. E., *Justice and the critique of pure psychology*.

9. Baars, B. J. (1986). *The cognitive revolution in psychology*. New York: Guilford; Friman, P. C., Allen, K. D., Kerwin, M. L. E., & Larzelere, R. (1993). Changes in modern psychology: A citation analysis of the Kuhnian displacement thesis. *American Psychologist*, *438*, 658–664; Gardner, H. (1985). *The mind's new science: A history of the cognitive revolution*. New York: Basic Books; Segal, E. M., & Lachman, R. (1972). Complex behavior or higher mental process: Is there a paradigm shift? *American Psychologist*, *27*, 46–55.

10. Sampson, E. E., *Justice and the critique of pure psychology*, p. 87.

11. Caplan, N., & Nelson, S. D. (1973). On being useful. *American Psychologist*, 199–211; Prilleltesky, I. (1989). Psychology and the status quo. *American Psychologist*, *44*, 795–802.

12. Hollander, E. P., & Offermannm, L. R. (1990). Power and leadership in organizations: Relationships in transition. *American Psychologist, 45*,179–189; p. 179.

13. Maton, K. (1993). *Researching the foundations of empowerment: Group-based belief systems, opportunity role structures, supportive resources, and leadership.* Paper presented at the Fourth Biennial Conference of the Society for Community Research and Action, Williamsburg, VA.

14. Lewis, D. (1994). *Race and educational reform in the American metropolis.* Albany: State University of New York Press.

15. Zimmerman, M. A., Israel, B. A., Schulz, A., & Checkoway, B. (1992). Further explorations in empowerment theory: An empirical analysis of psychological empowerment. *American Journal of Community Psychology*, 20, 707–727.

16. Chavis, D. M., & Wandersman, A. (1990). Sense of community in the urban environment: A catalyst for participation and community development. *American Journal of Community Psychology*, *18*, 159–162.

17. Hunter, A., & Riger, S. (1986). The meaning of community in community mental health. *Journal of Community Psychology*, *14*, 55–71.

18. Brenner, M. H. (1973). *Mental illness and the economy.* Cambridge, MA: Harvard University Press.

19. Molotch, H. (1973). *Social justice and the city.* Baltimore, MD: Johns Hopkins University Press.

20. Serrano-Garcia, I. (1984). The illusion of empowerment: Community development within a colonial context. *Prevention in Human Services, 3,* 173–200.

21. Serrano-Garcia, I., The illusion of empowerment: Community development within a colonial context, p. 195.

22. Serrano-Garcia, I., The illusion of empowerment: Community development within a colonial context, p. 198.

23. Gruber, J., & Trickett, E. J. (1987). Can we empower others? The paradox of empowerment in the governing of an alternative public school. *American Journal of Community Psychology*, *15*, 353–371.

24. Gutierrez, L. M. (1990). Working with women of color: An empowerment perspective. *Social Work*, 149–153.

25. Rappaport, J. (1990). Research methods and the empowerment social agenda. In P. Tolan, C. Keys, F. Chertok, & L. Jason (Eds.), *Researching community psychology* (pp. 51–63). Washington, DC: American Psychological Association.

26. Livert, D. E. (n.d.) Implications of an empowerment ideology for community psychology. Unpublished manuscript, George Peabody College of Vanderbilt University, Nashville, TN.

27. Bond, M., & Keys, C. (1993). Empowerment, diversity, and collaboration: Promoting synergy on community boards. *American Journal of Community Psychology*, *21*, 37–58.

28. For criticisms, see: Sarason, S. B. (1981). *Psychology misdirected*. New York: Free Press.

29. Gilligan, C. (1982). *In a different voice: Psychological theory and women's development*. Cambridge, MA: Harvard University Press.

30. Rappaport, J., Terms of empowerment/exemplars of prevention: Toward a theory for community psychology.

31. Sarason, S. B. (1974). *The psychological sense of community: Prospects for a community psychology*. San Francisco: Jossey-Bass.

32. Scherer, M. (1992). *Still loved by the sun: A rape survivor's journal*. New York: Simon and Schuster.

33. Fine, M. (1992). Coping with rape: Critical perspectives on consciousness. In M. Fine, *Disruptive voices: The possibilities of feminist research* (pp. 61–76). Ann Arbor: University of Michigan Press, pp. 62, 69.

34. Hare-Mustin, R. T., & Maracek, J. (1986). Autonomy and gender: Some questions for therapists. *Psychotherapy, 23*, 205–212.

35. Panzetta, A. F. (1973). The concept of community: The short-circuit of the mental health movement. In B. Denner & R. H. Price (Eds.), *Community mental health: Social action and reaction* (pp. 245–259). New York: Holt, Rinehart & Winston.

36. Sarason, S. B., *The psychological sense of community: Prospects for a community psychology*.

37. Stack, C. (1974). *All our kin*. New York: Harper & Row.

38. Chavis, D. M., & Wandersman, A., Sense of community in the urban environment: A catalyst for participation and community development.

39. Maton K., & Rappaport, J. (1984). Empowerment in a religious setting: a multivariate investigation. *Prevention in Human Services, 3*, 37–73.

40. Leavitt, J., & Saegert, S. (1990). *From abandonment to hope: Community households in Harlem* (p. 231). New York: Columbia University Press.

41. Zimmerman, M. A., Empowerment: Forging new perspectives in mental health.

42. Riger, S. (1994). Challenges of success: Stages of growth in feminist organizations. *Feminist Studies, 20*, 375–300.

CHAPTER 10

1. Women's Bureau, U.S. Dept. of Labor, Women in management. (1997, April). *Facts on Working Women, No. 97–3*.

2. Personal communication, *Catalyst,* Jan 31, 2000.

3. The Glass Ceiling Commission. (1995, March). Good for business: Making full use of the nation's human capital. Recommendations of the Federal Glass Ceiling Commission. Washington, DC: U.S. Government Printing Office.

4. Heider, F. (1958). *The psychology of interpersonal relations*. New York: Wiley.

5. Wallston, B. S. (1978, August). *Situation vs. person variables in research on women and employment*. Paper presented at the meeting of the American Psychological Association, Toronto, Canada.

6. Caplan, N., & Nelson, S. D. (1973). On being useful: The nature and consequences of psychological research on social problems. *American Psychologist, 28,* 199–211.

7. Ryan, W. (1971). *Blaming the victim.* New York: Pantheon.

8. Gutek, B. (1993). Changing the status of women in management. *Applied Psychology: An International Review, 42,* 301–311.

9. Horner, M. (1969, November). Fail: Bright women. *Psychology Today,* 36–38; 62; p. 38.

10. Tresemer, D. (1977). *Fear of success.* New York: Plenum; Zuckerman, M., & Wheeler, I. (1975). To dispel fantasies about the fantasy-based measure of fear of success. *Psychological Bulletin, 82,* 932–946.

11. Alper, T. G. (1974). Achievement motivation in college women: A now-you-see-it-now-you-don't phenomenon. *American Psychologist, 29,* 194–203.

12. Condry, J., & Dyer, S. (1976). Fear of success: Attribution of cause to the victim. *Journal of Social Issues, 32,* 63–83.

13. Lockheed, M. E. (1975). Female motive to avoid success: A psychological barrier or a response to deviancy? *Sex Roles, 1,* 41–50; Monahan, L., Kuhn, D., & Shaver, P. (1974). Intrapsychic versus cultural explanations of the "fear of success" motive. *Journal of Personality and Social Psychology, 29,* 60–64.

14. Ruddick, S., & Daniels, P. (1977). *Working it out.* New York: Pantheon.

15. Horner, M. (1972). Toward an understanding of achievement-related conflicts in women. *Journal of Social Issues, 28,* 157–176.

16. Hennig, M., & Jardim, A. (1977). *The managerial woman.* Garden City, NY: Anchor.

17. Hennig, M., & Jardim, A., (1977). *The managerial woman.*

18. Bartol, K. M., & Wortman, M. S. (1975). Male versus female leaders: Effects on perceived leader behavior and satisfaction in a hospital. *Personnel Psychology, 28,* 533–547; Chapman, J. (1975). Comparison of male and female leadership styles. *Academy of Management Journal, 18,* 645–650; Chapman, J., & Luthans, F. (1975). The female leadership dilemma. *Public Personnel Management, 4,* 175–179; Day, D. R., & Stogdill, R. M. (1972). Leader behavior of male and female supervisors: A comparative study. *Personnel Psychology, 25,* 353–360; Denmark, F. L. (1976, September). *Styles of leadership.* Paper presented at the meeting of the American Psychological Association, Washington, DC; Eagly, A. H., & Johnson, B. T. (1990). Gender and leadership style: A meta-analysis. *Psychological Bulletin, 108,* 233–256; Feild, H. S., & Caldwell, B. E. (1979). Sex of supervisor, sex of subordinate, and subordinate job satisfaction. *Psychology of Women Quarterly, 3,* 391–399; Megargee, E. I. (1969). Influence of sex roles on the manifestation of leadership. *Journal of Applied Psychology, 53,* 377–382; Muldrow, T. W., & Bayton, J. A. (1979). Men and women executives and processes related to decision accuracy. *Journal of Applied Psychology, 64,* 99–106; Renwick, P. A. (1977). The effects of sex differences on the perception and management of superior-subordinate conflict: An exploratory study. *Organizational Behavior and Human Performance, 19,* 403–415; Rosen, B., & Jerdee, T. H. (1973). The influence of sex-role stereotypes on eval-

uations of male and female supervisory behavior. *Journal of Applied Psychology, 57,* 44–48; Terborg, J. (1977). Women in management: A research review. *Journal of Applied Psychology, 62,* 647–664; Wexley, K., & Hunt, P. J. (1974). Male and female leaders: Comparison of performance and behavior patterns. *Psychological Reports, 35,* 867–872.

19. Osborn, R. N., & Vicars, W. M. (1976) Sex stereotypes: An artifact in leader behavioral and subordinate satisfaction analysis? *Academy of Management Journal, 19,* 439–449.

20. Eagly, A. H. & Johnson, B. T., Gender and leadership style: A meta-analysis.

21. Osborn, R. N., & Vicars, W. M., Sex stereotypes: An artifact in leader behavioral and subordinate satisfaction analysis?

22. Feild, H. S., & Caldwell, B. E., Sex of supervisor, sex of subordinate, and subordinate job satisfaction.

23. Eagly, A. H. & Johnson, B. T., Gender and leadership style: A meta-analysis.

24. Terborg, J., Women in management: A research review.

25. Osborn, R. N., & Vicars, W. M., Sex stereotypes: An artifact in leader behavioral and subordinate satisfaction analysis?

26. Bartol, K. M. (1976). Relationship of sex and professional training area to job orientation. *Journal of Applied Psychology, 61,* 368–370; Brief, A. P., & Oliver, R. L. (1976). Male-female differences in work attitudes among retail sales managers. *Journal of Applied Psychology, 61,* 526–528.

27. Feild, H. S., & Caldwell, B. E., Sex of supervisor, sex of subordinate, and subordinate job satisfaction.

28. Muldrow, T. W., & Bayton, J. A., Men and women executives and processes related to decision accuracy.

29. Bartol, K. M., & Butterfield, D. A. (1976). Sex effects in evaluating leaders. *Journal of Applied Psychology, 61,* 446–454; Haccoun, D. M., Haccoun, R. R., & Sallay, G. (1978). Sex differences in the appropriateness of supervisory styles: A non-management view. *Journal of Applied Psychology, 63,* 124–127; Petty, M. M., & Lee, G. K. (1975). Moderating effects of sex of supervisor and subordinate on relationships between supervisory behavior and subordinate satisfaction. *Journal of Applied Psychology, 60,* 624–628; Rosen, B., & Jerdee, T. H., The influence of sex-role stereotypes on evaluations of male and female supervisory behavior.

30. Eagly, A. H., Makhijani, M. G., & Klonsky, B. G. (1992). Gender and the evaluation of leaders: A meta-analysis. *Psychological Bulletin, 111,* 3–22.

31. Eagly, A. H. & Johnson, B. T., Gender and leadership style: A meta-analysis; Eagly, A. H., Makhijani, M. G. & Klonsky, B. G., Gender and the evaluation of leaders: A meta-analysis.

32. Eagly, A. H., Karau, S. J., & Makhijani, M. (1995). Gender and the effectiveness of leaders: A meta-analysis. *Psychological Bulletin, 117,* 125–145.

33. Freston, P., & Coleman, K. (1978, October). Managerial style in the marketplace. Paper presented at the National Feminist Therapy Conference, Pittsburgh.

34. Hennig, M., & Jardim, A., *The managerial woman.*

35. Kanter, R. M. (1977). *Men and women of the corporation.* New York: Basic Books.

36. Kanter, R. M. (1976, May). Why bosses turn bitchy. *Psychology Today,* 56–57, 59, 88–89, 91.

37. Taylor, S. E., Fiske, S. T., Close, N. M., Anderson, C. E., & Ruderman, A. J. (1977). *Solo status as a psychological variable: The power of being distinctive.* Unpublished manuscript, Harvard University, Cambridge, MA.

38. Crocker, J., & McGraw, K. M. (1984). What's good for the goose is not good for the gander: Solo status as an obstacle to occupational achievement for males and females. *American Behavioral Scientist, 27,* 357–369; Konrad, A. M., Winter, S., & Gutek, B. A. (1992). Diversity in work group sex composition: Implications for majority and minority members. *Research in the Sociology of Organizations, 10,* 115–140.

39. Larwood, L., O'Neal, E., & Brennan, P. (1977). Increasing the physical aggressiveness of women. *Journal of Social Psychology, 101,* 97–101; Larwood, L., Zalkind, D., & Legault, J. (1975). The bank job: A field study of sexually discriminatory performances on a neutral-role task. *Journal of Applied Social Psychology, 5,* 68–74; Megargee, E. I., Influence of sex roles on the manifestation of leadership; Zammuto, R. F., London, M., & Rowland, K. M. (1979). Effects of sex on commitment and conflict resolution. *Journal of Applied Psychology, 64,* 227–231.

40. Bartol, K. M., & Butterfield, D. A. (1976). Sex effects in evaluating leaders; Mai-Dalton, R. R., Feldman-Summers, S., & Mitchell, T. R. (1979). Effect of employee gender and behavioral style on the evaluation of male and female banking executives. *Journal of Applied Psychology, 64,* 221–226; Rosen, B., & Jerdee, T. H. (1974) Influence of sex role stereotypes on personnel decisions. *Journal of Applied Psychology, 59,* 9–14; Rosen, B., & Jerdee, T. H. (1975) Effects of employee's sex and threatening versus pleading appeals on managerial evaluations of grievance. *Journal of Applied Psychology, 60,* 442–445; Terborg, J., Women in management: A research review.

41. Heilman, M. E., & Saruwatari, L. R. (1979). When beauty is beastly: The effects of appearances and sex on evaluations of job applicants for managerial and nonmanagerial jobs. *Organizational Behavior and Human Performance, 23,* 360–372.

42. Kanter, R. M., Why bosses turn bitchy, p. 59.

43. O'Leary, V. E. Some attitudinal barriers to occupational aspirations in women. (1974). *Psychological Bulletin, 81,* 809–826.

44. Heilman, M. E., Block, C. J., Martell, R. F., and Simon, M. C. (1989). Has anything changed? Current characterizations of men, women, and managers. *Journal of Applied Psychology, 74,* 935–942.

45. Bass, B. M., Krusell, J., & Alexander, R. A. (1971). Male managers' attitudes toward working women. *American Behavioral Scientist, 15,* 221–236.

46. Bowman, G. W., Worthy, N. B., & Greyser, S. A. (1965). Are women executives people? *Harvard Business Review, 43,* 52–67.

47. Mayes, S. S. (1979). Women in positions of authority: A case study of changing sex roles. *Signs: Journal of Women in Culture and Society, 4*, 556–568; p. 566; Spence, J. T., Helmreich, R., & Stapp, J. (1975). Likability, sex-role congruence of interest, and competence: It all depends on how you ask. *Journal of Applied Social Psychology, 5*, 93–109.

48. Rosen, B., & Jerdee, T. H. (1975). The psychological basis for sex role stereotypes: A note on Terborg and Ilgen's conclusions. *Organizational Behavior and Human Performance, 14*, 151–153.

49. Lockheed, M. E. (1975). Female motive to avoid success: A psychological barrier or a response to deviancy?

50. Kiesler, S. B. (1975). Actuarial prejudice toward women and its implications. *Journal of Applied Social Psychology, 975*, 201–216.

51. Deaux, K., & Taynor, J. (1973). Evaluation of male and female ability: Bias works two ways. *Psychological Reports, 32*, 261–262.

52. Goldberg, P. (1968). Are women prejudiced against women? *Transaction, 5*, 28–30.

53. Levenson, H., Burford, B., Bonno, B., & Davis, L. (1975). Are women still prejudiced against women? A replication and extension of Goldberg's study. *Journal of Psychology, 89*, 67–71.

54. Cline, M. E., Holmes, D. S., & Werner, J. C. (1977). Evaluations of the work of men and women as a function of the sex of the judge and type of work. *Journal of Applied Social Psychology, 7*, 89–93.

55. Rosen, B., & Jerdee, T. H. (1974) Effects of applicant's sex and difficulty of job on evaluations of candidates for managerial positions. *Journal of Applied Psychology, 59*, 511–512.

56. Mischel, H. (1974). Sex bias in the evaluation of professional achievements. *Journal of Educational Psychology, 66*, 157–166.

57. Pheterson, G. I., Kiesler, S. B., & Goldberg, P. A. (1971). Evaluation of the performance of women as a function of their sex, achievement, and personal history. *Journal of Personality and Social Psychology, 19*, 114–118.

58. Bigoness, W. J. (1976). Effect of applicant's sex, race, and performance on employers' performance ratings: Some additional findings. *Journal of Applied Psychology, 61*, 80–84; Jacobson, M. B., & Effertz, J. (1974). Sex roles and leadership perceptions of the leaders and the led. *Organizational Behavior and Human Performance, 12*, 383–396; Taynor, J., & Deaux, K. (1973). When women are more deserving than men: Equity, attribution, and perceived sex differences. *Journal of Personality and Social Psychology, 28*, 360–367.

59. Hagen, R. L., & Kahn, A. (1975). Discrimination against competent women. *Journal of Applied Social Psychology, 5*, 362–376.

60. Deaux, K. (1976). Sex: A perspective on the attribution process. In J. H. Harvey, W. J. Ickes, & R. F. Kidd (Eds.), *New directions in attribution research* (pp. 335–352). Hillsdale, NJ: Erlbaum; Deaux, K., & Emswiller, T. (1974). Explanations of successful performance on sex-linked tasks. *Journal of Personality and Social Psychology, 29*, 80–85; Feldman-Summers, S., & Kiesler, S. B. (1974).

Those who are number two try harder: The effect of sex on attributions of causality. *Journal of Personality and Social Psychology, 30,* 846–855; Garland, H., & Price, K. H. (1977). Attitudes toward women in management and attributions for their success and failure in a managerial position. *Journal of Applied Psychology, 62,* 29–33; Terborg, J. R., and Ilgen, D. R. (1975). A theoretical approach to sex discrimination in traditionally masculine occupations. *Organizational Behavior and Human Performance, 13,* 352–376; Valian, V., *Why so slow? The advancement of women.*

61. Swim, J. K., & Sanna, L. J. (1996). He's skilled, she's lucky: A meta-analysis of observers' attributions for women's and men's successes and failures. *Personality and Social Psychology Bulletin, 22,* 507–519.

62. Taynor, J., & Deaux, K., When women are more deserving than men: Equity, attribution, and perceived sex differences.

63. Heilman, M. E., & Guzzo, R. A. (1978). The perceived cause of work success as a mediator of sex discrimination in organizations. *Organizational Behavior and Human Performance, 21,* 346–357.

64. Cohen, S. L., & Bunker, K. A. (1975). Subtle effects of sex role stereotypes on recruiters' hiring decisions. *Journal of Applied Psychology, 60,* 566–572; Dipboye, R. L., Fromkin, H. L., & Wiback, K. (1975). Relative importance of applicant sex, attractiveness and scholastic standing in evaluation of job applicant resumes. *Journal of Applied Psychology, 60,* 39–43.

65. Rosen, B., & Jerdee, T. H., Effects of applicant's sex and difficulty of job on evaluations of candidates for managerial positions.

66. Dipboye, R. L., Arvey, R. B., & Terpstra, D. E. (1977). Sex and physical attractiveness of raters and applicants as determinants of resume evaluations. *Journal of Applied Psychology, 62,* 288–294; Stroh, L. K., Brett, J. M., & Reilly, A. H. (1992). All the right stuff: A comparison of female and male managers' career progression. *Journal of Applied Psychology, 77,* 251–260.

67. Renwick, P. A., & Tosi, H. (1978). The effects of sex, marital status, and educational background on selection decisions. *Academy of Management Journal, 21,* 93–103.

68. Cohen, S. L., & Bunker, K. A., Subtle effects of sex role stereotypes on recruiters' hiring decisions.

69. Powell, G. N., & Butterfield, D. A. (1979). The "good manager": Masculine or androgynous? *Academy of Management Journal, 22,* 395–403; Schein, V. E. (1973). The relationship between sex role stereotypes and requisite management characteristics. *Journal of Applied Psychology, 57,* 95–100.

70. Hennig, M., & Jardim, A., *The managerial woman*; Roche, G. R. (1979). Much ado about mentors. *Harvard Business Review, 57,* 14–28.

71. Larwood, L., & Blackmore, J. (1978). Sex discrimination in managerial selection: Testing predictions of the vertical dyad linkage model. *Sex Roles, 4,* 365; Leong, F. T. L., Snodgrass, C. R., & Gardner, W. L., III. (1992). Management education: Creating a gender-positive environment. In Uma Sekaran & Frederick T. L. Leon (Eds.), *Woman-power: Managing in times of demographic turbulence* (pp. 192–220). Newbury Park, CA: Sage.

14. Nieva, V., & Gutek, B. Sex effects on evaluation.

15. Crosby, F. (1984). The denial of personal discrimination. *American Behavioral Scientist, 27,* 371–386.

16. Crosby, F., The denial of personal discrimination.

17. For a discussion of the circumstances under which this occurs, see Matlin, M. W. (1987). *The Psychology of Women* (pp. 132–137; 141–145). New York: Holt, Rinehart & Winston.

CHAPTER 12

1. For distinctions among feminist philosophies, see Jaggar, A., & Rothenberg, P. S. (1984). *Feminist frameworks: Alternative theoretical accounts of the relations between women and men* (2nd ed.). New York: McGraw-Hill; Offen, K. (1989). Defining feminism: a comparative historical approach. *Signs: Journal of Women in Culture and Society, 14,* 119–157; Black, N. (1989) *Social feminism.* Ithaca, NY: Cornell University Press; and Snitow, A. (1990). A gender diary. In Hirsch, M., & Fox Keller, E. (Eds.), *Conflicts in feminism.* New York: Routledge.

2. For a summary of these arguments, see Ferguson, K. E. (1984). *The feminist case against bureaucracy.* Philadephia: Temple University Press; Gould, M. (1979). When women create an organization: The ideological imperatives of feminism. In Dunkerley, D., & Salaman, G. (Eds.), *The international yearbook of organizational studies* (pp. 237–251). London: Routledge & Kegan Paul; Rodriguez, N. M. (1988). Transcending bureaucracy: Feminist politics at a shelter for battered women. *Gender and Society 2,* 214–27.

3. Friedman, D. (1977) Structuring a rape crisis center. *Feminist Alliance against Rape News, 8–10,* 8.

4. Joreen. (1973). The tyranny of structurelessness. In Koedt, A., Levine, E., & Rapone, A. (Eds.) *Radical feminism* (pp. 285–299). New York: Quadrangle.

5. Hartsock, N. (1981). Staying alive. In Quest staff (Eds.), *Building feminist theory: Essays from Quest* (pp. 111–122). New York: Longman.

6. Strobel, M. (1987). *The Chicago women's liberation union: A case study in feminist politics.* Paper presented at the Berkshire Women's History Conference, Wellesley, MA.

7. Morgen, S. (1990). Contradictions in feminist practice: Individualism and collectivism in a feminist health center. *Comparative Social Research, Suppl. 1,* 9–56.

8. Schechter, S. (1982). *Women and male violence* (p. 51). Boston: South End Press.

9. Katzenstein, M. F., & Mueller, C. M. (Eds.) (1987). *The women's movements of the United States and Western Europe: Consciousness, political opportunity, and public policy.* Philadelphia: Temple University Press.

10. Ferree, M. M. (1987). Equality and autonomy: Feminist politics in the U.S. In Katzenstein, M. F., & Mueller, C. M. (Eds.) *The women's movements of the United States and western Europe: Consciousness, political opportunity, and public policy,* pp. 172–195.

11. Martin, P. Y. (1990). Rethinking feminist organizations. *Gender and Society* 4, 182–206; p. 185.

12. Kimberly, J. R. (1980). The life cycle analogy and the study of organizations: Introduction. In Kimberley, J. R., & Miles, R. H. (Eds.) (1980). *The organizational life cycle: Issues in the creation, transformation, and decline of organizations* (pp. 1–14). San Francisco: Jossey-Bass. Theorists disagree about the presence of stages in the development of organizations. Noel M. Tichy argues that growth and development is cyclical rather than linear, with technical, political, and social problems continually needing adjustment in varying degrees throughout the life of the organization (Problem cycles in organizations and the management of change, in Kimberley & Miles, pp. 164–183). Some of the issues discussed here, such as the need for external resources, do arise in cyclical or even chronic fashion. However, other issues, such as the need for greater efficiency, can propel the organization into a qualitatively different mode of functioning that justifies the concept of stages.

13. Greiner, L. E. (1972). Evolution and revolution as organizations grow. *Harvard Business Review, 51*, 37–46.

14. Quinn, R. E., & Cameron, K. (1983). Organizational life cycles and shifting criteria of effectiveness: Some preliminary findings. *Management Science 29*, 33–51.

15. Quinn, R. E., & Andersen, D. F. (1984). Formalization as crisis: Transition planning for a young organization. In Kimberley, J. R., & Quinn, R. E. (Eds.), *Managing organizational transitions* (pp. 11–28). Homewood, IL: Irwin.

16. An emphasis on the organizational sources of conflict does not, of course, rule out the existence or importance of ideological or interpersonal sources.

17. In Quinn and Cameron's model, this stage is labeled "entrepreneurial," an appellation inappropriate for feminist organizations that often were avowedly anticapitalist.

18. Remington, J. (1989). *Women working together: How well is it working?* (p. 1). St. Paul: Minnesota Women's Press.

19. Bartunek, J. M., & Betters-Reeds, B. L. (1987). The stages of organizational creation. *American Journal of Community Psychology, 15*, 287–303.

20. Lippitt, G. L., & Schmidt, W. H. (1967). Crises in a developing organization. *Harvard Business Review, 45*, 102–112.

21. Ahrens, L. (1980). Battered women's refuges: Feminist cooperatives vs. social service institutions. *Radical America, 14*, 41–47.

22. Remington, J., *Women working together: How well is it working?*

23. Sealander, J., & Smith, D. (1986). The rise and fall of feminist organizations in the 1970s: Dayton as a case study. *Feminist Studies, 12*, (2), 320–341.

24. Quinn, R. E., & Andersen, D. F., Formalization as crisis: Transition planning for a young organization.

25. Schechter, S., *Women and male violence*, p. 49.

26. Adizes, A. (1979). Organizational passages: Diagnosing and treating life-cycle problems of organizations. *Organizational Dynamics, 1*, 3–24, 4.

27. Staggenborg, S. (1988). The consequences of professionalization and formalization in the pro-choice movement. *American Sociological Review, 53,* 585–606; Greiner, L. E., Evolution and revolution as organizations grow.

28. Schechter, S., *Women and male violence,* p. 49.

29. Quinn, R. E., & Cameron, K., Organizational life cycles and shifting criteria of effectiveness: Some preliminary findings.

30. Zald, M., & Ash, R. (1966). Social movement organizations: Growth, decay, and change. *Social Forces, 44,* 3, 327–341.

31. Mansbridge, J. J. (1986). *Why we lost the ERA* (p. 6). Chicago: University of Chicago Press.

32. Quinn, R. E., & Cameron, K., Organizational life cycles and shifting criteria of effectiveness: Some preliminary findings, p. 44.

33. Batchelder, E. O., & Marks, L. N. (1979). Creating alternatives: A survey of women's projects. *Heresies, 2,* 97–127.

34. hooks, b. (1984). *Feminist theory from margin to center* (p. 28). Boston: South End Press.

35. Mansbridge, J. J. (1979). Time, emotion, and inequality: Three problems of participatory groups. *Journal of Applied Behavioral Science, 9* (2–3), 351–368.

36. Freeman, J. (1973). The tyranny of structurelessness. In Koedt, A., Levine, E., & Rapone, A. (Eds.), *Radical feminism.* New York: Quadrangle.

37. Rothschild-Whitt, J. (1976). Conditions facilitating participatory-democratic organizations. *Sociological Inquiry, 46* (2), 75–86; Rothschild-Whitt, J. The collectivist organization: An alternative to rational-bureaucratic models (1979). *American Sociological Review, 44,* 509–527.

38. Riger, S. (1984). Vehicles for empowerment: The case of feminist movement organizations. *Prevention in Human Services, 3* (2–3), 99–117.

39. Rodriguez, N. M., Transcending bureaucracy: Feminist politics at a shelter for battered women.

40. Michels, R. (1962). *Political parties.* New York: Free Press. (Original work published 1911)

41. Mansbridge, J. (1979). The agony of inequality. In Case, J., & Taylor, R. C. R. (Eds.), *Coops, communes, and collectives: Experiments in social change in the 1960s and 1970s* (pp. 194–214). New York: Pantheon.

42. Iannello, K. P. (1992). *Decisions without hierarchy: Feminist interventions in organization theory and practice.* New York: Routledge.

43. Ferguson, K. E., *The feminist case against bureaucracy.*

44. Batchelder, E. O., & Marks, L. N., Creating alternatives: A survey of women's projects.

45. Martin, P. Y. (1987). A commentary on *The feminist case against bureaucracy* by Kathy Ferguson. *Women's studies international forum, 10,* (5), 543–548; p. 547.

46. Riger, S., & Keys, C. (1987, May). *Feminist organizations as organized anarchies: A portrait of consensus decision-making in action.* Paper presented at the meeting of the Midwest Psychological Association.

47. Greiner, L. E., Evolution and revolution as organizations grow.

48. Morgen, S. (1986). The dynamics of cooptation in a feminist health clinic. *Social Science and Medicine 23*, 201–210; p. 202.

49. Remington, J., *Women working together: How well is it working?*

50. Katz, D., & Kahn, R. (1978). *The social psychology of organizations* (2nd ed.). New York: Wiley.

51. Greiner, L. E., Evolution and revolution as organizations grow.

52. O'Sullivan, E. (1978). What has happened to rape crisis centers? A look at their structures, members, and funding. *Victimology: An International Journal, 3* (1–2), 45–62.

53. Remington, J., *Women working together: How well is it working?*

54. St. Joan, J. (1981). Female leaders: Who was Rembrandt's mother? In Quest staff (Eds.), *Building feminist theory: Essays from Quest*, pp. 223–235.

55. Eagly, A. H., & Johnson, B. T. (1990). Gender and leadership style: A meta-analysis. *Psychological Bulletin, 108*, 233–256. See Reed, B. G. (1983). Women leaders in small groups: Social-psychological perspectives and strategies. *Social Work With Groups, 6* (3–4), 35–42; Riger, S., & Galligan, P. (1980). Women in management: An exploration of competing paradigms. *American Psychologist 35*, 902–910.

56. Bernardez, T. (1983). Women in authority: Psychodynamic and interactional aspects. *Social Work with Groups, 6*, 42–49.

57. Fennell, M. L., Barchas, P. R., Cohen, E. G., McMahon, A. M., & Holdebrand, P. (1978) An alternative perspective on sex differences in organizational settings: The process of legitimation. *Sex Roles, 4*, 589–604.

58. Adizes, A., Organizational passages: Diagnosing and treating lifecycle problems of organizations.

59. Staggenborg, S., The consequences of professionalization and formalization in the pro-choice movement, p. 595.

60. Miles, R., & Randolph, W. A. (1980). Influence of organizational learning styles on early development. In Kimberley, J. R. & Miles, R. H. (Eds.), *The organizational life cycle: Issues in the creation, transformation, and decline of organizations* (pp. 44–82); Walton, R. E. (1980). Establishing and maintaining high commitment work systems. In Kimberley, J. R., & Miles, R. H. (Eds.), *The organizational life cycle: Issues in the creation, transformation, and decline of organizations*, pp. 208–290.

61. Morgen, S., The dynamics of cooptation in a feminist health clinic.

62. Meyer, J. W., & Rowan, B. (1977). Institutionalized organizations: Formal structure as myth and ceremony. *American Journal of Sociology 83*, 340–363.

63. Newman, K. (1980). Incipient bureaucracy: The development of hierarchies in egalitarian organizations. In Britan, G., & Cohen, R. (Eds.), *Hierarchy and society: Anthropological perspectives on bureaucracy*. Philadelphia: Institute for the Study of Human Issues, 143–163.

64. Rodriguez, N. M., Transcending bureaucracy: Feminist politics at a shelter for battered women.

65. Rodriguez, N. M., Transcending bureaucracy: Feminist politics at a shelter for battered women.

66. Piven, F. F., & Cloward, R. (1977). *Poor people's movements: Why they succeed,*

how they fail. New York: Pantheon. See also Morgen, S., The dynamics of cooptation in a feminist health clinic.

67. Morgen, S., The dynamics of cooptation in a feminist health clinic.

68. Remington, J., *Women working together: How well is it working?*, p. 14.

69. Matthews, N. (1989). Surmounting a legacy: The expansion of racial diversity in a local anti-rape movement. *Gender & Society, 3,* 518–532.

70. Staggenborg, S. (1989) Stability and innovation in the women's movement: A comparison of two movement organizations. *Social Problems, 36,* 75–92.

71. Kimberley, J. R. (1980). Initiation, innovation, and institutionalization in the creation process. In Kimberley, J. R., & Miles, R. H. (Eds.), *The organizational life cycle: Issues in the creation, transformation, and decline of organizations*, p. 39.

72. The classic analysis is Weber, M. (1946). On bureaucracy. In Gerth, H. H., & Mills, C. W. (Eds. and Trans.), *From Max Weber: Essays in sociology* (pp. 196–244). New York: Oxford University Press.

73. Katz, D., & Kahn, R., *The social psychology of organizations*, p. 73.

74. Martin, J. (1990). Deconstructing organizational taboos: The suppression of gender conflict in organizations. *Organization Science, 1,* (4), 339–359.

75. Ferguson, K. (1983). Feminism and bureaucratic discourse. *New Political Science, 11,* 53–73.

76. Reinelt, C. (1991). *Moving onto the terrain of the state: The battered women's movement and the politics of contradictory locations.* Unpublished manuscript: Brandeis University, Waltham, MA.

77. For a spirited defense of bureaucracy, see Perrow, C. (1979). *Complex organizations: A critical essay* (2nd ed.). Glenview, IL: Scott, Foresman & Co.

78. Kimberley, J. R., Initiation, innovation, and institutionalization in the creation process.

79. Meyer, J. W., & Rowan, B. (1977). Institutionalized organizations: Formal structure as myth and ceremony, pp. 342–344.

80. Martin, P. Y. (1990). Rethinking feminist organizations, p. 196.

81. Greiner, L. E., Evolution and revolution as organizations grow.

82. Child, J., & Kieser, A. (1981). Development of organizations over time. In Nystrom, P. & Starbuck, W. H. (Eds.), *Handbook of organizational design (vol. 1): Adapting organizations to their environments.* Oxford: Oxford University Press.

83. Gerlach, L. P., & Hine, V. H. (1970). *People, power, change: Movements of social transformation.* Indianapolis: Bobbs-Merrill Co, Inc.

84. Reinelt, C., *Moving onto the terrain of the state: The battered women's movement and the politics of contradictory locations*, p. 27.

85. Adizes, A., Organizational passages: Diagnosing and treating lifecycle problems of organizations.

86. Miner, V. (1985). Rumours from the cauldron: Competition among feminist writers. *Women's Studies International Forum, 8,* 45–50.

87. Keller, E. F., & Moglen, H. (1987). Competition and feminism: Conflicts for academic women. *Signs: Journal of Women in Culture and Society 12,* 493–511. See

also Miller, J. B. (1986). *Toward a new psychology of women* (2nd ed.). Boston: Beacon Press.

88. Douglas, M. A. (1979, May). *The dynamics of feminist in-fighting.* Paper presented at the First National Conference of the National Women's Studies Association, Lawrence, Kansas.

89. Mansbridge, J. J., *Why we lost the ERA*, p. 181.

90. Milkman, M. (1986). Women's history and the Sears case. *Feminist Studies*, *12*, 375–400.

91. Russo, A. (1987). Conflicts and contradictions among feminists over issues of pornography and sexual freedom. *Women's Studies International Forum 10* (2), 103–112. See, e.g., MacKinnon, C. (1987). On collaboration. In *Feminism unmodified: Discourses on life and law* (pp. 198–205). Cambridge, MA: Harvard University Press.

92. Mansbridge, J. J., *Why we lost the ERA*, p. 309.

93. Morgen, S. (1983). Toward a politics of "feelings": Beyond the dialectic of thought and action. *Women's Studies*, *10*, 203–223.

94. Keller, E. F., & Moglen, H. (1987). Competition and feminism: Conflicts for academic women. *Signs: Journal of Women in Culture and Society*, *12*, 493–511; p. 507–508.

95. Kennedy, F. (1970). Institutionalized oppression vs. the female. In Morgan, R. (Ed.), *Sisterhood is Powerful: An Anthology of Writings from the Women's Liberation Movement* (pp. 492–501). New York: Vintage Books.

96. hooks, b. (1984). *Feminist theory from margin to center*, p. 49.

97. Fisher-Manick, B. (1981). Race and class: Beyond personal politics. In Quest staff (Ed.), *Building feminist theory: Essays from Quest*, pp. 149–160.

98. Gruber, J., & Trickett, E. J. (1987). Can we empower others? The paradox of empowerment in the governing of an alternative school. *American Journal of Community Psychology*, *15*, 353–371; p. 370.

99. Murray, S. B. (1988). The unhappy marriage of theory and practice: An analysis of a battered women's shelter. *NWSA Journal*, *1*, 75–92, 81. For a discussion of problems with empowerment, see also Fine, M. (1983–84). Coping with rape: Critical perspectives on consciousness. *Imagination, Cognition, and Personality*, *3*, 249–267.

100. Ahrens, L., Battered women's refuges: Feminist cooperatives vs. social service institutions.

101. Miller, J. B., *Toward a new psychology of women.*

102. hooks, b., *Feminist theory from margin to center.*

103. Batchelder, E. O., & Marks, L. N., Creating alternatives: A survey of women's projects, p. 107.

104. Miller, J. B., *Toward a new psychology of women.*

105. Blake, R. R., & Mouton, S. S. (1981). *Managing intergroup conflict in industry* Houston: Gulf Publishing Co.; Fisher, R., & Uhry, W. (1981). *Getting to yes: Negotiating agreement without giving in.* Boston: Houghton Mifflin; Wheeler, C. E., & Chinn, P. L. (1984/1989). *Peace and power: A handbook of feminist process,* Publ. 15–2301. New York: National League for Nursing.

106. Paley, G. (1983). The Seneca stories: Tales from the women's peace encampment. *Ms.*, *12*, (6), 54–62; p. 58.

107. Jones, E. E., & Nisbett, R. E. (1971). *The actor and the observer: Divergent perceptions of the causes of behavior*. Morristown, NJ: General Learning Press.

CHAPTER 13

1. Brandwein, R. (1997). *Family violence and welfare reform: The Utah experience and national implications*. Paper presented at University of Utah, Salt Lake City.

2. Meier, J. (1997). Domestic violence, character, and social change in the welfare reform debate. *Law & Policy, 19*, 205–263.

3. Raphael, J. (1996). Domestic violence and welfare receipt: Toward a new feminist theory of welfare dependency. *Harvard Women's Law Journal, 19*, 201–227.

4. The Family Violence Option (1998, March). *Illinois welfare news*. Chicago: National Clearinghouse for Legal Services.

5. Kurz, D. (1997). Violence against women or family violence? Current debates and future directions. In O'Toole, L. L., & Shiffman, J. R. (Eds.), *Gender violence: Interdisciplinary perspectives* (pp. 443–453). New York: New York University Press; Raphael, J., & Haennicke, S. (1998). The family violence option: An early assessment. Chicago: The Taylor Institute.

6. Kurz, D. (1989). Social science perspectives on wife abuse: Current debates and future directions. *Gender & Society, 3*, 489–505; O'Neill, D. (1998). A post-structuralist review of the theoretical literature surrounding wife abuse. *Violence against Women, 4*, 457–490.

7. Crowell, N. A., & Burgess, A. W. (1996). *Understanding violence against women*. Washington, DC: National Academy Press; Koss, M. P., Goodman, L. A., Browne, A., Fitzgerald, L. F., Keita, G. P., & Russo, N. F. (1994). *No safe haven: Male violence against women at home, at work, and in the community*. Washington, DC: American Psychological Association.

8. Meier, J., Domestic violence, character, and social change in the welfare reform debate; Shepard, M., & Pence, E. (1988). The effect of battering on the employment status of women. *Affilia, 3*, 55–61.

9. Bowker, L. (1983). *Beating wife beating*. Toronto: D.C. Heath & Co.; Dobash, R. P., & Dobash, R. E. (1979). *Violence against wives: A case against the patriarchy*. New York: Free Press; Koss, M. P., Goodman, L. A., Browne, A., Fitzgerald, L. F., Keita, G. P., & Russo, N. F., *No safe haven: Male violence against women at home, at work, and in the community*; Martin, D. (1976). *Battered wives*. New York: Pocket Books.

10. Meier, J., Domestic violence, character, and social change in the welfare reform debate, p. 223.

11. Crenshaw, K. (1991). Mapping the margins: Intersectionality, identity politics, and violence against women of color. *Stanford Law Review, 43*, 1241–1299.

12. Meier, J., Domestic violence, character, and social change in the welfare reform debate; Merry, S. E. (1995). Gender violence and legally engendered selves.

Identities: Global studies in culture and power, 2, 49–73; Moore, A. M. (1997). Intimate violence: Does socioeconomic status matter? In A. P. Cardarelli (Ed.), *Violence between intimate partners: Patterns, causes, and effects* (pp. 90–100). Boston: Allyn & Bacon; Zawitz, M. W. (1994). *Violence between intimates.* Washington, DC: Bureau of Justice Statistics, U.S. Department of Justice.

13. Bachman, R., & Saltzman, L. E. (1995). *Violence against women: Estimates from the redesigned survey.* Washington, DC: Bureau of Justice Statistics, U.S. Department of Justice.

14. Nagel, M. V. (1998). *Domestic violence: Prevalence and implications for employment among welfare recipients* (Publication No. HEHS-99–12). Washington, DC: United States General Accounting Office.

15. Allard, M A., Albelda, R., Colten, M. E., & Cosenza, C. (1997). *In harm's way? Domestic violence, AFDC receipt, and welfare reform in Massachusets.* Boston, MA: Center for Social Policy Research, University of Massachusetts Boston.

16. Roper, P., & Weeks, G. (1993). *Over half of the women on public assistance in Washington State reported physical and sexual abuse as adults* (Issue Brief). Seattle: Washington State Institute for Public Policy.

17. Counts, D. A., Brown, J. K., & Campbell, J. C. (Eds.) (1992), *Sanctions and sanctuary: Cultural perspectives on the beating of wives.* Boulder, CO: Westview Press; Salomon, A., Bassuk, S. S., & Brooks, M. G. (1996). Patterns of welfare use among poor and homeless women. *American Journal of Orthopsychiatry*, 66, 510–525.

18. Gelles, R. J. (1993). Through a sociological lens: Social structure and family violence. In R. J. Gelles & D. R. Loseke (Eds.), *Current controversies on family violence* (p. 35). Newbury Park, CA: Sage.

19. Gelles, R. J., Through a sociological lens: Social structure and family violence.

20. Raphael, J., & Tolman, R. (1997). *Trapped by poverty, trapped by abuse: New evidence documenting the relationship between domestic violence and welfare reform.* Report of the Project for Research on Welfare, Work, and Domestic Violence. Chicago and Ann Arbor: The Taylor Institute and the University of Michigan Research Development Center on Poverty, Risk, and Mental Health.

21. Riger, S., Ahrens, C., Blickenstaff, A., & Camacho, J. (1998). *Obstacles to employment of welfare recipients with abusive partners.* Unpublished manuscript, University of Illinois at Chicago, Chicago.

22. Lloyd, S. (1995). *The effects of domestic violence on female labor force participation.* Paper presented at the 17th Annual APPAM Research Conference, Washington, DC.

23. Meier, J., Domestic violence, character, and social change in the welfare reform debate; Raphael, J., & Tolman, R., Trapped by poverty, trapped by abuse: New evidence documenting the relationship between domestic violence and welfare reform.

24. Raphael, J., Domestic violence and welfare: Toward a new feminist theory of welfare dependency.

25. Kenney, C. T., & Brown, K. R. (n.d.) *Report from the front lines: The impact of violence on poor women*. New York: NOW Legal Defense and Education Fund.

26. Axinn, J. M., & Hirsch, A. E. (1993). Welfare and the "reform" of women. *Families in society: The journal of contemporary human services, 74*, 563–572; Meier, Domestic violence, character, and social change in the welfare reform debate.

27. Kurz, D., Social science perspectives on wife abuse: Current debates and future directions; O'Neill, D., A post-structuralist review of the theoretical literature surrounding wife abuse.

28. Bailey, W. C., & Peterson, R. D. (1995). Gender inequality and violence against women: The case of murder. In J. Hagan & R. D. Peterson (Eds.), *Crime and inequality* (pp. 174–205). Stanford, CA: Stanford University Press; Brownmiller, S. (1975). *Against our will: Men, women, and rape*. New York: Simon & Schuster; Russell, D. (1975). *The politics of rape*. New York: Stein & Day.

29. Homans, G. C. (1974). *Social behavior: Its elementary forms* (Rev. ed.). New York: Harcourt Brace & World.

30. Smith, C. (1988). *Status discrepancies and husband-to-wife violence*. Unpublished manuscript, Family Research Laboratory, University of New Hampshire, Durham.

31. Homans, G. C., *Social behavior: Its elementary forms*.

32. Kurz, D., Violence against women or family violence? Current debates and future directions.

33. Coleman, D. H., & Straus, M. S. (1986). Marital power, conflict, and violence in a national representative sample of American couples. *Violence and Victims, 1*, 141–157; Straus, M. A., Gelles, R. J., & Steinmetz, S., (1980). *Behind closed doors: Violence in the American family*. Garden City, NY: Anchor.

34. Kalmuss, D. S., & Straus, M. A. (1982). Wife's marital dependency and wife abuse. *Journal of Marriage and the Family, 44*, 277–286.

35. Gelles, R. J. (1983). An exchange/social control theory. In D. Finkelhor, R. J. Gelles, G. T. Hotaling, & M. A. Straus (Eds)., *The dark side of families: Current family violence research* (pp. 151–165). Beverly Hills, CA: Sage; Gelles, R. J., & Straus, M. A. (1979). Determinants of violence in the family: Toward a theoretical integration. In W. R. Burr, R. Hill, F. I. Nye, & I. L. Reiss (Eds.), *Contemporary theories about the family* (Vol. 1). (pp. 449–581). New York: Free Press; Nye, F. I. (1979). Choice, exchange, and the family. In W. R. Burr, R. Hill, F. I. Nye, & I. L. Reiss (Eds.), *Contemporary theories about the family* (Vol. 2), pp. 1–41.

36. Gelles, R. J., An exchange/social control theory, p. 157.

37. Vogler, C. & Pahl, J. (1994). Money, power and inequality within marriage. *Sociological Review, 42*, 263–288.

38. Kalmuss, D. S., & Straus, M. A., Wife's marital dependency and wife abuse.

39. Aguire, B. E. (1985). Why do they return? Abused wives in shelters. *Social Work, 30*, 350–354. See also: Ehlers, T. B. (1991). Debunking marianismo: Economic vulnerability and survival strategies among Guatemalan wives. *Ethnology, 30*, 1–16; Johnson, I. M. (1992). Economic, situational, and psycholog-

ical correlates of the decision-making process of battered women. *Families in Society*, 73, 168–176.

40. Bachman, R., & Saltzman, L. E., *Violence against women: Estimates from the redesigned survey*.

41. Yllo, K. (1993). Through a feminist lens: Gender, power, and violence. In R. J. Gelles & D. R. Loseke (Eds.), *Current controversies on family violence* (pp. 47–62). Newbury Park, CA: Sage.

42. Bowker, L., *Beating wife beating*; Dobash, R. P., & Dobash, R. E., *Violence against wives: A case against the patriarchy*; Koss, M. P., Goodman, L. A., Browne, A., Fitzgerald, L. F., Keita, G. P., & Russo, N. F., *No safe haven: Male violence against women at home, at work, and in the community*; Pence, E. & Paymar, M. (1986). Power and control: Tactics of men who batter. Duluth: Minnesota Program Development; Russell, D., *The politics of rape*; Schechter, S. (1982). *Women and male violence: The visions and struggles of the battered women's movement*. Boston: South End Press.

43. Martin, D., *Battered wives*.

44. Frieze, I. H., & McHugh, M. C. (1992). Power and influence strategies in violent and nonviolent marriages. *Psychology of Women Quarterly*, 16, 449–465.

45. Schechter, S., *Women and male violence: The visions and struggles of the battered women's movement*, p. 291.

46. Dobash, R. P., & Dobash, R. E., *Violence against wives: A case against the patriarchy*, p. 57.

47. Russell, D., *The politics of rape*.

48. Lockhart, L. L., White, B. W., Causby, V., & Issac, A. (1994). Letting out the secret: Violence in lesbian relationships. *Journal of Interpersonal Violence*, 9, 469–492.

49. Renzetti, C. (1997). Violence and abuse among same-sex couples. In Cardarelli, A. P. (Ed.), *Violence between intimate partners: Patterns, causes, and effects* (pp. 70–89). Boston: Allyn & Bacon.

50. Brownmiller, S., *Against our will: Men, women, and rape*.

51. Counts, D. A., Brown, J. K., & Campbell, J. C., *Sanctions and sanctuary: Cultural perspectives on the beating of wives*.

52. Lenton, R. L. (1995). Power versus feminist theories of wife abuse. *Canadian Journal of Criminology*, 37, 305–330.

53. Smith, M. D. (1990). Patriarchal ideology and wife beating: A test of a feminist hypothesis. *Violence and Victims*, 5, 257–273.

54. Pratto, F. (1996). Sexual politics: The gender gap in the bedroom, the cupboard, and the cabinet. In D. M. Buss & N. M. Malamuth (Eds.), *Sex, power, and conflict* (pp. 179–230). New York: Oxford University Press.

55. Brown, B. W. (1980). Wife-employment, marital equality, and husband-wife violence. In M. A. Straus & G. T. Hotaling (Eds.), *The social causes of husband-wife violence* (pp. 176–187). Minneapolis: University of Minnesota Press.

56. Allen, C. M. & Straus, M. A. (1980). Resources, power, and husband-wife

violence. In M. A. Straus & G. T. Hotaling (Eds.), *The social causes of husband-wife violence*, pp. 188–210.

57. Forte, J. A., Franks, D. D., Forte, J. A., & Rigsby, D. (1996). Asymmetrical role-taking: Comparing battered and nonbattered women. *Social Work*, *41*, 59–73.

58. McCloskey, L. (1996). Socioeconomic and coercive power within the family. *Gender & Society, 10*, 449–463.

59. Campbell, R., Sullivan, C., & Davidson, W. S. (1995). Women who use domestic violence shelters: Changes in depression over time. *Psychology of Women Quarterly, 19*, 237–255.

60. McCloskey, L., Socioeconomic and coercive power within the family.

61. Hotaling, G. T., & Sugarman, D. B. (1986). An analysis of risk markers in husband to wife violence: The current state of knowledge. *Violence and Victims, 1*, 101–124.

62. Dugan, L., Nagin, D., & Rosenfeld, R. (1997). Explaining the decline in intimate partner homicide: The effects of changing domesticity, women's status, and domestic violence resources. Working paper, H. John Heinz III School of Public Policy and Management, Carnegie Mellon University, Pittsburgh.

63. McCloskey, L. (1996). Socioeconomic and coercive power within the family, p. 457.

64. Babcock, J. C., Waltz, J., Jacobson, N. S., & Gottman, J. M. (1993). Power and violence: The relation between communication patterns, power discrepancies, and domestic violence. *Journal of Consulting and Clinical Psychology, 61*, 40–50.

65. Yllo, K., & Straus, M. (1984). The impact of structural inequality and sexist family norms on rates of wife beating. *Journal of International and Comparative Social Welfare, 1*, 16–29.

66. Yllo, K., Through a feminist lens: Gender, power, and violence.

67. Straus, M. A., Gelles, R. J., & Steinmetz, S., *Behind closed doors: Violence in the American family*.

68. Smith, C., (1988). *Status discrepancies and husband-to-wife violence*.

69. McCord, J. (1992). Deterrence of domestic violence: A critical review of research. *Journal of Research in Crime and Delinquency, 29*, 229–239.

70. Babcock, J. C., Waltz, J., Jacobson, N. S., & Gottman, J. M., Power and violence: The relation between communication patterns, power discrepancies, and domestic violence.

71. Blood, R. O., & Wolfe, D. M. (1960). *Husbands and wives*. Glencoe, IL: Free Press.

72. Renzetti, C. (1997). Violence and abuse among same-sex couples. In Cardarelli, A. P. (Ed.), *Violence between intimate partners: Patterns, causes, and effects* (p. 82). Boston: Allyn & Bacon.

73. Cromwell, R. E., & Olson, D. H. (1975). *Power in families*. New York: Wiley.

74. Wardell, L., Gillespie, D. L., & Leffler, A. (1981, March). *The treatment of wife abuse in recent social science literature*. Paper presented at the annual convention of the Association for Women in Psychology, Boston.

75. Ferraro, K. J., & Johnson, J. M. (1983). How women experience battering: The process of victimization. *Social Problems, 30*, 325–339.

76. Cardarelli, A. P. (Ed.). (1997). *Violence between intimate partners: Patterns, causes, and effects*. Boston: Allyn & Bacon.

77. Koss, M. P., Goodman, L. A., Browne, A., Fitzgerald, L. F., Keita, G. P., & Russo, N. F., *No safe haven: Male violence against women at home, at work, and in the community*.

78. Jacobson, N., & Gottman, J. (1998). *When men batter women*. New York: Simon & Schuster; Saunders, D. (1992). A typology of men who batter: Three types derived from cluster analysis. *American Journal of Orthopsychiatry, 62*, 264–275.

79. Edin, K. & Lein, L. (1997). *Making ends meet: How single mothers survive welfare and low-wage work*. New York: Russell Sage Foundation.

80. Diller, M. (1998). Dismantling the welfare state: Welfare reform and beyond. *Stanford Law & Policy Review, 9*, 19–43.

81. *Get the facts: What the new welfare changes mean for me and my family*. (1997, October). Chicago, Chicago Jobs Council.

82. Salomon, A., Bassuk, S. S., & Brooks, M. G., Patterns of welfare use among poor and homeless women.

83. Meier, J., Domestic violence, character, and social change in the welfare reform debate.

84. Raphael, J., & Haennicke, S., The family violence option: An early assessment.

85. Meier, J., Domestic violence, character, and social change in the welfare reform debate.

86. Bertrand Russell (1938) as cited in Babcock, J. C., Waltz, J., Jacobson, N. S., & Gottman, J. M., Power and violence: The relation between communication patterns, power discrepancies, and domestic violence.

Name Index

Quinn, R. E., 126

Rappaport, J., 98, 105
Reinelt, Claire, 138, 139
Reinharz, Shulamit, 11
Remington, Judy, 133
Renzetti, Claire, 69, 154
Richardson, Laurel, 6
Rivers, C., 54
Rodriguez, Richard, 74
Rosenberg, M., 72
Rosenberg, Rosalind, 119
Rosenfeld, R., 152
Rossi, Alice, 28, 30, 35
Rothschild-Whitt, Joyce, 130
Rowan, B., 137
Russell, Bertrand, 156
Russell, D., 151

Saegert, S., 77, 78, 105
Sameroff, A., 31
Sampson, E. E., 98
Sarason, S. B., 104
Saruwatari, L. R., 112
Schechter, S., 150
Scherer, Migael, 103, 104
Scott, Joan, 46
Secord, P., 22
Seidman, E., 80
Serrano-Garcia, Irma, 100, 101
Sherif, C., 78
Shinn, M., 72
Smith, Dorothy, 13

Smith, C., 153
Snodgrass, Sara, 55, 56
Stack, Carol, 104
Staggenborg, Suzanne, 133, 136
Stanko, E., 67
Stewart, Abigail, 54
Straus, M. S., 149, 150
Sugarman, D. B., 152

Tanenbaum, A. S., 72
Tangri, S. S., 87
Tavris, C., 41
Taylor, S. E., 112
Thomas, Altavese, 103, 104
Thompson, Helen (Wooley), 19, 46
Thorne, B., 48
Trickett, E. J., 72, 101

Unger, Rhoda, 18, 19, 23, 25, 41, 54

Valian, Virginia, 114, 117

Wandersman, A., 100, 105
Weiner, L., 84, 95
Weisstein, Naomi, 8
Wellstone, Paul, 145
Wilkinson, S., 20
Wink, P., 41
Wittner, Judith, 49
Wolfe, D. M., 154
Wright, Robert, 39

Zimmerman, D. H., 98, 105

Subject Index